CW00402637

# welcome to the east of england

As I cycle along the back lane, the trees casting dappled shadows on the road, and the sweet scent of pine woods in the air, I listen to the sounds of this part of Suffolk. The gentle steady sound of my tyres on the road, bird song, and the chatter of friends cycling behind me. The rustle of the breeze in the leaves on the trees. It's peaceful and beautiful, and I remember how lucky I am to live in this part of England.

The East of England. We do have our "hot spots". At a Bank Holiday there are places which will be brimming over with visitors - and rightly so, because there are parts of this region so special that they are deservedly popular.

But for me, the delight of the East of England is that there are so many attractive places still to be discovered. Characterful towns and villages where nothing seems to change from one year to the next - or even from one decade to the next. Places of great beauty where it's still possible to be all alone, and to listen to the sound of silence.

If you know where to look, you can find special events or unusual things to see in the most unexpected places. All you need is a friendly local resident to give you a few tips - or failing that, keep a copy of the East of England Guide tucked in your saddlebag, your pocket or your glove compartment. The Guide is written by people who live in the East of England and who know exactly where it is all happening. We have put into it everything we think might be of interest to anyone planning a day out, a short break or a holiday. Keep this Guide beside you during your visit and you'll have all the information you need to ensure that you don't miss out on any of the fun.

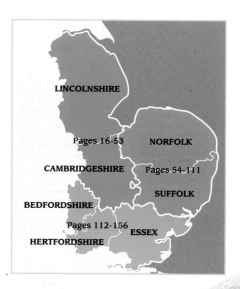

LINCOLNSHIRE

NORFOLK

Pages 16-53

CAMBRIDGESHIRE

Pages 54-111

SUFFOLK

BEDFORDSHIRE

Pages 112-156    ESSEX

HERTFORDSHIRE

## contents

This picture:   Castle Acre, Norfolk.
(photo by Robert Hallmann)

Front Cover:   Walberswick, Suffolk.
(Artist Clive Madgwick)

*Great Ouse, Ely, Cambridgeshire*

# How to use this guide

The information in the Guide is divided into three areas, each with its own distinctive character.

*Cambridgeshire and Lincolnshire* will surprise you. Probably you immediately think of Cambridge city, fascinating for university life which has continued for centuries, for architecture and history, for the rush of bicycles and the buzz of activity. Or of Lincoln, with its awe inspiring Cathedral on a vantage point above the historic city. But look further. Here are the Fens - unique wetland landscape, rich in wildlife, and perfect for cycling. Here are the Lincolnshire Wolds - who said this area is flat? And here are fine towns and cities, and cathedrals to take your breath away.

*Norfolk and Suffolk* - the traditional holiday area with glorious beaches, fascinating towns and villages. There's space here, and the countryside is home to masses of birdlife, some common, some rare. Many nature reserves preserve the variety of different habitats. The wide skies of this landscape inspired paintings by Constable and Gainsborough. Come here to unwind, and find your own inspiration!

*Bedfordshire, Essex and Hertfordshire* have a wealth of irresistible places to visit, ideal for a big day out or as the highlight of a short break. Grand houses, wild animals, roman treasures, vintage aircraft... turn the pages to find out more. And what's more, you may be surprised to discover a wealth of unspoilt countryside with ancient woodlands, chalk downlands and creeks and inlets along the coastline.

Within each of these areas we have listed every place that we think you might like to visit. To help you select what may be of interest, places to visit are grouped together in four categories: History & Heritage; Bloomin' Beautiful; Family Fun and Countryside Activities & Sport. Within each of these sections, places are listed alphabetically by town name, and each one has a map reference to help you locate them. The map reference can be found in brackets at the end of each entry and is to be used with the relevant map featured at the beginning of each area section. If you already know the name and want more detail, turn to the index at the back of this guide.

Prices appear in the order of Adult/Child/Senior Citizen. In some instances prices were not available at the time of going to press, so we therefore recommend you contact the place you wish to visit to confirm prices.

For each area you can also read about the specialities of regional food, and where to eat it, in a selection of restaurants and tea shops, featured in our 'Food and Drink' section. And if you're looking for that 'something special' to take home, consult our 'Stop and Shop' section for some of the best places to indulge in some speciality shopping.

We've also included a few ideas to help you plan your day out in our 'Discovery Tours', featured at the end of each area section. These tours give some suggestions on what to see how to fit it all in!

*Danbury, Essex*

Of course these are only a selection of the places you can visit in the East of England. Why not make up your own Discovery Tour with a little bit of help from the information in this Guide. When using one of our Tours, please remember to contact the establishments featured, to check they'll be open when you plan to visit them.

You will find a detailed contents listing at the beginning of each area section, to assist you in finding the information you require. There is also a comprehensive alphabetical index at the back of this Guide, featuring all of the establishments, places to visit etc, that are included in this publication.

# Our promise of quality

Every eligible attraction in this Guide has signed the National Code of Practice for Visitor Attractions so we are confident that you will find quality and good value for money at the places you visit.

⊛ In addition, more than 1000 attractions, tea rooms, hotels and guest houses are members of the East of England Tourist Board.

*Lavenham, Suffolk*

*Pull's Ferry, Norwich, Norfolk*

You will recognise them by the Rose symbol in the pages of this Guide and by the membership sticker in the window. These establishments are all dedicated to providing the highest standard of courtesy, cleanliness and service. Look out for the rose. It means you're welcome.

The information contained in this Guide is given in good faith, based on the information supplied by the individual establishments listed. Whilst every care has been taken to ensure accuracy of the information published herein, the East of England Tourist Board cannot accept responsibility in respect of any error or omission which may have occurred. Visitors are advised to check details of opening times, admission prices, etc, as changes do occur after press date.

EAST OF ENGLAND TOURIST BOARD

Published by East of England Tourist Board, Toppesfield Hall, Suffolk IP7 5DN.
Tel: (01473) 822922. Fax: (01473) 823063.
Internet:
http://www.visitbritain.com/east-of-england/
e-mail:
eastofenglandtouristboard@compuserve.com

| | |
|---|---|
| Editor and Production Manager: | Emma Rush |
| Production Assistant: | Claire Walker |
| Editorial Assistant: | Cara Myall |
| Editorial Contribution: | Elizabeth Woolnough |
| Graphic Design by | PRS, Ipswich |
| Printed in Great Britain by | Warners Midlands plc |

ISBN: 1 873246 28 5

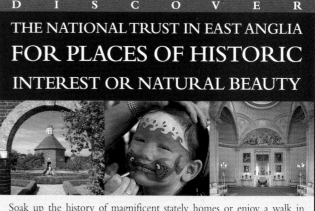

*events 1999*

The East of England offers a range of exciting and varied events to suit all tastes, from air shows to arts festivals, from historical re-enactments and cheese rolling contests to craft fairs and agricultural shows. Or for the more unusual, try the World Snail Racing and Pea Shooting Championships, all held in the region throughout the year. On the following pages we have brought together a selection of events taking place during 1999. For information on the events listed or other events taking place during 1999, please call the East of England Tourist Board on (01473) 822922.

\* - Provisional

**January**

6 Jan — Haxey Hood Game, Haxey, nr. Epworth, Lincs

8-10 Jan — Whittlesey Straw Bear Festival, Town Centre, Whittlesey, Cambs

29-31 Jan — The Harwich Film Festival, Electric Palace Cinema, King's Quay Street, Harwich, Essex

**February**

4-7 Feb — Springfields Horticultural Exhibition, Springfields Exhibition Centre, Camelgate, Spalding, Lincs

13-27 Feb — King's Lynn Mart, Tuesday Market Place, King's Lynn, Norfolk

16 Feb — Lowestoft Pancake Races, The Triangle Market Place, Lowestoft, Suffolk

27 Feb-6 Mar — Bedfordshire Festival of Music, Speech & Drama, Corn Exchange, St. Pauls Square, Bedford, Beds

**March**

20-21 Mar — National Shire Horse Show, East of England Showground, Alwalton, nr. Peterborough, Cambs

27-28 Mar — Thriplow Daffodil Weekend, Thriplow, Cambs

**April**

2-5 Apr — Aldeburgh Easter Festival, Snape Maltings, Snape, Suffolk

2-5 Apr — Blickling Craft Show, Blickling Hall, Blickling, Norfolk

2-5 Apr — Great Easter Egg Quiz & Re-creation of Tudor Life at Eastertide, Kentwell Hall, Long Melford, Suffolk

4-5 Apr — Elton Hall Garden Show, Elton, nr. Peterborough, Cambs

4-5 Apr — The Saxon Market, West Stow Anglo-Saxon Village, West Stow, Suffolk

8-10 Apr — Bury St. Edmunds Beer Festival, Corn Exchange, Cornhill, Bury St. Edmunds, Suffolk

17-18 Apr — Belton Horse Trials, Belton House, Park & Garden, Belton, nr. Grantham, Lincs

21-25 Apr\* — Leap Festival of Dance, Various venues, Norwich, Norfolk

24-25 Apr — St. George's Day Festival, Wrest Park Gardens, Silsoe, Beds

24 Apr-3 May\* — South Holland Church Flower Festivals, Various churches throughout South Holland District, Lincs

30 Apr-3 May — Lincoln Folk Festival, The Lawn, Lincoln, Lincs

30 Apr-8 May — Newmarket Guineas Festival, Town Centre, Newmarket, Suffolk

**May**

Throughout May — Hertford Music Festival, Various venues, Hertford, Herts

May to Oct — The Shuttleworth Collection Flying Displays (normally first Sun in month), Old Warden, nr. Biggleswade, Beds

1 May — King's Lynn May Garland Procession, Town Centre, King's Lynn, Norfolk

1-3 May — Re-creation of Tudor Life at May Day, Kentwell Hall, Long Melford, Suffolk

1-3 May — Spalding Flower Festival & Springfields Country Fair (parade on 1st), Town Centre & Springfields, Camelgate, Spalding, Lincs

1-3 May — Woburn Spring Craft Show, Woburn Abbey, Woburn, Beds

2 May — Duxford Airshow \*, Imperial War Museum, Duxford, Cambs

2 May — Mayfair Bazaar, RAF Mildenhall, Mildenhall, Suffolk

2-3 May \* — Knebworth Country Show, Knebworth House, Gardens & Park, Knebworth, nr. Stevenage, Herts

2-3 May — Truckfest, East of England Showground, Alwalton, nr. Peterborough, Cambs

3 May — Ickwell May Festival, Ickwell Green, nr. Biggleswade, Beds

3 May — Mendlesham Street Fayre, Mendlesham, Suffolk

3 May — Spilsby Grand May Day Carnival, Various venues, Spilsby, Lincs

3 May — Stilton Cheese Rolling Contest, Stilton, nr. Peterborough, Cambs

3 May \* — Tour de Tendring (Cycle Race), Various venues, Tendring district, Essex

3 May — Woodbridge Horse Show, Suffolk Showground, Bucklesham Road, Ipswich, Suffolk

6-9 May — Living Crafts at Hatfield House, Hatfield House, Hatfield, Herts

9 May — The Colchester Classic Vehicle Show, Colchester Institute, Sheepen Road, Colchester, Essex

9 May — South Suffolk Show, Ampton Park, Ingham, nr. Bury St. Edmunds, Suffolk

| | |
|---|---|
| 12-22 May | Chelmsford Cathedral Festival, Chelmsford, Essex |
| 14-30 May | Bury St. Edmunds Festival, Various venues, Bury St. Edmunds, Suffolk |
| 15 May | Hadleigh Farmers' Agricultural Association May Show, Holbecks Park, Hadleigh, Suffolk |
| 15-16 May * | Hertfordshire Garden Show, Knebworth House, Gardens & Park, Knebworth, nr. Stevenage, Herts |
| 15-23 May | Rickmansworth Week, Bury Grounds, Bury Lane, Rickmansworth, Herts |
| 19-22 May | Tallington Beer Festival, Barholm Road Showground, Tallington, Lincs |
| 22-23 May | BMF Bike Show, East of England Showground, Alwalton, nr. Peterborough, Cambs |
| 22-23 May | Tallington Steam & Country Festival, Barholm Road Showground, Tallington, Lincs |
| 29-30 May | Air Fete '99, RAF Mildenhall, Mildenhall, Suffolk |
| 29-30 May | Hertfordshire County Show, Hertfordshire County Showground, Dunstable Road, Redbourn, Herts |
| 29-31 May | Alford Craft Market Spring Festival, Alford Manor House Museum Grounds, Alford, Lincs |
| 29-31 May | Country and Western Craft Fayre, Aldenham Country Park, Elstree, Herts |
| 29-31 May | Felbrigg Coast & Country Show, Felbrigg Hall, Felbrigg, Norfolk |

| | |
|---|---|
| 29-31 May | Re-creation of Tudor Life at Whitsuntide, Kentwell Hall, Long Melford, Suffolk |
| 29-31 May * | Woburn Garden Show, Woburn Abbey, Woburn, Beds |
| 29 May-5 Jun* | Felixstowe Drama Festival, Spa Pavilion Theatre, Seafront, Felixstowe, Suffolk |
| 30 May | Bury in Bloom Flower Market, The Buttermarket, Bury St. Edmunds, Suffolk |
| 30-31 May | Carrington Steam & Vintage Rally, White House Farm, Carrington, Lincs |
| 30-31 May | Southend Air Show, Seafront, Western Esplanade, Southend-on-Sea, Essex |
| 30 May-6 Jun | Downham Market Carnival & Festival (carnival on 31st), Various venues, Downham Market, Norfolk |

| | |
|---|---|
| 31 May | Luton Carnival & Procession, Various venues, Luton, Beds |
| 31 May | Woodhall Spa Agricultural Show, Jubilee Park, Stixwould Road, Woodhall Spa, Lincs |

| | |
|---|---|
| 31 May | Woolpit Street Fair, Woolpit, nr. Bury St. Edmunds, Suffolk |

**June**

| | |
|---|---|
| Jun-Aug | The Gardens of the Rose 'Season of Music & Theatre', The Gardens of the Rose, Chiswell Green, nr. St. Albans, Herts |
| 1 Jun-29 Aug* | Rutland Open Air Theatre - Shakespeare Season, Tolethorpe Hall, nr. Stamford, Lincs |
| 2-3 Jun | Suffolk Show, Suffolk Showground, Bucklesham Road, Ipswich, Suffolk |
| 5-6 Jun | Thaxted Morris Ring, Various venues in Thaxted and surrounding villages, Essex |
| 5-6 Jun | Woolpit Steam Rally, Warren Farm, Wetherden, nr. Stowmarket, Suffolk |
| 6 Jun | Evening Telegraph Motor Show, Normanby Hall Country Park, Normanby, nr. Scunthorpe, Lincs |
| 6 Jun | Messingham Show, Holme Meadow, Holme Lane, Messingham, Lincs |
| 11-13 Jun | Orchestrella, Christchurch Park, Ipswich, Suffolk |
| 11-26 Jun | Aldeburgh Festival of Music & the Arts (52nd), Snape Maltings, Snape, Suffolk |
| 11-27 Jun | Hunstanton & District Festival of Arts, Various venues, Hunstanton, Norfolk |
| 12-13 Jun | East Anglian Daily Times Country Fair, Melford Hall, Long Melford, Suffolk |

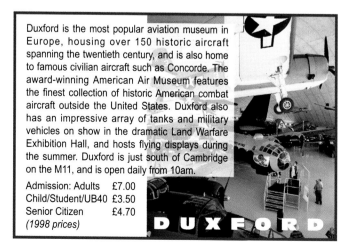

12-13 Jun — Southend Water Festival, Seafront, Southend-on-Sea, Essex

13 Jun — 9th Euston Park Rural Pastimes Show, Euston Hall, Euston, nr. Thetford, Norfolk

13 Jun — Luton Festival of Transport, Stockwood Country Park, Farley Hill, Luton, Beds

18 Jun-11 Jul — Thaxted Festival, Various venues, Thaxted, Essex

18-20 Jun — Essex County Show, Essex Showground, Great Leighs, Essex

19-20 Jun — Festival of Gardening, Hatfield House, Hatfield, Herts

19-20 Jun — Maritime Ipswich, Wet Dock and Cliff Quay area, Ipswich, Suffolk

19-27 Jun — Harwich Festival, Various venues, Harwich, Essex

20 Jun — The Hidden Gardens of Bury St. Edmunds, Various venues, Bury St. Edmunds, Suffolk

20 Jun — Nowton Park Country Fair, Nowton Park, Bury St. Edmunds, Suffolk

20 Jun-11 Jul — Great Annual Re-creation of Tudor Life, Kentwell Hall, Long Melford, Suffolk

23-24 Jun — Lincolnshire Show, Lincolnshire Showground, Grange-de-Lings, Lincoln, Lincs

23-28 Jun — Cambridge Midsummer Fair, Midsummer Common, Cambridge, Cambs

25-27 Jun — The Anglian Flower & Garden Show, Bourn Airfield, Bourn, Cambs

25-27 Jun — Midsummer Folk Festival, Various venues, Southend-on-Sea, Essex

25 Jun-3 Jul — Peterborough Cathedral Festival, Peterborough, Cambs

25 Jun-24 Jul — Theatre in the Parks, Various venues, Norwich, Norfolk

26-27 Jun * — Sandringham Country Weekend, Sandringham Estate, Sandringham, Norfolk

26-27 Jun — Eye Gardens, Various venues, Eye, Suffolk

26-27 Jun — RAF Waddington International Air Show, RAF Waddington, nr. Lincoln, Lincs

27 Jun — Chelsworth Gardens Open Day, Various venues, Chelsworth, Suffolk

27 Jun * — Hunstanton Carnival, Various venues, Hunstanton, Norfolk

27 Jun — Lowestoft Classic Vehicle Run, Lowestoft, Suffolk

27 Jun * — Walsworth Festival Family Fun Day, Walsworth Common, Walsworth, Herts

27 Jun-13 Jul — Hitchin Festival, Various venues, Hitchin, Hertfordshire

30 Jun-1 Jul — Royal Norfolk Show, Norfolk Showground, Dereham Road, New Costessey, Norwich, Norfolk

30 Jun-4 Jul — Wisbech Rose Fair, St. Peter's Parish Church, Wisbech, Cambs

## July

1-4 Jul — Cambridge Music Festival, King's College & St. John's College, Cambridge, Cambs

2-4 Jul * — PFA International Air Rally 1999, Cranfield Airfield, Cranfield, Beds

3 Jul — Meadow Park Families Day, Meadow Park, Borehamwood, Herts

3-4 Jul — Festival of Gardening, Fulbeck Hall, Fulbeck, nr. Grantham, Lincs

3-4 Jul * — Pre-50 American Auto Club "Rally of the Giants", Knebworth House, Gardens & Park, Knebworth, nr. Stevenage, Herts

3-4 Jul — Winterton Agricultural Show, New Showground, Town End, Winterton, nr. Scunthorpe, Lincs

4 Jul — Aquafest, Riverside (Willow Walk/Maltings area), Ely, Cambs

4 Jul — Clacton Classic Vehicle Show, West Road, Clacton-on-Sea, Essex

4 Jul — Ipswich Music Day, Christchurch Park, Ipswich, Suffolk

4 Jul * — Woodbridge Summer Street Fair, Town Centre, Woodbridge, Suffolk

9-11 Jul — Lord Mayor's Weekend Celebrations (parade on 10th), Various venues, Norwich, Norfolk

9-17 Jul — International Organ Festival, Cathedral & Abbey Church of St. Albans, St. Albans, Herts

10 Jul — Tendring Hundred Show, Lawford House Park, Lawford, nr. Manningtree, Essex

10 Jul — World Pea Shooting Championships, Village Green, Witcham, Cambs

10-11 Jul * — Duxford Airshow, Imperial War Museum, Duxford, Cambs

10-11 Jul — The Mayor of Lincoln's Water Carnival, Brayford Pool, Lincoln, Lincs

10-11 Jul * — Watford Rainbow Festival, Cassiobury Park, Watford, Herts

10-11 Jul — Wings & Wheels Model Spectacular, North Weald Airfield, Epping, Essex

10 Jul-1 Aug — 21st East Anglian International Summer Music Festival, The Old School, Bridge Street, Hadleigh, Suffolk

11 Jul * — Fireworks & Laser Symphony Concert, Knebworth House, Gardens & Park, Knebworth, nr. Stevenage, Herts

11 Jul — Normanby Show, Normanby Hall Country Park, Normanby, nr. Scunthorpe, Lincs

15-25 Jul * — Cressing Temple Festival, Cressing, nr. Braintree, Essex

16 Jul — Summer in the City '99 - 'Pop in the Park', Parker's Piece, Cambridge, Cambs

16-18 Jul * — Hacheston Rose Festival, All Saint's Church & surrounding fields, Hacheston, Suffolk

16-18 Jul — Weeting Steam Engine Rally, Fengate Farm, Weeting, Brandon, Suffolk

17 Jul — Armada Special '99, Sparrow's Nest Gardens, Lowestoft, Suffolk

17 Jul — Framlingham Horse Show, Castle Meadow, Framlingham, Suffolk

17 Jul * — Skegness Illuminations Switch-on, The Clock Tower, Skegness, Lincs

17 Jul — Summer in the City '99 - 'The Big Day Out' (fireworks in evening), Parker's Piece, Cambridge, Cambs

17 Jul — World Snail Racing Championships, The Cricket Field, Grimston, nr. King's Lynn, Norfolk

17-18 Jul — A10 Vintage Vehicle Rally & Country Fair, St. Edmunds College Park, Puckeridge, Herts

17-18 Jul * — Holkham Country Fair, Holkham Hall, Holkham, nr. Wells-next-the-Sea, Norfolk

17-18 Jul — Lakeside Jazz Festival, Blickling Hall, Blickling, Norfolk

18 Jul * — Mablethorpe District Show, Tennyson High School, Seaholme Road, Mablethorpe, Lincs

20-22 Jul — East of England Show, East of England Showground, Alwalton, nr. Peterborough, Cambs

22-31 Jul — King's Lynn Festival, Various venues, King's Lynn, Norfolk

23-24 Jul * — Lincoln Street Fest, Various venues, Lincoln, Lincolnshire

24-25 Jul — 132nd Heckington Show, The Showground, Eastgate, Heckington, Lincs

24-25 Jul * — NSRA Hot Rod Supernationals, Knebworth House, Gardens & Park, Knebworth, nr. Stevenage, Herts

25 Jul — London to Southend Classic Car Run, Southend-on-Sea Pier, Western Esplande, Southend-on-Sea, Essex

25 Jul — Mablethorpe Illuminations Switch On, Central Pullover, Mablethorpe, Lincs

28 Jul — Sandringham Flower Show, Sandringham Park, Sandringham, Norfolk

28 Jul-8 Aug — Sheringham Carnival (parade on 4th), Various venues, Sheringham, Norfolk

29-30 Jul — Lowestoft Seafront Air Festival, Seafront, Lowestoft, Suffolk

29 Jul-2 Aug — Lincoln Cathedral Flower Festival, Lincoln Cathedral, Lincoln, Lincs

30 Jul-1 Aug — 35th Charles Wells Cambridge Folk Festival, Cherry Hinton Hall Grounds, Cherry Hinton, Cambs

30 Jul-2 Aug — Beccles Carnival, Beccles Quay, Beccles, Suffolk

30 Jul-1 Aug * — Southend Jazz Festival, Various venues, Southend-on-Sea, Essex

30 Jul-1 Aug — Worstead Festival, Various venues, Worstead, Norfolk

**August**

1 Aug — Revesby Country Fair, Revesby Park, nr. Horncastle, Lincs

1 Aug — Annual British Open Crabbing Championships, Ferry Car Park, Walberswick, Suffolk

1 Aug — Waterloo Park Music Festival, Waterloo Park, Norwich, Norfolk

1-8 Aug — Lowestoft Carnival Week, Various venues, Lowestoft, Suffolk

1-31 Aug — Snape Proms, Snape Maltings Concert Hall, Snape, Suffolk

1-7 Aug — 15th Mundesley Festival, Coronation Hall, Cromer Road, Mundesley-on-Sea, Norfolk

5 Aug * — Brigg Fair, Various venues, Brigg, Lincs

5 Aug * — Cromer Lifeboat Day, The Promenade, Cromer, Norfolk

7-8 Aug — The National Show for Miniature Roses, The Gardens of the Rose, Chiswell Green, nr. St. Albans, Herts

7-8 Aug — Re-creation of Tudor Life at Lammastide, Kentwell Hall, Long Melford, Suffolk

7-8 Aug — Thurlow Steam Rally & Show, Haverhill Showground (on A143), Haverhill, Suffolk

8 Aug * — Broxbourne Folk Festival, Various venues, Broxbourne, Herts

8-13 Aug — Skegness Carnival, Various venues, Skegness, Lincs

8-15 Aug — Mablethorpe Carnival Week, Various venues, Mablethorpe, Lincs

10-15 Aug — Felixstowe Carnival Week (parade on 14th, fireworks on 15th), Various venues, Felixstowe, Suffolk

13-15 Aug — Medieval Craft Fayre, Aldenham Country Park, Elstree, Herts

14 Aug — Illuminated Carnival Procession & Firework Spectacular, Seafront, Southend-on-Sea, Essex

| | |
|---|---|
| 14 Aug * | Ipswich Carnival, Town Centre & Christchurch Park, Ipswich, Suffolk |
| 14 Aug | Proms in the Park '99, Bedford Park, Park Avenue, Bedford, Beds |
| 14-15 Aug * | De Havilland Moth Fly-in (20th Anniversary), Woburn Abbey, Woburn, Beds |
| 14-15 Aug | Oulton Broad & Lowestoft Horticultural Show, Royal Green, Lowestoft, Suffolk |
| 14-20 Aug | Cromer Carnival (parade on 18th), Various venues, Cromer, Norfolk |
| 14-21 Aug | Great Yarmouth & Gorleston Carnival (parade on 15th), Various venues, Great Yarmouth/ Gorleston, Norfolk |
| 15 Aug | Westleton Barrel Fair, Westleton, Suffolk |
| 16 Aug | Aldeburgh Carnival & Fireworks, Seafront & High Street, Aldeburgh, Suffolk |
| 19-20 Aug | Thorpeness Regatta & Fireworks, Thorpeness, Suffolk |
| 20-21 Aug | Blickling Fireworks & Laser Concert, Blickling Hall, Blickling, Norfolk |
| 21-22 Aug * | Hertfordshire Craft Fair, Knebworth House, Gardens & Park, Knebworth, nr. Stevenage, Herts |
| 21-22 Aug | Lincolnshire Steam & Vintage Rally, Lincolnshire Showground, Grange-de-Lings, nr. Lincoln, Lincs |
| 21-22 Aug * | V99, Hylands Park, Chelmsford, Essex |
| 24-29 Aug | Peterborough CAMRA Beer Festival, The Embankment, Bishop's Road, Peterborough, Cambs |
| 26-27 Aug | Clacton Airshow, West Greensward, Clacton-on-Sea, Essex |
| 27-30 Aug * | The Chelmsford Spectacular, Hylands Park, Chelmsford, Essex |
| 27-30 Aug | Clacton Jazz Festival, Various venues, Clacton-on-Sea, Essex |

| | |
|---|---|
| 27-30 Aug | High Summer Re-creation of Tudor Life, Kentwell Hall, Long Melford, Suffolk |
| 28 Aug* | Watford Show, High Street, Watford, Herts |
| 28 Aug | Southend Sailing Barge Race, Seafront, Southend-on-Sea, Essex |
| 28-29 Aug | Fenland Country Fair, Quy Park, Stow Cum Quy, Cambs |
| 28-30 Aug | Alford Craft Market August Festival, Alford Manor House Museum Grounds, Alford, Lincs |
| 28-30 Aug | Bedfordshire Millennium Festival, Shuttleworth Park, Old Warden, nr. Biggleswade, Beds |
| 28-30 Aug | Mildenhall Cycling Rally, Jubilee Fields, Recreation Way, Mildenhall, Suffolk |
| 29-30 Aug | The Countess of Warwick Country Show, Little Easton, nr. Dunmow, Essex |
| 29-30 Aug | Eye Show, Eye Showground, Dragon Hill, Eye, Suffolk |
| 29-30 Aug * | Knebworth '99 - The Classic Car Show, Knebworth House, Gardens & Park, Knebworth, nr. Stevenage, Herts |
| 30 Aug | Aylsham Agricultural Show, Blickling Park, Blickling, Norfolk |
| 30 Aug | Oulton Broad Charity Gala Day, Nicholas Everitt Park, Oulton Broad, Suffolk |
| 30 Aug | St. Albans Carnival, Various venues, St. Albans, Herts |

## September

| | |
|---|---|
| 2-5 Sept | Burghley Horse Trials, Burghley House & Park, nr. Stamford, Lincs |
| 4-5 Sept | Boston Horticultural Show, Central Park, Boston, Lincs |

| | |
|---|---|
| 5 Sept * | Herring Festival, Hemsby Beach, nr. Great Yarmouth, Norfolk |
| 11-12 Sept | Essex Steam Rally & Country Fair, Barleylands Farm Museum, Barleylands Road, Billericay, Essex |
| 11-12 Sept | Haddenham Steam Engine Rally, Haddenham, nr. Ely, Cambs |
| 12 Sept | Duxford Airshow*, Imperial War Museum, Duxford, Cambs |
| 12 Sept | Thornham Country Fair, Thornham Walks, Thornham Magna, Suffolk |
| 18-19 Sept | Bedfordshire Steam & Country Fayre, Shuttleworth Park, Old Warden, nr. Biggleswade, Beds |
| 18-19 Sept | Great Henham Steam Rally (Silver Jubilee), Henham Park, nr. Blythburgh, Suffolk |
| 18-19 Sept | Re-creation of Tudor Life at Michaelmas, Kentwell Hall, Long Melford, Suffolk |
| 18-19 Sept | Somerleyton Horse Trials, Somerleyton Hall & Gardens, Somerleyton, nr. Lowestoft, Suffolk |
| 21-22 Sept | English Wine Festival & Country Craft Fair, New Hall Vineyards, Purleigh, Essex |
| 24-26 Sept | The Craft Show, Chilford Halls, Linton, nr. Cambridge, Cambs |
| 24-26 Sept | Woodhall Spa Festival, Various venues, Woodhall Spa, Lincs |
| 25 Sept | Soham Pumpkin Fayre, Recreation Ground, Soham, Cambs |

## October

| | |
|---|---|
| 1-17 Oct | Norfolk & Norwich Festival, Various venues, Norwich, Norfolk |
| 2-17 Oct * | Watford Autumn Festival, Various venues, Watford, Herts |
| 6-9 Oct | Bedford Beer Festival, Corn Exchange, Bedford, Beds |
| 9-11 Oct * | Corby Glen Sheep Fair, Corby Glen, nr. Grantham, Lincs |
| 10 Oct | World Conker Championships, The Village Green, Ashton, Cambs |
| 17 Oct | Duxford Airshow *, Imperial War Museum, Duxford, Cambs |

| | |
|---|---|
| 23-30 Oct | 21st CAMRA Norwich Beer Festival, St. Andrews & Blackfriars Halls, Norwich, Norfolk |
| 29-31 Oct | Saffron Walden Folk Festival, Various venues, Saffron Walden, Essex |

**November**

| | |
|---|---|
| 5 Nov | 31st Big Night Out, Melford Hall Park, Long Melford, Sudbury, Suffolk |
| 5 Nov | Cambridge 'Grafton Centre' Fireworks Display, Midsummer Common, Cambridge, Cambs |
| 5 Nov * | Luton Fireworks Spectacular, Popes Meadow, Old Bedford Road, Luton, Beds |
| 5-7 Nov | The Craft Show, Marks Hall Estate, nr. Coggeshall, Essex |
| 6 Nov | Gala & Firework Celebration at St. Albans, Verulamium Park, St. Albans, Herts |
| 6 Nov * | Ipswich Firework Display, Christchurch Park, Ipswich, Suffolk |
| 12-28 Nov * | East Coast Jazz Festival 1999, Various venues, throughout Norfolk |
| 20 Nov-23 Dec | The Thursford Christmas Spectacular's, The Thursford Collection, Thursford, Norfolk |

| | |
|---|---|
| 27-28 Nov | Alford Craft Market Christmas Festival, Corn Market, Alford, Lincs |
| 27-28 Nov * | Southend Victorian Christmas, High Street, Southend-on-Sea, Essex |

**December**

| | |
|---|---|
| From Dec | (2nd week) Christmas Nostalgia Shows, The Village, Fleggburgh, nr. Great Yarmouth, Norfolk |
| 2-5 Dec | Lincoln Christmas Market, City Centre, Lincoln, Lincs |
| 6 Dec * | Woodbridge Christmas Street Fair, Town Centre, Woodbridge, Suffolk |
| 9-11 Dec * | Bedford Victorian Christmas Fair, Town Centre, Bedford, Beds |
| 9 & 16 Dec * | Victorian Evenings in Maldon, High Street, Maldon, Essex |
| 11-12 Dec * | Boston Christmas Craft Market, Town Centre, Boston, Lincs |
| 10-12 Dec | Crafts for Christmas, Blickling Hall, Blickling, Norfolk |
| 12 Dec | Hitchin Winter Gala, Various venues, Hitchin, Herts |
| 31 Dec | Lincoln Millennium 2000 Celebrations (including fireworks), Lincoln City Football Ground, Sincil Bank, Lincoln, Lincs |

**Horseracing**
(contact relevant racecourse for events list)
Fakenham - (01328) 862388
Great Yarmouth - (01493) 842527
Huntingdon - (01480) 453373
Market Rasen - (01673) 843434
Newmarket - (01638) 663482

**Motor Racing**
(contact relevant venue for events list)
Cadwell Park, nr. Louth, Lincs - motorcycle racing from Mar-end Oct. Tel: (01507) 343248
Santa Pod Raceway, Santa Pod, Beds - Europe's premier drag racing strip. Tel: (01234) 782828
Snetterton Circuit, Snetterton, Norfolk - motorcar and bike racing events. Tel: (01953) 887303

**The National Trust & English Heritage**
Both organise a wide and varied range of special events at their properties in the East of England.
Contact: The National Trust - (01263) 733471
English Heritage - (0171) 973 3396.

# Lights, Camera, Action

## Cambridgeshire and Lincolnshire

Discover the scenes of your favourite film and television programmes in the East of England. From Chariots of Fire, Lovejoy, Dad's Army and Vanity Fair to James Bond, Eastenders, Star Wars and Middlemarch, you'll find them all here, plus lots more.

Eastern Screen - is the Screen Commission for the East of England. Since the organisation was formed in 1993, the Commission's staff have assisted many film and television production companies with finding locations in the region. Eastern Screen is proud to have assisted a number of prestigious productions - some of which are featured here - and endeavours to bring the East of England to cinema and television screens around the world.

The Tourist Board would like to thank Eastern Screen for their help with this special feature.

*Below:*
*James Bond-Goldeneye*

## Film

**Chariots of Fire (1981)**
- oscar-winning film based on the true story of the Olympic runners Harold Abrahams and Eric Liddell, and the 1924 games. Street scenes were filmed in Cambridge. The famous race around the college precinct was based on the actual event at Trinity College, but filmed at Eton College in Berkshire.

**Dad Savage (1998)** - kidnap & revenge film starring Patrick Stewart (Star Trek), shot in the Fens.

**GoldenEye (1995) and Octopussy (1983)** - two James Bond adventure's with scenes filmed at the Nene Valley Railway at Peterborough in Cambs.

**Peter's Friends (1992)** - scenes filmed at the Nene Valley Railway at Peterborough in Cambs.

**Waterland (1992)** - intense and intriguing drama starring Jeremy Irons, filmed in the Fens.

## Television

**An Unsuitable Job for a Lady (ITV)** - detective drama with an episode filmed in Cambridge.

**Bliss (ITV)** - set in Cambridge, Simon Shepherd takes the lead as a scientific investigator.

**The Buccaneers (BBC)** - drama based on Edith Wharton's unfinished novel. Scenes were filmed at Burghley House, nr. Stamford and Grimsthorpe Castle, nr. Bourne (both in Lincolnshire).

**Cold Enough for Snow (BBC)** - drama with Maureen Lipman. Scenes filmed in Cambridge.

**Honey for Tea (BBC)** - Clare College in Cambridge provided scenes for this comedy series.

**Ivanhoe (BBC)** - classic tale, filmed at Boothby Pagnall Manor House, nr. Grantham in Lincs.

**The Life & Crimes of William Pardoner (ITV)** - starring Keith Allen. Scenes filmed in Lincoln.

**London's Burning (ITV)** - scenes filmed at the Nene Valley Railway at Peterborough in Cambs.

**Middlemarch (BBC)** - George Eliot's classic novel set in 19th century Georgian England, against the backdrop of the Industrial Revolution. Filmed on location in Stamford, Lincolnshire. Other locations used include Grimsthorpe Castle, nr. Bourne and Straggleworth Hall, nr. Grantham.

**Moll Flanders (ITV)** - drama, which used the estate of Grimsthorpe Castle, near Bourne to depict Virginia in the USA. The Red Hall in Bourne & St. George's Church at Galtho were also used.

**Pride and Prejudice (BBC)** - Jane Austen's classic tale, shown in 1995 and starring Colin Firth. Belton House, near Grantham in Lincolnshire was the home of the aunt, Catherine De Bourgh.

**A Sense of Guilt (BBC)** - controversial drama with Trevor Eve, featuring scenes of Cambridge.

**Silent Witness (BBC)** - drama set in Cambridge, with Amanda Burton as pathologist Sam Ryan.

*Tom Jones- Max Beesley*

**Tom Jones (BBC)** - written by Henry Fielding, the tale charts the life/loves of rogue Tom Jones. Scenes were filmed at Belton House & Straggleworth Hall, near Grantham in Lincs.

**The Student Prince (BBC)** - drama with Robson Green. Filmed at Queens' College, Cambridge.

**Wings (USA)** - 80s American mini-series set during the war, and starring Robert Mitcham. Scenes were filmed at the Cambridge American Cemetery.

## Norfolk and Suffolk

### Film

**The Care of Time (1990)** - with Christopher Lee. Hemsby in Norfolk became Miami Beach USA.

*Wind in the Willows*

**Dad Savage (1998)** - kidnap & revengefilm shot in Norfolk at Hunstanton and Wells.

**The Dambusters** - classic film which used Langham Airfield in Norfolk for some scenes.

**Eyes Wide Shut (1999)** - forthcoming film directed by Stanley Kubrick, and starring Tom Cruise and Nicole Kidman. Filmed partly at Elveden Hall and Thetford Forest in Norfolk.

**The Fourth Protocol (1987)** - with Michael Caine. Scenes shot in Ipswich and along the River Orwell.

**The Go Between (1971)** - with Alan Bates. Used Melton Constable Hall and Norwich in Norfolk.

**The Grotesque (1997)** - starring Sting and Alan Bates. Filmed at Heydon Hall in Norfolk.

**Julia (1977)** - filmed at Winterton in Norfolk, which doubled as an 1930's Cape Cod, USA.

**Out of Africa (1985)** - oscar-winning film, starring Robert Redford. The opening shots which seem to show Denmark, were actually filmed at Castle Rising in Norfolk.

**Revolution (1985)** - King's Lynn in Norfolk became 18th c. New York for the filming of this film starring Al Pacino, and set against the background of the American War of Independence.

**Shakespeare in Love (1999)** - forthcoming romantic comedy starring Gwyneth Paltrow. Scenes based around a dramatic shipwreck were filmed at Holkham Beach in Norfolk.

**The Wind in the Willows (1995)** - Kentwell Hall at Long Melford in Suffolk became Toad Hall for the latest film adaptation of Kenneth Cranham's animal adventures.

### Television

**The Adventures of Sherlock Holmes (ITV)** - drama series based on the Baker Street detective. Part of 'The Sign of Four' story was filmed at Burgh Castle in Norfolk.

**A Fatal Inversion (BBC) and Gallowglass (BBC)** - two chilling tales from East Anglian writer, Ruth Rendall. Both were filmed at locations in the Norfolk and Suffolk areas.

**Allo Allo (BBC)** - comedy series set in France during the Second World War. Scenes were filmed in Thetford Forest, Norfolk (including Lynford Hall, nr. Mundford).

**Between the Lines (BBC)** - police series, mainly based in London. One storyline had scenes filmed in the town of Felixstowe and at the riverside hamlet of Pin Mill in Suffolk.

**Dad's Army (BBC)** - comedy classic, following the exploits of the Home Guard. Eighty episodes were filmed over nine years during the 1960/70's, and nearly all featured locations in Norfolk and Suffolk, including:- All Saints' Church, Honington; The MoD's Stanford Training Ground, nr. Thetford; High Lodge in Thetford Forest; Lynford Hall, nr. Mundford; North Norfolk Railway, Sheringham; Oxburgh Hall, Oxborough and Winterton beach. Bressingham Steam Museum (nr. Diss) is home to vehicles used in the series including a vintage traction engine.

**The Chief (ITV)** - drama set around the head of the regional police and filmed throughout the area.

**Dangerfield (BBC)** - medical/police drama, which for two episodes used the North Norfolk coast.

**Eastenders (BBC)** - soap opera which recently featured episodes filmed in the Norfolk Broads.

**Jonathan Creek (BBC)** - one of the episodes from the first series of this comedy drama was filmed in Suffolk at The Bell pub in Middleton, and at locations in Wangford and Wrentham.

**Kavanagh QC (ITV)** - courtroom drama starring John Thaw. Scenes shot at Norwich in Norfolk.

**Keeping up Appearances (BBC)** - comedy series which in 1995 filmed scenes in Gt. Yarmouth.

**Love on a Branch Line (BBC)** - nostalgic drama, filmed at Oxburgh Hall, nr. Oxborough and on the North Norfolk Railway at Sheringham, both in Norfolk.

**Lovejoy (BBC)** - based on the books by Essex writer Jonathan Gash, this comedy drama was set around the adventures of antiques rogue 'Lovejoy' played by Ian McShane. Filmed throughout Suffolk including Bury St. Edmunds, Hadleigh, Kersey, Lindsey, Lavenham, Long Melford and Pin Mill. Felsham Hall (home of Lady Jane) can be found in the village of Belchamp Walter.

**Martin Chuzzlewit (BBC)** - classic Dicken's tale brought to life in 1996, and filmed in the town of King's Lynn in Norfolk (which was designed to represent London at the time).

**The Mill on the Floss (BBC)** - latest adaptation filmed at Bintree Mill, nr. Dereham in Norfolk.

**The Moonstone (BBC)** - costume drama, filmed at Heydon and Elveden Hall's in Norfolk.

**P.D. James Mysteries (ITV)** - drama series based on the novels written by East Anglian writer P.D. James, and featuring detective Adam Dalglish. Filmed throughout Norfolk and Suffolk, including the coastline, Norfolk Broads, Norwich and Ipswich.

**September Song (ITV)** - comedy drama starring Russ Abbot. Filmed at Cromer in Norfolk.

**The Uninvited (ITV)** - sci-fi drama starring Leslie Grantham, and filmed throughout Norfolk

**Vanity Fair (BBC)** - the latest adaptation of William Thackeray's tale. Filmed in Norfolk at Rainthorpe Hall, nr. Flordon; Barningham Hall, nr. Holt and Thelveton Hall, nr. Diss. These three though will appear on screen as one property, the grand Elizabethan Queens Crawley.

## Bedfordshire, Essex and Hertfordshire

Hertfordshire - Britain's very own Hollywood
The town of Borehamwood is home to several famous studios. The historic Neptune Studio opened in 1914, and over the years has seen many different owners. In the 1960's it became ATV Television, home of The Saint, The Persuaders and Robin Hood, plus big entertainment specials with Shirley Bassey and Tom Jones. In the 1980's the studio was sold to the BBC and became their Elstree Centre, home to Top of the Pops, Grange Hill, and the set of Eastenders.

The British National Studios, built in 1926 are home to over 500 famous feature films, with hundreds of well-known stars passing through its gates. Today they are owned by Hertsmere Borough Council. Recent productions have included:- Jane Eyre (ITV), My Summer with Des (BBC), Kavanagh QC (ITV) and Watch that Man (1996) starring Bill Murray. Some of the famous films to come out of the studios at Borehamwood include:- Star Wars, The Empire Strikes Back, Return of the Jedi, Raiders of the Lost Ark, Indiana Jones and the Last Crusade, 2001: A Space Odyssey, Get Carter, Monty Python's Meaning of Life and The Dambusters.

Leavesden Studios at Abbots Langley (just off the M25) are Britain's most exciting new film-making complex. Here a former wartime plane factory and airfield, once owned by Rolls Royce, has been transformed into over one million square feet of studio space and over hundred acres of back lot. The James Bond adventure 'Goldeneye' was filmed here, and more recently George Lucas filmed the first in the new prequel to the original Star Wars trilogy.
Coming soon.... in 2004, Leavesden will open a major film-based tourist attraction with a studio tour and entertainment centre, allowing us all to experience the magic of the movies.

## Film

**Batman (1990)** - directed by Tim Burton, and starring Jack Nicholson and Michael Keaton. Wayne Manor in the film was Knebworth House in Herts.

**Boston Kickout (1998)** - film shot on location in Stevenage, Herts.

**Chitty Chitty Bang Bang (1968)** - classic family film, scenes were filmed at Cardington in Beds.

*Mill on the Floss-*
*'Maggie' Emily Watson*

**Clockwork Mice (1995)** - starring Art Malik and Ian Hart. Shot at Chipping Ongar in Essex.

**Empire of the Sun (1987)** - directed by Steven Spielberg. Scenes shot at Luton Hoo in Beds.

**Eyes Wide Shut (1999)** - forthcoming film directed by Stanley Kubrick, starring Tom Cruise and Nicole Kidman. Partly filmed at Woburn Abbey in Beds.

**The Fourth Protocol (1987)** - starring Michael Caine and Pierce Brosnan. Shot in Essex at Colchester and Chelmsford (where there is a memorable car chase scene).

**First Knight (1995)** - romantic King Arthur adventure with Sean Connery and Richard Gere. Scenes were filmed at the Ashridge Estate and the Abbey Church of St. Albans in Herts.

**Four Weddings and a Funeral (1994)** - romantic comedy, with scenes shot at Luton Hoo in Beds, and at St. Clement's Church, West Thurrock in Essex.

**GoldenEye (1995)** - James Bond adventure, filmed at Leavesden Studios in Herts. Scenes were also shot at Stansted Airport in Essex.

**The Great Escape (1963)** - classic wartime drama. Scenes were filmed at Luton Hoo in Beds.

**Haunted Honeymoon (1986)** - comedy with Gene Wilder. Filmed at Knebworth House in Herts.

**Killing Dad** - starring Richard E. Grant. Filmed at the Pier and Palace Hotels in Southend, Essex.

**Lair of the White Worm (1988)** - Ken Russell film shot at Knebworth House in Herts.

**Merlin (1999)** - film set in AD800, and partially shot at the Ashridge Estate in Herts.

**Never Say Never Again (1983)** - James Bond film with scenes shot at Luton Hoo in Beds.

**Peter's Friends (1992)** - directed by Kenneth Branagh, and filmed at Wrotham Park in Herts.

**Princess Caraboo (1994)** - scenes shot at both Luton Hoo in Beds and Wrotham Park in Herts.

*Jonathan Creek-*
*Caroline Quentin and Alan Davies.*

**Saving Private Ryan (1998)** - directed by Steven Spielberg, this wartime epic was shot on vast sets constructed on the former British Aerospace facility at Hatfield in Herts.

**Those Magnificent Men in their Flying Machines** - classic film which used many of the planes now displayed at The Shuttleworth Collection, Old Warden in Beds.

**Tomorrow Never Dies (1997)** - James Bond adventure shot at Frogmore Studio's, nr. St. Albans.

**The Wings of the Dove (1997)** - drama by Henry James. Filmed at Luton Hoo in Beds.

## Television

**The Alchemist (Channel 5)** - four part thriller filmed at Leavesden Studios and in Herts.

**Brothers in Trouble (BBC)** - screen two film shot at Clacton and Mistley Quay in Essex.

**Bugs (BBC)** - hi-tech adventure series which filmed at locations throughout Herts.

**The Canterville Ghost (ITV)** - two versions of this tale have been filmed at Knebworth House in Herts. The most recent starring comedian Rik Mayall.

**Eastenders (BBC)** - soap opera, filmed at the BBC Elstree Studios in Borehamwood, Herts. Storylines are sometimes filmed at outside locations, such as Shenley (Michelle and Lofty's marriage) and Watford (where Arthur Fowler is buried). In Essex, both Southend-on-Sea and Clacton-on-Sea have featured in past episodes.

**Hi-de-Hi (BBC)** - comedy series centred around Maplin's Holiday Camp. Scenes for the show were filmed on the Essex Sunshine Coast at Dovercourt.

**Ivanhoe (BBC)** - classic tale, filmed at Hedingham Castle, Castle Hedingham in Essex.

**Jane Eyre (ITV)** - the recent adaptation of this story, filmed scenes at Knebworth House in Herts.

**Jonathan Creek (BBC)** - comedy drama. One episode featured Stansted Airport in Essex.

**Lady Chatterley (BBC)** - recent version of D.H. Lawrence novel, shot at Wrotham Park in Herts.

**Lovejoy (BBC)** - based on the books by Essex writer Jonathan Gash, this comedy drama was set around the adventures of antiques rogue 'Lovejoy' played by Ian McShane. Filmed throughout Essex including Braintree, Chelmsford, Coggeshall, Colchester, Finchingfield, Gosfield Hall, Halstead, Hedingham Castle, Ingatestone Hall, Kelvedon, Layer Marney Tower, Maldon, Moyns Park, Saffron Walden, Thaxted and Wakes Colne.

**Pie in the Sky (BBC)** - the restaurant exterior used can be found at Hemel Hempstead Old Town.

**Playing the Field (BBC)** - drama about a woman's football team, filmed in the Herts area.

**Plotlands (BBC)** - drama filmed at Wivenhoe in Essex.

**Porridge (BBC)** - classic comedy set in Slade Prison, and starring Ronnie Barker. The opening shot features the gatehouse of the old prison in Victoria Road, St. Albans in Herts.

**Sharpe's Regiment (ITV)** - starring Sean Bean. Scenes filmed at Tilbury Fort in Essex.

**Some Mothers do have em' (BBC)** - classic comedy, with scenes filmed at Short Street in Bedford, Beds.

**Trial and Retribution II (ITV)** - Lynda La Plante drama filmed in South Herts.

# Cambridgeshire & Lincolnshire

There are fascinating stories from the past to discover through the historic cities and towns in these parts. The stories of Oliver Cromwell, and of the Pilgrim Fathers, and the poetry of Alfred Lord Tennyson will emerge through your explorations of this part of England.

There are attractive areas of countryside too, including the unusual landscape of *Fenland* with its rich peaty soil, waterways and ingenious drainage system, the gentle hills of the *Lincolnshire Wolds*, and the coastline with its mixture of wild beauty and sandy beaches. Let's begin with a look at the cities and towns and their rich history.

*Left: Hemingford Abbots, Cambridgeshire*
*Below: Grantchester, Cambridgeshire*

## Cambridge – University City

The river and the Roman road made *Cambridge* an important settlement and market from early times and the mound built by William the Conqueror for his castle still survives. The city is famous for its university which was established in the 13th century, and for connections with many famous people including sixty-two Nobel prize winners, thirteen prime ministers and nine archbishops of Canterbury!

The first college was founded in 1284, and other colleges including Kings and Trinity were built in medieval times. Kings College Chapel is a place of great beauty, with fabulous carved woodwork and a bold fan-vaulted ceiling. It is interesting to visit, particularly if you have the chance to attend a service or concert. The 'Backs' (at the back of the colleges) are lush and green and a peaceful place to wander as a break from shopping. You can try your hand at punting here - or hire a chauffeur to do the hard work for you!

*continued*

## contents

# CAMBRIDGE

When in Cambridge, make the most of your visit, join a
Walking Tour accompanied by a Blue Badge Guide.

Tours leaves the Tourist Information Centre daily
throughout the year.

For further information or details regarding the special
arrangements necessary for groups.

Please contact:

The Tourist Information Centre
Wheeler Street
Cambridge CB2 3QB
Tel: (01223) 322640/457574
Fax: (01223) 457588

Few cathedrals in England are as awe inspiring as *Lincoln* Cathedral and none so

### Two Fine Cathedrals

spectacularly placed. Approaching *Lincoln* from any direction, the sight of the Cathedral on the hill is unforgettable. There are many unforgettable buildings too, and a good way to see everything, and to discover the city's history, is to follow the Heritage trail. This takes you to the Cathedral and castle, and remains of the Bishops Palace, as well as the aptly named Steep Hill with shops and eating places. A river cruise will show you Lincoln at a more leisurely pace.

*Peterborough* combines old and new so well that its cathedral is right at its heart, in the midst of the shopping area and next door neighbour to the excellent Queensgate shopping centre. There are plenty of leisure and sporting facilities to enjoy.

The third cathedral of this area is *Ely* - a masterpiece of building skill, and such a

### Cromwell Country

landmark standing out on the Fenland skyline that it is known as the "ship of the Fens". It would have been a familiar sight to Oliver Cromwell, who spent most of his life in this part of the world.

This year we celebrate the 400th anniversary of the birth of this famous statesman whose career began as Member of Parliament for Cambridge in 1640. He fought at the outbreak of the Civil War two years later, rising through the ranks to become second in command of the new Parliamentary Army. In 1653, he was declared Lord Protector, the most powerful man in the land, and King in all but name. How much of the area which he knew so well would Cromwell recognise today? He would be surprised to come back to *Ely*, to recognise his family home imaginatively restored and furnished to show his life and times, complete with the sounds and smells of the period. He would be even more surprised to join visitors on a favourite riverside walk where the view of the Cathedral is unchanged, but the to and fro of pleasure cruisers would be a most unexpected novelty.

*Huntingdon*, nearby, is his birthplace, and if he visited the Cromwell Museum he would find many of his personal belongings as exhibits, as well as portraits of himself and his family. The ancestral home, Hinchingbrook House, is on the outskirts of *Huntingdon* and is open to the public. He would also be familiar with *St Ives*, notable

now for its stone bridge with bridge chapel which provided a religious retreat for weary travellers and is one of only three remaining in the country.

*Stamford* still retains its medieval street pattern, so has an attractive mix of narrow

### Scene set for Drama

passageways and cobbled streets opening into more spacious squares. There are many fine medieval and Georgian buildings, and indeed many streets and squares have no 20th century buildings, or even Victorian ones. For this reason *Stamford* was chosen as the location for the costume drama "Middlemarch", where with modern street lamps, road signs and aerials removed, the town took on a convincing 18th century appearance. If you need a rest from architecture, relax by the river. The water meadows are right in the centre of town.

The town of *Gainsborough* has stories to tell. It was here in the medieval Old Hall,

### Passionate beliefs

that Henry VIII met Catherine Parr, his sixth and final wife. And in the same Old Hall, the Pilgrim Fathers met to worship in the early days when passionate beliefs led to the formation of

*continued*

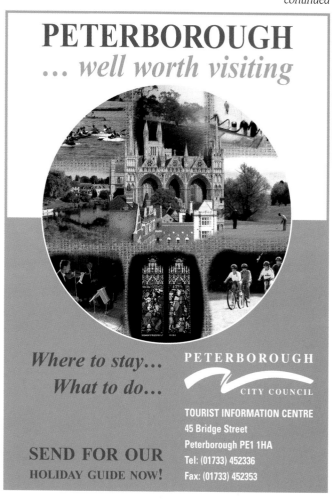

# LINCOLNSHIRE

## SHORT BREAKS
Heritage towns, picturesque villages, rural peace and unspoilt countryside.

## SHOP WITH STYLE
Speciality Foods, the Best Places to Eat and Shop, Antiques, Crafts and Market Days.

## LINCOLN AND STAMFORD
One of England's great historic cities and "the best stone town in England".

## GARDENS AND NURSERIES
Stately gardens, specialist nurseries and over 100 private gardens to visit.

*TELEPHONE NOW FOR YOUR FREE BROCHURES - 01522 526450*

☐ *Holiday Guide*

☐ *Shop with Style*

☐ *Lincoln City Short Breaks*

☐ *Countrylife Short Breaks*

☐ *Gardens and Nurseries*

☐ *Places to Visit*

Name

Address

Post Code

**Send to Lincolnshire Tourism, Dept EETB, Lincoln Castle, Lincoln, LN1**

their Separatist religion, some 40 years before the "Mayflower" took them out to colonise America.

This determined and principled group of people believed that the simple faith of Christ had been corrupted by the Church of England. To escape persecution they fled to Holland, but a first attempt at flight resulted in betrayal and trial at *Boston* and *Lincoln*. The Boston Guildhall is now open as a museum and you can see the cells where the men were imprisoned.

In 1620, after several years in Holland, 40 pilgrims and 66 other sectarians braved the 67 day journey in the small crowded "Mayflower" to establish a new way of life in North America. Some of the pilgrim leaders are now well respected figures in American history.

There's character to be found in many of the towns in this area, - far too many to mention each one. Four

### Towns of Character

market towns worth visiting are *Horncastle*, noted for antique shops, *Sleaford* with many fine buildings and the site of a medieval castle, and *Alford* with its thatched manor house and five sailed windmill, as well as *Brigg*, known through Percy Grainger's setting of the folk song "Brigg Fair".

*Grantham*, once a coaching town on the Great North Road, is built of red brick and stone and has many surviving old inns from these times. *St Neots* too, was on the Great North Road, and its handsome rectangular market place and surviving coaching inns and hostelries are a reminder of this important time in the life of the town which originally grew up around a Benedictine Priory.

*Ramsey* was built around a Benedictine Abbey too, and part of the Abbey Gatehouse can be seen today. *Crowland* is known for

*Steep Hill, Lincoln, Lincolnshire*

its medieval abbey and the curious triangular bridge, but *Whittlesey's* fame is even more curious - it is the strange tradition of the Straw Bear Festival for which this town is known!

The chalk hills of the *Lincolnshire Wolds* may come as a surprise if you believe that this

### Climb those Hills!

area is all flat. The gentle hilly countryside with its spectacular views far across the county, is good territory for walkers and cyclists. Indeed, riders on the long distance *Hull* to *Harwich* cycle route will travel right through the Wolds. The market town of *Louth* with lovely Georgian architecture is set on the edge of the *Wolds*, and just south, the Edwardian Spa resort of *Woodhall Spa* is pleasantly surrounded by pine and birch woodland.

There's good cycling too, at the water playgrounds of *Grafham Water* and *Rutland Water*, as well as windsurfing, sailing,

*Lincoln Castle, Lincolnshire*

*Cambridgeshire ● Lincolnshire*

fishing, nature trails and more. *Rutland Water* is the largest man made lake in Europe, covering a huge 3,100 acres.

We should mention Lord Alfred Tennyson before we leave the *Wolds*, as he was born here, at *Somersby*, and most of his childhood was spent in the Wolds. His poem "The Brook" is loosely based on the stream that passes through his home village, and just down the road is Harrington Hall where "Maud" was invited to "come into the garden". Tennyson also stayed at *Mablethorpe* on occasions. In *Lincoln*, a statue of him with his wolfhound stands outside the chapter house at the Cathedral.

*Fenland* is a uniquely special part of England. Before the *Fens* were drained, this

## Misty Marshes, Web-footed Folk and Witches

was a different world of misty marshes and bogs. Of small islands, inhabited by strange independent folk, their livelihood the fish and wildfowl of this eerie, watery place. There are legends of web-footed people, of ghosts and witchcraft.

Today's *Fen* landscape is the result of man's determination to tame the wet wilderness and create more farmland. Ever since Domesday, attempts have been made to gradually reclaim the land. In the early 17th century Dutch experts were called in to help, and Cornelius Vermuyden undertook the greatest scheme, constructing the Old and New Bedford Rivers which stretch across the Fens for 21 miles.

Drainage schemes continued, but unexpectedly the land began to shrink at an alarming rate as the soil dried out. As the level of the land dropped, water could no longer drain into the rivers which were by now higher than the fields. Windpumps were introduced to pump water off the land and into the rivers but their reliance on adequate wind and continued shrinkage of the land saw the task become increasingly difficult. It was not until steam power was introduced in the 1820's that the *Fens* were effectively drained.

Today the *Fens* have a sophisticated network of drains, embankments and pumps to protect the land from the ever present threat of rain and tide. To see how the fen landscape would have looked before modern drainage, come to *Wicken Fen*, managed by the National Trust to preserve the native flora and fauna. Here you will also see the last example of a Fen windpump - once these dominated the skyline in their hundreds.

*Fenland* has many habitats for wildlife. Along the coastal marshes of the *Wash*, the Peter Scott Walk, the Gedney Drove End and Frampton Marsh Nature Reserves all provide opportunities for birdwatching and the quiet contemplation of nature. Inland the creation of the Old and New Bedford Rivers left an area between known at the *Ouse Washes*, a unique wetland environment of international significance. The wildfowl and wetland plants of this area can best be appreciated from the excellent reserves at *Welney* and *Welches Dam*.

The draining of the *Fens* in the 17th and 18th centuries created rich areas of

## Towns prosper

farmland and brought great trade and prosperity to the *Fenland* towns. The fine Georgian architecture of *Wisbech* is testimony to this wealth. The North Brink, the Crescent and Museum Square must be among the finest examples of Georgian street architecture in the country.

The River Welland flows through the peaceful town of *Spalding* and to either side of it are grand Georgian buildings. Also beside the river is the restored medieval manor house of Ayscoughfee Hall, now a museum and Tourist Information Centre. The town is now renowned as the centre of Britain's flower and bulb industry, celebrated every year in the famous Spalding Flower Parade.

*Boston* has long traditions as a port as well as the tallest working windmill in Britain, and the easily recognised landmark, the 'Boston Stump' tower of St Botolph's church. In March, the impressive church of St Wendreda has a breathtaking roof of flying angels.

## Jolly Good Fun

There are wide, safe, sandy beaches along the length of the coast where children can paddle, build sandcastles and enjoy donkey rides.

The three traditional resorts have all the attractions and entertainment you would expect. *Skegness* has six miles of sandy beach, two fun fairs, gardens and golf courses. It is known for its "Jolly Fisherman" character who originated on a railway poster of 1908 and has been used to promote the town ever since.

*Cleethorpes* is a long established family resort, famous for its miles of clean golden sands, beautiful parks and restful gardens. From here there are fine views of shipping entering the Humber, much of it destined for neighbouring *Grimsby*, which has one of the largest fish markets in the country. Go behind the scenes on a fish market tour and try the best fish and chips around!

*Mablethorpe* is a lively resort with plenty of childrens' activities to keep everyone amused. Take a trip along the beach on the sand train or ride the road train - or try out the excellent range of sporting facilities in the town.

Quieter resorts include *Sutton on Sea*, *Chapel St Leonard's* and *Ingoldmells*. Here you will find sandy beaches, gardens and attractions set against the village atmosphere of these smaller towns.

The Lincolnshire coastline is not so lively that it does not have space and quiet places for birds such as shelduck and short eared owls that nest in watery slacks behind the dunes at places like *Gibraltar Point*. Sand dune plants flourish too, and the natterjack toad is quite at home in these parts.

*Centre of Cambridge, Cambridgeshire*

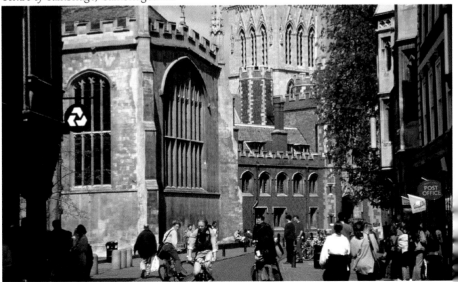

# Tourist Information Centres

With so much to see and do in this area, it's impossible for us to mention all of the places you can visit. You will find Tourist Information Centres (TICs) throughout Cambridgeshire and Lincolnshire, with plenty of information on all the things that you can do and the places you can visit. TICs can book accommodation for you in their own area, or further afield using the 'Book A Bed Ahead Scheme'. They can be the ideal place to purchase locally made crafts or gifts, as well as books covering a wide range of local interests. A list of the TICs in this area can be found below together with a map reference to help you locate them.

\* Not open all year.

## Cambridgeshire

**Cambridge**, Wheeler Street,
Tel: (01223) 322640 *(K/L23/24)*
**Ely**, Oliver Cromwell's House,
29 St Mary's Street,
Tel: (01353) 662062 *(M20)*
**Huntingdon**, The Library, Princes Street,
Tel: (01480) 388588 *(I21)*
**Peterborough**, 45 Bridge Street,
Tel: (01733) 452336 *(H18)*
**St Neots**, The Old Court, 8 New Street,
Tel: (01480) 388788 *(H23)*
**Wisbech**, 2-3 Bridge Street,
Tel: (01945) 583263 *(L16/17)*

## Lincolnshire

\* **Alford**, Manor House Museum,
West Street, Tel: (01507) 462143 *(L8)*
**Boston**, The Market Place,
Tel: (01205) 356656 *(J12)*
**Brigg**, The Buttercross, Market Place,
Tel: (01652) 657053 *(E/F3/4)*
\* **Horncastle**, Trinity Centre, Spilsby Road,
Tel: (01507) 526636 *(I/J9/10)*
**Lincoln**, 9 Castle Hill, Tel: (01522) 529828
*(I8)*
**Louth**, The New Market Hall,
off Cornmarket, Tel: (01507) 609289 *(J6)*
**Mablethorpe**, Dunes Family
Entertainment, Central Promenade,
Tel: (01507) 472496 *(L6)*
**Skegness**, Embassy Centre, Grand Parade,
Tel: (01754) 764821 *(M9)*
**Spalding**, Ayscoughfee Hall, Churchgate,
Tel: (01775) 725468 *(I15)*
\* **Woodhall Spa**, The Cottage Museum,
Iddesleigh Road, Tel: (01526) 353775 *(H9)*

## Blue Badge Guides:

There are also experts available to help you explore some of our towns and cities. These Registered Blue Badge Guides have all attended a training course sponsored by the East of England Tourist Board. Below are some of the tours offered by these Guides - you can obtain further information by contacting the appropriate Tourist Information Centre, unless otherwise indicated. Some Blue Badge Guides have a further qualification to take individuals or groups around the region for half day, full day or longer tours if required.

## Cambridgeshire

### Cambridge
**Regular Walking Tours:** Individual visitors may join tours which leave the Tourist Information Centre daily and up to 4 times a day in summer. Colleges are included as available: not those which charge admission.

**City Centre Tours:** These tours do not go into the colleges, but explore the street scenes and the historic past of the city. Evening drama tours take place during mid-summer.

**Group Tours:** Guides can be booked at any time for private groups, except Christmas Day. Tours last one or two hours, extensions are possible. One guide can escort up to 20 people. Some guides are trained to accompany groups throughout the East of England; many speak languages other than English. For bookings and enquiries contact us by telephone (01223) 457574) or fax (01223) 457588.

**College Tours for Groups:** All parties of 10 or more who intend to tour the colleges, should be accompanied by a Cambridge registered Blue Badge Guide. Colleges which charge admission are only included on request (cost added to tour price). Most colleges are closed to the public during University examination time, mid Apr-end Jun.

### Ely
**Cathedral and City Tours and City only Tours:** Guides available for pre-booked groups all year. Tours can include the cathedral and city or Oliver Cromwell's House.

**Oliver Cromwell's House: Tours and Visits:** Available for pre-booked groups all year round. Evening tours can be arranged. Special rate for school parties.

**Ghost Tours and Alternative Ely Tours:** With costumed guides can be arranged. Please telephone: (01353) 662062.

### Peterborough
**Group Tours:** Guides are available for city and cathedral tours at any time for private groups, each tour lasts approximately one and a half hours. Contact the Tourist Information Centre. Tel: (01733) 452336.

## Lincolnshire

Pre-bookable tours for Lincolnshire, including Lincoln. Contact: Pearl Wheatley, Tel: (01522) 595114.

### Stamford
**Regular Town Tours:** These are held periodically during the summer season. Details available from the Tourist Information Centre.

**Group Tours:** Guided tours can be arranged for groups by contacting the Blue Badge Guide direct on Tel: (01780) 410780.

*Royal Oak, Aubourn,
Lincolnshire*

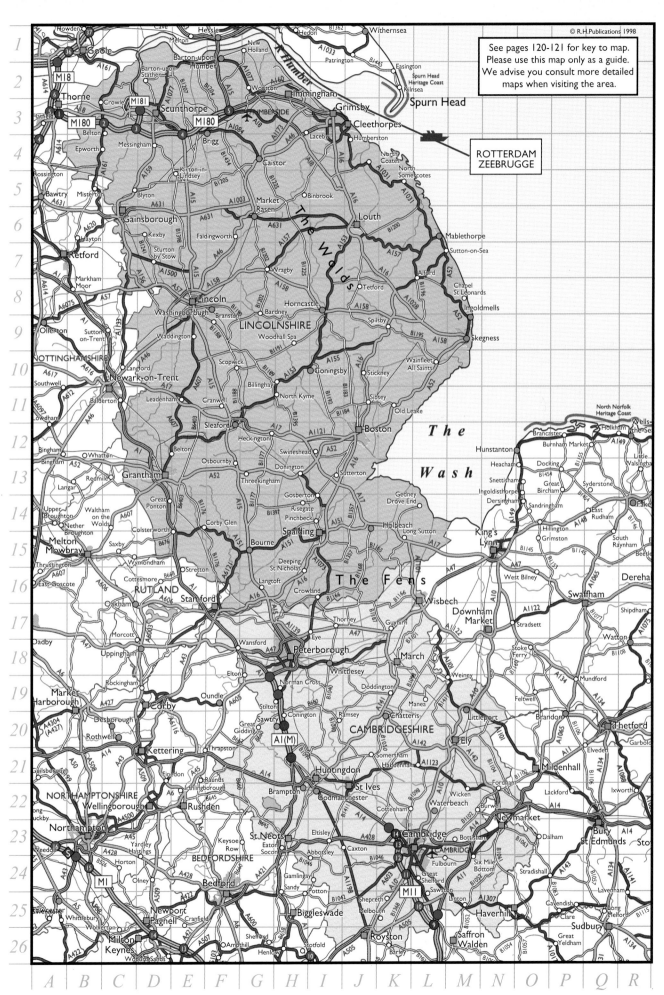

© R.H.Publications 1998

See pages 120-121 for key to map.
Please use this map only as a guide.
We advise you consult more detailed
maps when visiting the area.

ROTTERDAM
ZEEBRUGGE

The Imperial War Museum is Europe's top aviation museum and it has over 120 historic aircraft, many in flying condition. It is appropriate that it is in this part of England which has such a long association with flying, dating right back to the First World War when this was the base for many military aerodromes. During the Second World War, again this became home to many bomber squadrons, the best known being the famous Dambuster Squadron based at Woodhall Spa. In the village, visitors will see the memorial appropriately made in the shape of a dam. There are RAF airfields still operating from this part of England and at RAF Coningsby, at the Battle of Britain Memorial Flight Visitor Centre, you may see the famous and unique Lancaster Bomber. The home of the Red Arrows is here too, so look out for them flying overhead.

Wind power has always been valued here, and many windmills are open to view. You might think of windmills as having four sails, but here you can see mills with six sails, eight sails, or even five sails.

To better understand the ecology and ingenious feats of engineering used in draining the Fens, visit some of our local museums which explain this clearly. Pinchbeck Engine and Land Drainage Museum at Spalding, despite its unromantic name, does make interesting viewing.

This area has relied heavily on the sea for food, and at Grimsby's National Fishing Heritage Centre, your respect for trawlermen will be sealed for ever when you experience the feel of the icy deck beneath your feet, hear the roar of the engines, and witness the awful conditions of life at sea.

*historic houses*

# Cambridgeshire

### Arrington
### ⊚ Wimpole Hall and Home Farm
The National Trust Tel: (01223) 207257
An 18thC house in a landscaped park with a folly, Chinese bridge, plunge bath and yellow drawing room in the house, the work of John Soane. Home Farm has a rare breeds centre. *Please contact for details of opening times. Hall: £5.70/£2.50/£5.70. (J24/25)*

### Elton
### ⊚ Elton Hall
Tel: (01832) 280468
An historic house and gardens open to the public with a fine collection of paintings, furniture, books and Henry VIII's prayer book. There is also a restored rose garden. *Open 30, 31 May, Sun, Bank Hol Mon, 1400-1700; 2-30 Jun, Wed, 1400-1700; 1 Jul-30 Aug, Wed, Thu, Sun, Bank Hol Mon, 1400-1700. House and Garden: £4.50/free/£4.50. (G18/19)*

### Ely
### ⊚ Oliver Cromwell's House
29 St Marys Street Tel: (01353) 662062
The family home of Oliver Cromwell with a 17thC kitchen, parlour, a 'haunted bedroom', a Tourist Information Centre, souvenirs and a craft shop. *Open 2 Jan-31 Mar, Mon-Sat, 1000-1700; 1 Apr-30 Sep, daily, 1000-1730; 1 Oct-31 Dec, Mon-Sat, 1000-1700; closed 25, 26 Dec, 1 Jan. £2.50/£2.10/£2.10. (M20)*

### Godmanchester
### ⊚ Island Hall
Tel: (0171) 491 3724
A mid-18thC mansion of architectural importance on the Great Ouse river. A family home with interesting ancestral possessions. *Open 4, 11, 18, 25 Jul, Sun, 1430-1700; last admission 1630. £3.50/£2.00/£3.50. (I22)*

### Huntingdon
### Hinchingbrooke House
Brampton Road Tel: (01480) 451121
A large country house with its origins in a 12thC nunnery. It was the home of the Cromwell family and the Earls of Sandwich. *Open 2 May-29 Aug, Sun, 1400-1700. £2.00/£1.00/£1.00. (H22)*

### Kimbolton
### Kimbolton Castle
Tel: (01480) 860505
A Tudor house, remodelled by Vanburgh with Pelligrini mural paintings, an Adam gatehouse and fine parklands. The Castle is now occupied by an independent school. *Open 4, 5 Apr, 30, 31 May, 25 Jul, 1, 8, 15, 22, 29, 30 Aug, 1400-1800. £2.50/£1.50/£1.50. (G22)*

*Oliver Cromwell's House, Ely, Cambridgeshire*

### Lode
### ⊚ Anglesey Abbey
Gardens and Lode Mill
Tel: (01223) 811200
A 13thC abbey with a later Tudor house and the famous Fairhaven collection of paintings and furniture. There is also an outstanding 100-acre garden and arboretum. *Please contact for details of opening times. House and Gardens: (Wed-Sat) £6.00/£3.00/£6.00. (M23)*

### Wisbech
### ⊚ Peckover House
North Brink Tel: (01945) 583463
A merchant's house on the north brink of the River Nene, built in 1722 with a plaster and wood rococo interior and a notable and rare Victorian garden with unusual trees. *Open 29 Mar-2 Nov, Wed, Sat, Sun, Bank Hol Mon, 1230-1700; Gardens only, Mon, Tue, 1230-1700. House and Garden: £3.50/£1.50/£3.50. (L16/17)*

*Cambridgeshire* ● *Lincolnshire*

# Lincolnshire

### Aubourn
**Aubourn Hall**
Tel: (01522) 788270
A beautiful redbrick manor-house, built about 1600 and attributed to the architect J Smythson Junior with a unique carved oak staircase and panelled rooms. *Open 7, 14, 21, 28 Jul, 4, 11, 18, 25 Aug, 1400-1730; see local press for details. £2.50/free/£2.00. (D9)*

### Billinghay
**Billinghay Cottage**
(The Old Vicarage), Bridge Street
A 'mud and stud' thatched cottage, dating from 1650 with a display of old village photographs. *Please contact for details of opening times. (G/H10)*

### Boston
**Fydell House, South Square**
Tel: (01205) 351520
A small town house, built before 1720 and occupied by members of the Fydell family, prosperous 18thC merchants and local politicians, with a fine 18thC staircase. *Open all year, Mon-Fri, 0930-1230, 1330-1630 during university term time. (J12)*

### Doddington
**Doddington Hall**
Tel: (01522) 694308
An Elizabethan mansion, gatehouse and walled gardens with good furniture, pictures, porcelain and textiles. The gardens are an exceptional feature with spring bulbs. *Open Gardens 7 Mar-25 Apr, Sun, 1400-1800; House and Gardens 5 May-29 Sep, Wed, Sun, Bank Hol Mon, 1400-1800. £3.80/£1.90/£3.80. (D8)*

### Fulbeck
**Fulbeck Hall**
Tel: (01400) 272205
The Fane family home since 1632. The house is mainly 18thC with alterations and additions, furniture, pictures and items from India and the Far East and 11 acres of gardens. *Open 4-7, 11-14 Apr, 3-5, 31 May, 3-7, 12-14, 19-21, 25-28 Jul, 1400-1700; 30 Aug, 1400-1700. £3.50/£1.50/£3.00. (E11)*

### Gainsborough
**Gainsborough Old Hall**
Parnell Street Tel: (01427) 612669
A late medieval timber-framed manor-house, built about 1460 with a fine medieval kitchen and many special events held throughout the year. *Open 2 Jan-27 Mar, Mon-Sat, 1000-1700; 29 Mar-31 Oct, Mon-Sat, 1000-1700; Sun, 1400-1730; 26 Oct-31 Dec, Mon-Sat, 1000-1700; closed 2 Apr, 25, 26 Dec. £2.50/£1.00/£1.50. (C6)*

### Grimsthorpe
**Grimsthorpe Castle**
Tel: (01778) 591205
The Castle covers 4 periods of architecture with a collection of portraits and furniture which are mainly 18thC. *Open 4 Apr-26 Sep, Thu, Sun, Bank Hol; 3-31 Aug, Sun-Thu, Park, 1100-1800; Castle and Gardens, 1300-1700; last admission 1630. £3.00/£1.50/ £2.00. (F15)*

### Harlaxton
**Harlaxton Manor**
Tel: (01476) 564541
Historic garden restored by TV gardener Alan Mason. Formal gardens built on seven levels with Italian, French and Dutch features surround 'Fairytale' Harlaxton Manor (not open). Six acre walled garden with show gardens. *Please contact for details of opening times. £4.00/£2.00/£3.50. (D13)*

### Lincoln
**Lincoln Guildhall**
The Stonebow, Saltergate
Tel: (01522) 526454
The Guildhall has a fine open timber roof with carved bosses of the 15th and 16thC. The civic insignia include Richard II and Henry VII swords, maces and a cap of maintenance. *Open 2 Jan, 6 Feb, 6 Mar, 3, 18 Apr, 1, 16, 31 May, 5, 20 Jun, 3, 18 Jul, 7, 22, 30 Aug, 4, 26 Sep, 2 Oct, 6 Nov, 4, 11, 12 Dec, guided tours, 1030, 1330. (E8)*

### Normanby
**Normanby Hall**
Tel: (01724) 720588
A Regency mansion by Sir Robert Smirke, architect of the British Museum, furnished and decorated in period with displays of costumes. *Open all year, daily, 0900-1700; Hall and Farming Museum, 1 Apr-30 Sep, 1300-1700; Walled Garden, daily, 1100-1700. Please contact for details of admission prices. (D2)*

### Stamford
**Browne's Hospital**
Broad Street Tel: (01780) 51226
A museum of almshouse life, founded around 1483 by William Browne, wool merchant. *Open 8 May-26 Sep, Sat, Sun, Bank Hol Mon, 1100-1600. £1.50/50p/£1.00. (F17)*

### Stamford
**Burghley House**
Tel: (01780) 752451
The largest and grandest house of the first Elizabethan age. Built between 1565 and 1587, it features fine paintings tapestries, ceramics and works of art. *Open 1 Apr-4 Oct, daily, 1100-1630. Please contact for details. (F17)*

### Tattershall
**Tattershall College**
Off Market Place.
Built in the mid-15thC by the builder of Tattershall Castle, Ralph, Lord Cromwell, as a grammar school for the church choristers. The building is now a ruin. *Open all year, daily, 1000-1700; please phone to confirm. (H10)*

*Burghley House, Stamford, Lincolnshire.*

# Ancient Monuments

## Cambridgeshire

### Cambridge
**Kings College Chapel**
Kings College
Tel: (01223) 331100
The chapel, founded by Henry VI includes the breathtaking fan-vault ceiling, stained glass windows, a carved oak screen and Ruben's masterpiece 'The Adoration of the Magi'. *Please contact for details. £3.00/£2.00/£3.00. (K/L23/24)*

### Coton
**Cambridge American Cemetery**
Tel: (01954) 210350
A cemetery with a visitor reception for information, the graves area and a memorial chapel, operated and maintained by The American Battle Monuments Commission. *Open 1 Jan-15 Apr, daily, 0800-1700; 16 Apr-30 Sep, daily, 0800-1800; 1 Oct-31 Dec, daily, 0800-1700. (K23/24)*

### Chittering
**⊛ Denny Abbey**
Ely Road
Tel: (01223) 860489
The remains of a 12thC Benedictine abbey and a 14thC dining hall of a religious house. It was run as a hospital by the Knights Templar and became a Franciscan Convent in 1342. *Open 22 Mar-31 Oct, daily, 1200-1700. £3.30/£1.20/£2.40. (L22)*

### Ely
**⊛ Ely Cathedral**
Chapter House, The College
Tel: (01353) 667735
One of England's finest cathedrals with fine buildings, guided tours and tours of the Monastic Octagon and West Tower, also a brass rubbing centre and stained glass museum. *Please contact for details of opening times. £3.50/free/£3.00. (M20)*

### Fengate
**⊛ Flag Fen Bronze Age Excavations**
Fourth Drove Tel: (01733) 313414
A semi-floating visitor centre with a museum of the Bronze Age, a gift shop and cafe. There is a landscaped park with roundhouses, primitive animals and important excavations. *Open all year, daily, 1000-1700; guided tours available from 10 Apr-31 Oct; closed 25 Dec-2 Jan. £3.50/£2.50/£3.00. (H18)*

### Isleham
**⊛ Isleham Priory Church**
A rare example of an early Norman church with much 'herringbone' masonry. It has been little altered despite later conversion to a barn. *Open at any reasonable time. (N21)*

### Longthorpe
**⊛ Longthorpe Tower**
Thorpe Road Tel: (01733) 268482
The 14thC tower of a fortified manor-house with wall paintings which form the most complete set of domestic paintings of the period in northern Europe. *Open 27 Mar-31 Oct, Sat, Sun, Bank Hols, 1000-1300, 1400-1800/1800 or dusk in Oct. £1.10/60p/£1.10. (G18)*

### March
**Saint Wendreda's Church,**
Church Street Tel: (01354) 654783
This church is noted for its exceptional double hammerbeam timber roof which contains 120 carved angels. *Open all year, daily, 0900-1700; key obtainable at nearby shop which is signed on the church notice board. (K18)*

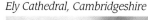

*Ely Cathedral, Cambridgeshire*

*Peterborough Cathedral, Cambridgeshire*

### Peterborough

#### ⊛ Peterborough Cathedral

Minster Precincts Tel: (01733) 343342
A Norman cathedral with an early English west front, a 13thC painted nave ceiling and the tomb of Catherine of Aragon. It was also the former burial place of Mary Queen of Scots. *Open all year, Mon-Fri, 0830-1715; Sat, 0830-1745; Sun,1200-1745. Donations requested. (H18)*

### Ramsey

#### Ramsey Abbey Gatehouse

Abbey School
Tel: (01263) 733471
The ruins of a 15thC gatehouse. *Open 1 Apr-31 Oct, daily, 1000-1700. (I20)*

### St Ives

#### Saint Ives Bridge Chapel

Bridge Street
Tel: (01480) 465101
A 15thC chapel built onto the bridge, in midstream. One of only 4 in England with a balcony over the river. *Please contact for details of opening times. (J21/22)*

### Thorney

#### Thorney Abbey Church

Tel: (01733) 270388
Abbey church with a Norman nave (c1100), a fine church organ originally built in 1787-1790 and a stained glass east window depicting the miracles of St Thomas Becket. *Open all year, daily, 1000-dusk. (I17)*

### Whittlesford

#### ⊛ Duxford Chapel

Tel: (01799) 522842
A 14thC chapel which was once part of the Hospital of St John. *Please contact key keeper Tel: (01223) 443180. (L25)*

# Lincolnshire

### Bardney

#### ⊛ The Tupholme Abbey Ruins

Off the B1190
Situated in 20 acres of grassland is the site and ruins of a 12thC Premonstratensian abbey with the refectory wall standing to eaves height and a unique reader's pulpit. There is also a picnic site. *Open all year, daily, dawn-dusk. (G8/9)*

### Crowland

#### Croyland Abbey

East Street
Tel: (01733) 210499
The preserved ruins of a large Benedictine abbey with statues on the 13thC west front. The complete north aisle serves as a parish church with a 12thC Norman arch. *Open all year, daily, 0900-dusk. (I16)*

### Grantham

#### Saint Wulfram's Parish Church

Church Street
Tel: (01476) 561342
A large parish church with a 282ft spire, a chained library, crypt chapel, 12th-15thC work, 19thC and more recent stained glass. *Open all year, Mon, Thu-Sat, 0900-1230, 1400-1730; Tue, 0900-1230; Sun, 0730-1200, 1800-2000. (D13)*

### Lincoln

#### ⊛ Lincoln Castle

Castle Hill  Tel: (01522) 511068
A medieval castle including towers and ramparts with a Magna Carta exhibition, a prison chapel experience, reconstructed Westgate and popular events throughout the summer. *Please contact for details of opening times. £2.50/£1.00/£1.50. (E8)*

### Lincoln

#### ⊛ Lincoln Cathedral

Tel: (01522) 544544
A medieval Gothic cathedral of outstanding historical and architectural merit.
*Open 1 Jan-31 May, Mon-Sat, 0715-1800; Sun, 0715-1700; 1 Jun-31 Aug, Mon-Sat, 0715-2000; Sun, 0715-1800; 1 Sep-31 Dec, Mon-Sat, 0715-1800;Sun, 0715-1700. £3.00/£1.00/£1.00. (E8)*

### Old Bolingbroke

#### ⊛ Bolingbroke Castle

The remains of a castle where Henry IV was born with excellent interpretation panels with artists' impressions and text. *Open 1 Jan-31 Mar, daily, 0900-1900; 1 Apr-30 Sep, daily, 0900-2100; 1 Oct-31 Dec, daily, 0900-1900. (J9)*

### Stow

#### Saint Mary's Church

Normanby Road
Tel: (01427) 788251
One of the most complete Saxon churches surviving in the country, founded around 975 with a 12thC chancel and one of the largest Saxon arches in the country. *Open all year, daily, 0900-dusk. (D7)*

### Tattershall

#### Collegiate Church of the Holy Trinity

Sleaford Road
Tel: (01526) 342223
Founded in 1439 by Ralph, 3rd Baron Cromwell, the Lord High Treasurer of England with an east window of priceless medieval glass and a collection of medieval brasses. *Open all year, Mon-Sat, 1000-1730; Sun, 1200-1730. (H/I10)*

*Lincoln Cathedral, Lincolnshire*

# museums &heritage Centres

## Cambridgeshire

### Burwell
**Burwell Museum Trust**
Mill Close
A rural village museum housed in a re-erected 18thC timber-framed barn with a smithy and wheelwright's shop. There are also wagon sheds with displays of wagons. *Open 11 Apr-26 Sep, Thu, Sun, Bank Hol Mon, 1400-1700. £1.50/free/£1.50. (M22)*

### Cambridge
**Cambridge and County Folk Museum**
2-3 Castle Street Tel: (01223) 355159
The building was a 16thC farmhouse. From the 17thC to 1934 it was an inn. It now houses a wide variety of objects relating to the everyday life of people in the city and country. *Open 2 Jan-31 Mar, Tue-Sat, 1030-1700; Sun, 1400-1700; 1 Apr-30 Sep, Mon-Sat, 1030-1700; Sun, 1400-1700; 1 Oct-23 Dec, Tue-Sat, 1030-1700; Sun, 1400-1700; closed 2 Apr. £2.00/50p/£1.00. (K/L23)*

### Cambridge
**Fitzwilliam Museum**
Trumpington Street Tel: (01223) 332900
A large, internationally-renowned collection of antiquities, applied arts and fine arts. The original buildings are mid-19thC with later additions. *Open all year, Tue-Sat, Bank Hol Mon, 1000-1700; Sun, 1415-1700; closed 2 Apr, 24 Dec-1 Jan. (K/L23/24)*

### Cambridge
**Kettle's Yard**
Castle Street Tel: (01223) 352124
A major collection of 20thC paintings and sculpture exhibited in a house of unique character. Also temporary contemporary art exhibitions in the gallery. *Open 2 Jan-1 Apr, Tue-Sun, 1400-1600; 11 Apr-30 Aug, Tue-Sat 1330-1630; Sun, Bank Hol Mon, 1400-1630; 1 Sep-31 Dec, Tue-Sun, 1400-1600; closed 23-26 Dec, 1 Jan. (K/L23)*

### Cambridge
**Sedgwick Museum**
Department of Earth Sciences, Downing Street Tel: (01223) 333456
A large collection of fossils from all over the world, both invertebrate and vertebrate with some mounted skeletons of dinosaurs, reptiles and mammals. *Open all year, Mon-Fri, 0900-1300, 1400-1700; Sat, 1000-1300; closed 2-5 Apr, 24 Dec-3 Jan. (K/L23/24)*

### Cambridge
**University Museum of Archaeology and Anthropology**
Downing Street Tel: (01223) 337733
Displays relating to world prehistory and local archaeology with anthropology displays. *Open all year, Tue-Fri, 1400-1600; Sat, 1000-1230; summer, Tue-Fri, 1030-1630; closed 9-15 Apr; please telephone for Christmas closing. (K/L23/24)*

### Cambridge
**Whipple Museum of the History of Science**
Free School Lane Tel: (01223) 334545
Recently designated as a museum with a pre-eminent collection. The Whipple Museum houses an extensive collection of scientific instruments and related ephemera. *Open all year, Mon-Fri, 1330-1630; please telephone to confirm during university vacations. (K/L23/24)*

### Ely
**Ely Museum**
The Old Gaol, Market Street Tel: (01353) 666655
A chronological account of the history of Ely and the Isle from prehistory to the present day. The collections consist of archaeology, social and military history. *Open all year, Tue-Sun, Bank Hol Mon, 1030-1630. £1.80/£1.25/£1.25. (M20)*

*Fitzwilliam Museum, Cambridge*

### Ely
**Stained Glass Museum**
The Cathedral Tel: (01353) 660347
A museum housing examples of stained glass from the 13thC to the present day in specially lighted display boxes with models of a modern workshop. *Open summer, Mon-Fri, 1030-1700, Sat, 1030-1730, Sun, 1200-1800; winter, Mon-Fri, 1030-1630, Sat, 1030-1700, Sun, 1200-1615; closed 2 Apr, 25 Dec. £2.50/£1.50/£1.50. (M20)*

### Fengate
**Flag Fen Bronze Age Excavations**
See Ancient Monuments Section.

### Huntingdon
**Cromwell Museum**
Grammar School Walk Tel: (01480) 375830
A museum with portraits, signed documents and other articles belonging to Cromwell and his family. *Please contact for details of opening times and admission prices. (H/I21/22)*

### March
**March and District Museum**
High Street Tel: (01354) 655300
A general collection of artefacts relating to social history, agricultural tools, many local photographs and 19thC record material and a restored blacksmith's forge. *Open all year, Wed, 1000-1200; Sat, 1030-1530; 2 May, 6 Jun, 4 Jul, 1 Aug, 5 Sep, 1430-1700; closed 22 Dec-1 Jan. (I20)*

### Peterborough
**⊛ Peterborough Museum and Art Gallery**
Priestgate Tel: (01733) 343329
Museum of local history, geology, archaeology, natural and social history, a world-famous collection of Napoleonic POW work, a period shop and many temporary exhibitions. *Open all year, Tue-Sat, 1000-1700; closed 2 Apr; 20-28 Dec. (H18)*

*Oliver Cromwell*
*Cromwell Museum, Ely, Cambridgeshire*

### Ramsey
**Ramsey Rural Museum**
The Wood Yard, Cemetary Road
Tel: (01487) 815715
Rebuilt farm buildings housing a collection of old farm implements of the Fens and Victorian life in the home. Now including a chemist's and a cobbler's shop. *Open 4 Apr-26 Sep, Thu, Sun, 1400-1700. £1.00/50p/50p. (I20)*

### St Ives
**Norris Museum**
The Broadway Tel: (01480) 465101
Museum displaying the history of Huntingdon from earliest times to the present day with fossils, archaeology, history, an art gallery and library. *Please contact for details of opening times. (J21/22)*

### St Neots
**Saint Neots Museum**
The Old Court, 8 New Street
Tel: (01480) 388788
A former police station and Magistrates' Court, now housing the local history museum. *Open 2 Jan, 20 Jan-31 Dec, Wed-Sat, 1030-1630; closed 25 Dec, 1 Jan. £1.50/75p/75p. (H23)*

### Thorney
**Thorney Heritage Museum**
Station Road Tel: (01733) 270780
Showing the development from monastic days, Walloon and Flemish influence after Vermuydens drainage; also 19thC model housing by the Duke of Bedford showing village life. *Open 3 Apr-25 Oct, Sat, Sun, 1400-1700. (I17)*

### Waterbeach
**Farmland Museum**
Denny Abbey, Ely Road
Tel: (01223) 860988
An agricultural estate since medieval times with an abbey and an interactive museum. Lots of fun for families with animal, medieval and craft events throughout the year. *Open 1 Apr-31 Oct, daily, 1200-1700. Please contact for details of admission prices. (L22)*

### Wisbech
**Octavia Hill Birthplace Museum**
1 South Brink Place Tel: (01945) 476358
A museum in the Grade II Georgian building in which Octavia Hill, social reformer and co-founder of the National Trust, was born, commemorating her life, work and legacy. *Open 3 Mar-31 Oct, Wed, Sat, Sun, Bank Hol Mon, 1400-1730; last admission 1700. £1.50/free/£1.50. (L16/17)*

### Whittlesey
**Whittlesey Museum**
Town Hall, Market Street
Tel: (01733) 840986
Museum of archaeology, agriculture, hand tools, brickmaking, local photographs, a Sir Harry Smith exhibition, railways, costume display and temporary exhibitions. *Open all year, Fri, Sun, 1430-1630; Sat, 1000-1200; closed 25, 26 Dec, 1 Jan. 50p/20p/50p. (I18)*

### Wisbech
**Elgood's Brewery and Garden**
North Brink Brewery Tel: (01945) 583160
Independent family brewery established in 1795. Visitors can watch traditional methods of brewing and sample a range of real ales. A 4-acre garden contains many features and maze. *Open 1 May-10 Oct, Wed-Sun, Bank Hol Mons, 1300-1700; Brewery Tours, Wed-Fri, 1430. £4.00/£1.50/£4.00. (L16/17)*

### Wisbech
**Skylark Studios**
Hannath Road, Tydd Gote
Tel: (01945) 420403
An art gallery showing monthly exhibitions by local and national artists along with a permanent display of art and crafts. *Open 6 Jan-24 Dec, Wed-Fri, 1000-1700; Sat, 1100-1700; Sun, 1100-1600; 5 Apr, 1200-1600; closed 4 Apr. (L16/17)*

### Wisbech
**Wisbech and Fenland Museum**
Museum Square Tel: (01945) 583817
A purpose-built Victorian local history museum with a reconstruction of a shop, a Post Office, Roman and Fenland finds, decorative and fine art, natural history and geology. *Open 2 Jan-27 Mar, Tue-Sat, 1000-1600; 1 Apr-30 Sep, Tue-Sat, 1000-1700; 1 Oct-24 Dec, Tue-Sat, 1000-1600. (L16/17)*

*The Farm Museum,*
*Denny Abbey, Cambridgeshire*

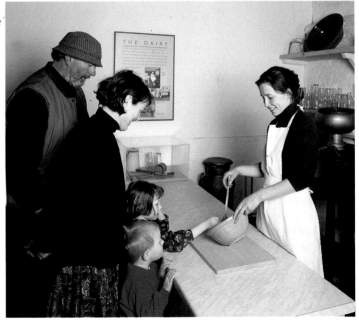

*Cambridgeshire ● Lincolnshire*

# Lincolnshire

### Alford

**Alford Manor-House Museum**

The Manor House, West Street
Tel: (01507) 463073

A thatched 17thC manor-house housing a museum which includes the history of the manor-house and general local history. Victorian room, school room and USA connections. *Open 2 Apr-30 Sep, Mon-Sat, 1000-1700; last admission 1630; Sun, 1330-1630; last admission 1600. Please contact for details. (L8)*

### Boston

**⊛ Boston Guildhall Museum**

South Street  Tel: (01205) 365954

A 15thC building with 16thC kitchens, the original cells which imprisoned the early Pilgrim Fathers in 1607, a museum shop, maritime exhibits, pictures, firemarks and farm tools. *Open 2 Jan-31 Mar, Mon-Sat, 1000-1700; 1 Apr-30 Sep, Mon-Sat, 1000-1700; Sun, 1330-1700; 1 Oct-31 Dec, Mon-Sat, 1000-1700; closed 25, 26 Dec. £1.25/free/80p. (J12)*

### Brant Broughton

**⊛ Brant Broughton Heritage Room**

Meeting House Lane

An exhibition venue with exhibitions arranged every eight weeks. Open all year, daily, 1000-1600; Bank Hols. *Please contact Tourist Information Centre, Tel: (01529) 414294. (D10/11)*

*The Lawn, Lincoln*

*The Incredibly Fantastic Old Toy Show, Lincoln*

### Corby Glen

**Willoughby Memorial Trust Gallery**

Moreley's Lane  Tel: (01476) 550380

A 17thC grammar school which is now a library, reading room and gallery. Exhibitions are run from Easter to November, changing each month. *Open 2 Apr-28 Nov, Tue, 1200-1900; Wed-Sun, 1200-1700; closed Mon except Bank Hol Mon. (E/F14/15)*

### Cranwell

**Cranwell Aviation Heritage Centre**

Heath Farm, North Rauceby
Tel: (01529) 488490

An exhibition featuring the history of the Royal Air Force College, Cranwell which became the first military air academy in the world when opened in February 1920. *Open 1 Apr-30 Sep, daily, 1000-1630. (F11)*

### Grantham

**⊛ Grantham Museum**

St Peter's Hill  Tel: (01476) 568783

A collection relating to the history, natural history and archaeology of Grantham and district with special displays on Sir Isaac Newton, Mrs Thatcher and the 617 Squadron. *Open all year, Mon-Sat, 1000-1700; closed 25 Dec and 1 Jan. (D13)*

### Lincoln

**The Incredibly Fantastic Old Toy Show**

26 Westgate  Tel: (01522) 520534

Over 2000 toys displayed in the former church hall with cars, trains, dolls, dolls' houses, rocking horses, games, teddies and much more. *Open 3 Apr-30 Sep, Tue-Sat, 1100-1700; Sun, Bank Hol Mon, 1200-1600; 9 Oct-26 Dec, Sat, 1100-1700; Sun, 1200-1600. £1.90/£1.00/£1.50. (E8)*

### Lincoln

**⊛ The Lawn**

Union Road  Tel: (01522) 560330

A visitor centre including a tropical glasshouse, an archaeology centre, shops, a pub, restaurant, conference and function rooms with a children's play area and picnic site. *Open 2 Jan-31 Mar, Mon-Fri, 0900-1600; Sat, Sun, 1000-1600; 1 Apr-30 Sep, Mon-Fri, 0900-1700; Sat, Sun, 1000-1700; 1 Oct-31 Dec, Mon-Fri, 0900-1600; Sat, Sun, 1000-1600; closed 25, 26 Dec, 1 Jan. (E8)*

### Lincoln

**⊛ Museum of Lincolnshire Life**

Burton Road  Tel: (01522) 528448

The region's largest social history museum showing the agricultural, industrial and social history of Lincolnshire from a teapot to a World War I tank and a Victorian room. *Open 2 Jan-30 Apr, Mon-Sat, 1000-1730; Sun, 1400-1730; 1 May-30 Sep, daily, 1000-1730; 1 Oct-31 Dec, Mon-Sat, 1000-1730; Sun, 1400-1730; closed 2 Apr, 24-27 Dec, 1 Jan. £2.00/60p/£2.00. (E8)*

### Lincoln

**⊛ Tales of the River Bank Visitor Centre**

Walcott Bank, Tattershall Bridge
Tel: (01526) 345718

An interpretation centre 'Tales of the River Bank' relates the history of fen drainage and the pumping station which stands on the banks of the River Witham. *Open 1 Apr-31 Oct, Tue-Sun, 1400-1700. (E8)*

### Lincoln
#### ⬡ Usher Gallery
Lindum Road  Tel: (01522) 527980
Paintings, ceramics, silver and a special collection of paintings by Peter de Wint, local topographical paintings, a large collection of English coins and a Tennyson collection. *Open all year, Mon-Sat, 1000-1730; Sun, 1430-1700; closed 24-26 Dec, 1 Jan. £2.00/50p/£2.00. (E8)*

### Louth
#### Louth Museum
4 Broadbank  Tel: (01507) 601211
A museum with butterflies, moths, sketches by a local 19thC artist, local history documents and photographs, fossils, local carpets and tapestry of the 19thC, dresses and gloves. *Open 2 Apr-24 Jul, Wed, 1000-1600; Fri, Sat, 1400-1600; 26 Jul-31 Aug, Mon-Sat, 1000-1600; 1 Sep-30 Oct, Wed, 1000-1600; Fri, Sat, 1400-1600. 50p/20p/20p. (J6)*

### Mablethorpe
#### Ye Olde Curiosity Museum
61 Victoria Road  Tel: (01507) 472406
A collection of 4500 old glass lampshades, memorabilia and bygones during the last 100 years such as a Morris Minor estate, irons, kettles, bed warmers and dollypegs. *Open all year, daily, 1000-1700; closed 25, 26 Dec, 1 Jan. (L6)*

### Metheringham
#### Metheringham Airfield Visitor Centre
Westmoor Farm, Martin Moor
Tel: (01526) 378270
A fascinating exhibition of photographs which recall life on the World War II airfield of RAF Metheringham and the history of 106 Squadron who served there. *Open 31 Mar-31 Oct, Sat, Sun, Bank Hols, 1200-1700; Wed, 1200-1600. (E9)*

*Church Farm Museum, Skegness, Lincolnshire*

*Ayscoughfee Hall, Spalding, Lincolnshire*

### Navenby
#### ⬡ Mrs Smith's Cottage
3 East Cottage  Tel: (01529) 414155
Built in the early 19th it is a remarkable survival of a bygone age. The cottage was lived in by Mrs Smith until she was 102 years old. *Please contact Sleaford Tourist Information Centre Tel: (01529) 414294. (E10)*

### Normanby
#### Normanby Park Farming Museum
Tel: (01724) 720588
A museum of rural life including farming, rural crafts, industries, set in 300 acres of parkland with a Regency mansion and a walled Victorian kitchen garden. *Open 1 Apr-30 Sep, daily, 1300-1700. Please contact for details of admission prices. (D2)*

### Osbournby
#### The Barn Gallery
18 West Street  Tel: (01529) 455631
An art gallery with seasonal exhibitions of wildlife and country pictures and prints featuring local and international artists. *Open all year, Sun-Tue, 1100-1700; closed 26-29 Dec. (F13)*

### Pinchbeck
#### Spalding Bulb Museum and Horticultural Exhibition
Birchgrove Garden Centre,
Surfleet Road  Tel: (01775) 680490
Museum with a slide presentation theatre with undercover exhibits and artefacts. There are also outdoor exhibits. *Open 1 Apr-31 Oct, daily, 1000-1630; closed 12 Apr. (I14)*

### Skegness
#### ⬡ Church Farm Museum
Church Road South
Tel: (01754) 766658
The Bernard Best collection of agricultural objects in a 19thC farmhouse and buildings with a late 18thC timber framed re-erected thatched cottage and Sunday demonstrations. *Open 1 Apr-31 Oct, daily, 1030-1730; closed 2 Apr. £1.00/50p/£1.00. (M9)*

### Spalding
#### The Gordon Boswell Romany Museum
Clay Lake  Tel: (01775) 710599
A collection of Romany vardos (caravans), carts and harness, all horse-drawn. The largest collection of Romany photographs and sketching covering the last 150 years. *Open 6-28 Mar, Sat, Sun, 1030-1700; 1 Apr-30 Sep, Wed-Sun, Bank Hol Mon, 1030-1700; 2-31 Oct, Sat, Sun, 1030-1700. £2.75/£2.00/£2.50. (I15)*

### Spalding
#### ⬡ Ayscoughfee Hall, Museum and Gardens
Churchgate  Tel: (01775) 725468
A museum with displays on land drainage, agriculture, horticulture, wildfowling, local history and Spalding, a restored library and with 17thC yew tree walks. *Please contact for details of opening times. (I15)*

*Lincoln from the South West by Peter De Wint, 1784-1849, Usher Gallery, Lincoln*

## Whaplode St Catherine
### Museum of Entertainment
### (Rutland Cottage Music Museum)
Millgate Tel: (01406) 540379
The official museum of the Fairground Society with music boxes, fairground and church organs, theatre, radio and television collections. *Open 2-5 Apr, 1300-1700; 11 Apr-27 Jun, Sun, 1300-1700; 1 Jul-30 Sep, Sun-Thu, 1300-1700. £2.50/£2.00/£2.00. (J15)*

## Woodhall Spa
### Woodhall Spa Cottage Museum
Iddesleigh Road Tel: (01526) 353775
The Victorian Boulton and Paul sectional bungalow houses displays on Woodhall Spa history plus an ancillary exhibition on the 617 Squadron, 'The Dambusters'. *Open 2 Apr-1 Oct, Mon-Sat, 1000-1700; Sun, 1100-1700; 2-31 Oct, Sat, 1000-1700; Sun, 1100-1700. £1.00/free/£1.00. (H9)*

## Stamford
### ❀ Stamford Museum
Broad Street Tel: (01780) 766317
Displays to illustrate the development of Stamford, an important historic town, including customs, trades and the people. There are also temporary exhibitions. *Open 1 Jan-31 Mar, Mon-Sat, 1000-1700; 1 Apr-30 Sep, Mon-Sat, 1000-1700; Sun, 1400-1700; 1 Oct-31 Dec, Mon-Sat, 1000-1700; closed 25, 28, 29 Dec, 1 Jan. (F17)*

## Stamford
### ❀ Stamford Theatre and Arts Centre
27 St Mary's Street Tel: (01780) 763203
An historic theatre and assembly room converted into a fully equipped arts centre with a full programme of film, plays, poetry, contemporary art exhibitions, coffee and snacks. *Open all year, Mon-Fri, 0915-1700; Sat, 1030-1400; closed 25 Dec. (F17)*

## Stickford
### Allied Forces Museum
Main Road (Church Road)
Tel: (01205) 480317
A museum housing a private collection including a display of military motorcycles, heavy vehicles, weaponry, uniforms, medals and a guard room. *Open all year, Mon-Fri, 0930-1630. (J10)*

## Tattershall
### Dogdyke Steam Pumping Station
Bridge Farm Tel: (01526) 342352
A beam engine by Bradley and Craven, Wakefield 1855 with a 28ft in diameter scoop wheel; the only known land drainage engine worked in steam. Also a Ruston diesel engine and pump. *Open 4 Apr, 2 May, 6 Jun, 4 Jul, 1 Aug, 5 Sep, 3 Oct, Sun, 1400-1700. £2.00/50p/£1.00. (H10)*

## Wainfleet
### Magdalen Museum
St John's Street Tel: (01754) 880343
A museum with exhibits of local history, all donated or lent by people living locally. There is also the original charter lent by Magdalen College, Oxford. *Open 30 Mar-30 Sep, Tue, Thu-Sun, Bank Hol Mon, 1330-1630. £1.00/20p/£1.00. (L10)*

*Museum of Entertainment, Whaplode St Catherine, Lincolnshire*

# machinery & transport

"Concorde" at the Imperial War Museum, Duxford, Cambridgeshire

### Duxford
#### ⊛ Imperial War Museum
Imperial War Museum
Tel: (01223) 835000
Over 140 aircraft on display with tanks, vehicles and guns, a ride on the simulator, an adventure playground, shops and a restaurant. *Open 1 Jan-14 Mar, daily, 1000-1600; 15 May-25 Oct, daily, 1000-1800; 26 Oct-31 Dec, daily, 1000-1600; closed 24-26 Dec. £7.00/£3.50/£4.70. (L25)*

### Peterborough
#### ⊛ Railworld
Oundle Road Tel: (01733) 344240
Railworld has train exhibitions, mainly modern rail travel and worldwide with some historic items and locomotives. *Open 1 Jan-26 Feb, Mon-Fri, 1100-1600; 1 Mar-31 Oct, daily, 1100-1600; 3 Nov-23 Dec, Mon-Fri, 1100-1600. £2.00/£1.00/£1.50. (H18)*

## Cambridgeshire

### Burwell
#### Burwell Museum Trust
See entry in Museums section.

### Cambridge
#### Museum of Technology
The Old Pumping Station, Cheddars Lane
Tel: (01223) 368650
A Victorian pumping station housing unique Hawthorn Davey steam pumping engines, electrical equipment and a working letterpress print shop. *Open 3 Jan, 7 Feb, 7 Mar, 1400-1700; 4 Apr-24 Oct, Sun, 1400-1700; 7 Nov, 5 Dec, 1400-1700; please phone for dates of steam days. £1.50/50p/50p. (K/L23/24)*

### Prickwillow
#### Prickwillow Engine Museum
Main Street
Tel: (01353) 688360
A museum housing a Mirrlees Bickerton and Day diesel engine, a 5-cylinder, blast injection, 250 bhp working unit and a Vicker-Petter, 2-cylinder, 2-stroke diesel and others. *Open 6-28 Mar, Sat, Sun, 1100-1600; 1 Apr-31 Oct, daily, 1100-1700; 6-28 Nov, Sat, Sun, 1100-1600. £2.00/£1.00/£1.00. (M/N20)*

### Stibbington
#### ⊛ Nene Valley Railway
Wansford Station Tel: (01780) 784444
A 7.5-mile track between Wansford and Peterborough via Yarwell Mill and Nene Park with over 28 steam and diesel locomotives. Regular steam trains operate over the line. *Open all year, daily, 0930-1630; closed 25 Dec; please phone for train services. £2.50/£1.50/£2.50. (F/G18)*

## Lincolnshire

### Coningsby
#### Battle of Britain Memorial Flight
RAF Coningsby
Tel: (01526) 344041
A hangar containing the only flying Lancaster bomber in Europe, 5 Spitfires, 2 Hurricanes and other memorabilia, a souvenir shop and in addition, 1 Douglas Dakota. *Please contact for details of opening times. £3.50/£1.50/£2.00 (with effect from April 1999). (H/I10)*

Battle of Britain Memorial Flight, Coningsby, Lincolnshire

### Cranwell
**Cranwell Aviation Heritage Centre**
See entry in Museums
and Heritage section.

### Dorrington
**North Ings Farm Museum
and Railway**
North Ings Farm
Tel: (01526) 833100
A working narrow-gauge railway with static exhibits, a working windpump, static working industrial plant, working vintage tractors, pet's corner and railway ride around site. *Open 4 Apr-31 Oct, Sun, 1000-1700. £2.00/£1.00/£2.00. (F/G11)*

### East Kirkby
 **Lincolnshire
Aviation Heritage Centre**
The Airfield
Tel: (01790) 763207
Part of the wartime airfield including the restored control tower, aircraft and artefacts depicting the history of flying in Lincolnshire and RAF Escaping Society exhibits. *Open 1 Jan-27 Mar, Mon-Sat, 1000-1600; 29 Mar-30 Oct, Mon-Sat, 1000-1700; 2 Nov-31 Dec, Mon-Sat, 1000-1600; last admission 1 hour before closing; closed 25, 26 Dec. £3.50/£1.50/£3.25. (J9/10)*

*Imperial War Museum, Duxford, Cambridgeshire*

### Metheringham
**Metheringham Airfield Visitor Centre**
See entry in Museums section.

### South Witham
**Geeson Brothers Motor Cycle
Museum and Workshop**
2,4 Water Lane
Tel: (01572) 767280
A museum showing 80 British motorcycles dating back to 1913. Most restored to new condition. There is also a workshop showing work in progress. *Please contact for details of opening times. £2.00/free/£2.00. (D/E15)*

### Spalding
**Pinchbeck Engine and Land
Drainage Museum**
Off West Marsh Road
Demonstrations are given in this restored steam pumping station with a collection of rare hand tools and displays on land reclamation, drainage and modern conservation work. *Open 1 Apr-31 Oct, daily, 1000-1600. (I14)*

### Stickford
**Allied Forces Museum**
See entry in Museums section.

*Cambridgeshire ● Lincolnshire*

## Cambridgeshire

### Bourn
#### Bourn Windmill
Caxton Road

An interesting example of a very early type of windmill. *Open 28 Mar-26 Sep, last Sun in each month, National Mills Day, 1400-1700; £1.00/25p/£1.00. (G15)*

### Hinxton
#### Hinxton Watermill
Mill Lane

A 17thC watermill restored to working order with working machinery which grinds flour. *Open 6 Jun, 4 Jul, 1 Aug, 5 Sep, Sun, 1430-1730. £1.00/25p/£1.00. (L25)*

### Houghton
#### ⊛ Houghton Mill
Tel: (01480) 301494

A large timber-built watermill on an island in the River Ouse with much of the 19thC mill machinery intact and some restored to working order. *Open 3 Apr-27 Jun, Sat, Sun, Bank Hol Mon, 1400-1730; 22 Jun-31 Aug, Mon-Wed, Sat, Sun, Bank Hol Mon, 1400-1730; 12 Sep-10 Oct, Sat, Sun, Bank Hol Mon, 1400-1730. £2.50/£1.25/£2.50. (I21/22)*

### Soham
#### Downfield Windmill
Fordham Road  Tel: (01353) 720333

A working windmill, dating back to 1726. Flour is produced for sale to visitors and local shops. *Open all year, Sun, Bank Hol Mon, 1100-1700; closed 27 Dec. 70p/30p/70p. (M/N21)*

## Lincolnshire

### Aby
#### Claythorpe Watermill and Wildfowl Gardens
Claythorpe  Tel: (01507) 450687

A restored 1720s watermill in a picturesque setting with trout in the mill pond, various species of waterfowl, poultry and birds in landscaped gardens and bygone exhibits. *Please contact for details of opening times. £3.00/£2.00/£2.50. (K7)*

*Ellis Mill, Lincoln, Lincolnshire*

### Alvingham
#### Alvingham Watermill
Church Lane  Tel: (01507) 327544

An authentic 18thC working water cornmill. *Open 2, 4, 5 Apr, 1100-1700; 3, 23, 24 May, 1100-1700; 5 Jul-26 Aug, Mon, Thu, 1400-1630; 30, 31 Aug, 1100-1700; 12, 26 Jul, 1400-1700; 9, 23 Aug, 1400, 1700. £1.20/70p/80p. (J6)*

### Burgh-le-Marsh
#### ⊛ Burgh-le-Marsh Windmill
46 High Street  Tel: (01754) 810609

A 5-sailed towermill, built in 1813, in full working order. Stoneground wholemeal flour is available and there is a milling museum. *Open 14 Mar-31 Oct, 2nd and last Sun of each month, Bank Hol Mon, 1300-1600. 50p/25p/50p. (L9)*

### Hagworthingham
#### Stockwith Mill
Harrington Road  Tel: (01507) 588221

A 17thC watermill containing a permanent exhibition of the possessions and works of the poet, Tennyson. There is also a craft shop and country walks. *Open 2 Mar-31 Dec, Tue-Sun, Bank Hol Mon, 1030-1800. (J8/9)*

### Lincoln
#### ⊛ Ellis Mill
Mill Road  Tel: (01522) 523870

The last surviving windmill in Lincoln, restored by Lincoln Civic Trust with 4 sails which grind wheat. Wholemeal flour is on sale. *Open 3 Jan-25 Apr, Sun, 1400-dusk; 1 May-26 Sep, Sat, Sun, 1400-1800; 3 Oct-19 Dec, Sun, 1400-dusk. 70p/30p/70p. (F8)*

### Sibsey
#### ⊛ Sibsey Trader Windmill
Frithville Road  Tel: (01205) 750036

Restored in 1982, this 1877, 6-sailed cornmill is working on open days, weather permitting. Visitors can watch the grain being turned into flour. There is also a museum and tearooms. *Open 30 May, 13, 27 Jun, 11, 25 Jul, 8, 22 Aug, 12 Sep, Sun, 1100-1700. £1.60/80p/£1.20. (J11)*

### Sleaford
#### ⊛ Cogglesford Watermill
East Road  Tel: (0966) 400634

A watermill dating from the 18th and 19thC with an exhibition telling its history and that of the river upon which it depends. *Open 2 Jan-28 Mar, Sat, Sun, 1000-1600; 2 Apr-31 Oct, daily, 1000-1700; 6 Nov-26 Dec, Sat, Sun, 1000-1600. (F12)*

The fertile soil of Fenland and the surrounding area makes excellent growing country, as any journey through these counties will reveal. Fields of vegetables and crops are intermingled with fields of flowers. Gardens and nurseries, large and small abound. One such, Bay Tree Nursery near Spalding, specialises in roses. This thriving enterprise started life as a smallholding with a hut on the roadside for selling produce, but now grows some 100,000 roses a year.

Spalding is renowned, of course, as the centre of bulb growing, and in spring it proudly shows off its skill in the Spalding Flower Parade - a rich riot of glorious colour.

At Normanby Hall there is much of interest, in particular the recently restored working Victorian Kitchen Garden. The garden at Peckover House is Victorian too, and has many unusual trees.

And if you love gardens but have missed the spring and summer displays, don't despair - Cambridge University Botanic Garden is open all year round. It looks magnificent in every season, and even has a special winter garden providing colour and interest to cheer us through the depths of winter.

## Cambridgeshire

### Arrington
**⊛ Wimpole Hall and Home Farm**
See entry in Historic Houses section.

### Cambridge
**University of Cambridge Botanic Garden**
Cory Lodge, Bateman Street
Tel: (01223) 336265
Situated near the centre of Cambridge the Botanic Garden covers 40 acres and has many notable features including glasshouses and lake, scented, dry and genetic garden. *Please contact for details of opening times. £2.00/£1.50/£1.50. (K/L23/24)*

### Coton
**Coton Orchard and Vineyard**
Madingley Road  Tel: (01954) 210234
An orchard and vineyard with pick-your-own throughout the year. There is a coffee shop and gift shop. The garden centre is open all week and function rooms are available. *Open all year, daily, 0900-1700; closed 25, 26 Dec. (K23)*

### Elton
**⊛ Elton Hall**
See entry in Historic Houses section.

### Godmanchester
**⊛ Island Hall**
See entry in Historic Houses section.

### Huntingdon
**Hinchingbrooke House**
See entry in Historic Houses section.

### Linton
**⊛ Chilford Hall Vineyard**
Chilford Hundred Limited,
Balsham Road  Tel: (01223) 892641
A winery housed in interesting old buildings with a collection of sculptures on view. There is a vineyard, cafe and shop. *Open 10 Apr-2 Nov, daily, 1100-1730. £4.50/free/£4.50. (M25)*

### Lode
**⊛ Anglesey Abbey Gardens and Lode Mill**
See entry in Historic Houses section.

### Shepreth
**Crossing House**
78 Meldreth Road  Tel: (01763) 261071
The crossing keeper's cottage and a small plantsman's garden with a very wide variety of plants. *Open all year, daily, dawn-dusk. (K25)*

### Shepreth
**Docwra's Manor Garden**
2 Meldreth Road  Tel: (01763) 261473
Walled gardens round an 18th C red-bricked house approached by 18th C wrought iron gates. There are barns a 20th C folly, unusual plants and plants for sale. *Open all year. Wed, Fri, 1000-1600; 7 Mar, 4 Apr, 2 May, 6 Jun, 4 Jul. 1 Aug, 5 Sep, 3 Oct, Sun 1400-1700. (K25)*

### Warboys
**Grays Honey Farm Tearoom and Garden**
Cross Drove  Tel: (01354) 693798
Grays Honey Farm has a tearoom and garden. Picnic area where children can visit the guinea piggery and aviary or play in the miniature black forest house. *Open 1 Apr-30 Oct, Tue-Sat, Bank Hol Mon, 1130-1700; closed 2 Apr. (J20/21)*

### Wilburton
**Herb Garden, Nigel House**
High Street  Tel: (01353) 740824
A herb garden laid out in collections: culinary, aromatic, medical, biblical, Shakespearean, dye bed and astrological. *Open 8 May-26 Sep, Sat, Sun, 1000-1900; during week by appointment only. (L21)*

### Wisbech
**⊛ Peckover House**
See entry in Historic Houses section.

## Lincolnshire

### Aubourn
**Aubourn Hall**
See entry in Historic Houses section.

### Billinghay
**⊛ Billinghay Cottage**
See entry in Historic Houses section.

### Boston
**Fydell House**
See entry in Historic Houses section.

*Anglesey Abbey, Cambrige*

### Candlesby
**Candlesby Herbs**
Cross Keys Cottage
Tel: (01754) 890211
A herb nursery and herbal workshop. *Open all year, Tue-Sun, Bank Hol Mon, 1000-1700; closed 25 Dec. (K/L9)*

### Doddington
**Doddington Hall**
See entry in Historic Houses section.

### Fulbeck
**Fulbeck Hall**
See entry in Historic Houses section.

### Gainsborough
⊛ **Gainsborough Old Hall**
See entry in Historic Houses section.

### Grimsthorpe
⊛ **Grimsthorpe Castle**
See entry in Historic Houses section.

### Harlaxton
⊛ **Harlaxton Manor Gardens**
The Garden House Tel: (01476) 592101
A magnificent 'fairytale' chateau in 110 acres of gardens and grounds, currently underrestoration. *Open 1 Apr-31 Oct, Tue-Sun, Bank Hol Mon, 1100-1700. £3.00/£1.25/£2.00. (D13)*

### Lincoln
⊛ **Lincoln Guildhall**
See entry in Historic Houses section.

### Pinchbeck
**Spalding Tropical Forest and Rose Cottage Water Garden Centre**
Glenside North Tel: (01775) 710882
A 0.5-acre glasshouse enclosing a tropical environment with 4 zones including a tropical rain forest, Japanese and Australian tropical plants and Mediterranean temperate zone. *Open all year, daily, summer, 1000-1730; winter, 1000-1600; closed 25, 26 Dec. £2.45/£1.40/£1.99.*

### Spalding
⊛ **Ayscoughfee Hall, Museum and Gardens**
See entry in Museums section.

### Spalding
⊛ **Springfields**
Camelgate Tel: (01775) 724843
One of Britain's premier show gardens. In spring there is a spectacle of tulips, daffodils and hyacinths and in summer, a bedding plant display. *Open 19 Mar-9 May, daily, 1000-1800. £2.00/free/£2.70.*

### Stamford
**Browne's Hospital**
See entry in Historic Houses section.

# Nurseries & Garden Centres

## Cambridgeshire

### Elton
⊛ **Bressingham Plant Centre**
Elton Hall, Elton, Peterborough
Tel: (01832) 280058
8 miles west of Peterborough on A605. This appealing Plant Centre is set within the old kitchen garden of romantic Elton Hall. It has opened up the 'Bressingham Experience' to more northern customers, offering the famous Bressingham range of thousands of varieties - many introduced by founder Alan Bloom MBE, VMH. Enjoy friendly, expert advice, top quality and value with exciting events and inspiring displays. The accent is on roses from the traditional to the newest of varieties. *Open: Daily including Sun, 0900-1730 except Christmas Day/Boxing Days. See also entry for Elton Hall under Historic Houses & Monuments and the Bressingham Tea Room under Afternoon Teas. (G18/19)*

### Stamford
⊛ **Burghley House**
See entry in Historic Houses section.

### Tattershall
⊛ **Tattershall College**
See entry in Historic Houses section.

*Fulbeck Hall Plant Fair, Lincolnshire*

### Orton Waterville
⊛ **Notcutts Garden Centres**
Oundle Road, Orton Waterville, Peterborough *(H18)*
Tel: (01733) 234600
Notcutts Garden Centres are wonderlands for gardeners. Over 2000 varieties of guaranteed hardy plants. No need to be a specialist. There's plenty of help on hand. Why not spend some time wandering at leisure. There's so much to see - display borders, pools, furniture, stoneware, books, gift ideas and pot plants, plus lots of tips on how to improve your garden. Whatever your interests, there's plenty for you at Notcutts. Also at Woodbridge Tel: (01394) 445400.
Ardleigh Tel: (01206) 230271.
Norwich Tel: (01603) 453155.
St.Albans Tel: (01727) 853224.

For family days out, there's plenty of choice. Mablethorpe Animal Gardens tells the story of the wildlife of this area. You will see the animals who live here today - including owls, seals and seabirds, and also animals which lived here way back in the Ice Age, like the lynx, the arctic fox and snowy owls.

To see a modern farm typical of this area, and with lots of farm animals and exhibits which you are actually encouraged to use and examine, go to Sacrewell Farm and Country Centre or Rand Farm Park near Wragby.

Or for the more exotic, Linton Zoo has tigers, tapirs, toucans and plenty more, and at the Butterfly and Wildlife Park, there are the most fabulously painted butterflies in a tropical paradise setting.

Looking for excitement? Hop along to Fantasy Island. Ride the Volcanic Eruption if you dare! Sail with Captain Rhombus and marvel at his collection of fish and mystical sea creatures. Ride a rocket powered train, spin on the Hoola Kula. And, due to open this summer, is one of the world's first wonders of the 21st century, the Millennium Rollercoaster. The ride will loop its way around the entire Fantasy Island, towering above its main pyramid building. Come and try it!

## Cambridgeshire

### Godmanchester
#### Wood Green Animal Shelters
King's Bush Farm, London Road
Tel: (01480) 830014
Europe's most progressive shelter for unwanted animals, including farm animals, cats, dogs and small animals. Some permanent residents, others awaiting caring new homes. *Open all year, daily, 0930-1530. (I22)*

### Hamerton
#### Hamerton Zoo Park
Tel: (01832) 293362
A wildlife park with lemurs, marmosets, meerkats, wallabies and a unique bird collection with rare and exotic species from around the world. Also an adventure playground. *Open 1 Jan-26 Mar, daily, 1030-1600; 27 Mar-25 Oct, daily, 1030-1800; 26 Oct-31 Dec, daily, 1030-1600; last admission 1 hour before closing. £4.50/£3.50/£4.00. (G20)*

*Farmland Museum, Denny Abbey, Cambridgeshire (see page 30)*

### Linton
#### Linton Zoo
Hadstock Road  Tel: (01223) 891308
The zoo has big cats, lynx, wallabies, llamas, toucans, parrots and reptiles. A wonderful combination of beautiful gardens and wildlife. *Open all year, daily, 1000-1800/dusk; closed 25 Dec. £4.00/£3.00/£3.75. (M25)*

### Peakirk
#### Peakirk Waterfowl Gardens
Deeping Road Tel: (01733) 252271
A flock of Chilean flamingos and some 137 species of duck, geese and swans in 20 acres of water gardens with a refreshment room, a shop and a children's play area. *Open all year, summer, daily, 0930-1730; winter, daily, 0930-dusk; closed 24, 25 Dec. £3.50/£1.75/£2.50. (H17)*

### Peterborough
#### Activity World
Padholme Road Tel: (01733) 314446
An indoor adventure playground with giant chess, draughts and crazy golf. *Open all year, daily, 0930-1930; closed 25, 26 Dec. For admission prices, please contact for details. (H18)*

### Shepreth
#### Willers Mill Wildlife Park
Station Road  Tel: (01763) 262226
Wildlife Sanctuary started in 1979 for unwanted pets, road or accident casualties etc. Fish farm also open to public. Fully fledged wildlife park with wolves, monkeys and otters. *Open all year, summer, 1000-1800; winter, 1000-dusk; closed 25 Dec. £3.95/£2.95/£3.50. (K25)*

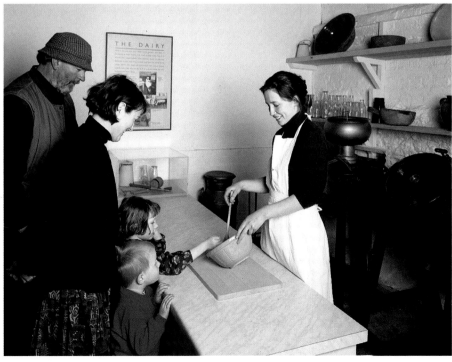

*All the fun of the Fair, Skegness*

### Woodston
**Big Sky Adventure Play**
24 Wainman Road, Shrewsbury Avenue
Tel: (01733) 390810
An indoor children's soft play activities centre with electric mini go-karts and a monorail rocket ship ride. *Open all year, daily, 0930-1900; closed 25, 26 Dec, 1 Jan. For admission prices, please contact for details. (H18)*

## Lincolnshire

### Chapel St Leonards
**Lakeside Leisure Limited**
Boating Lake  Tel: (01754) 872631
There are 3.5 acres of coarse fishing lakes next to a beach with ample parking, boats, crazy golf, an indoor play area and gardens. *Open 14 Mar-26 Oct, daily, 1000-dusk. (M8)*

### Thornhaugh
**⊛ Sacrewell Farm and Country Centre**
Sacrewell Tel: (01780) 782254
A 500-acre farm with a working watermill, farmhouse gardens, shrubberies, farm, nature and general interest trails, 18thC buildings, displays of the farm and bygones. *Open all year, daily, summer, 0930-1800; winter, 0900-1700; closed 25 Dec. £3.00/£1.00/£2.00. (F17/18)*

### Woodhurst
**⊛ The Raptor Foundation**
The Heath, St Ives Road
Tel: (01487) 741140
A collection of injured birds of prey and wild birds. Hand-reared owls used for fund raising for the hospital. Tearoom, gift shop, craft village and falconry flying area. *Open all year, daily, 1030-1700; closed 24-26 Dec, 1 Jan. (J21)*

### Great Steeping
**Northcote Heavy Horse Centre**
Tel: (01754) 830286
Heavy horses, dray rides, a horse-drawn vehicle collection, rare breeds farm, dalmatian carriage dogs, field walk, talks and demonstrations. A unique hands-on experience. *Open 1 Apr-30 Jun, Tue-Thu, Sun, Bank Hol Mons, 1100-1600; 1 Jul-31 Aug, daily except Sat, 1100-1600; 1-30 Sep, Tue-Thu, Sun, 1130-1600. Please contact for details of admission prices. (K/L9)*

*Punting on the River Cam, Cambridge*

*Cambridgeshire ● Lincolnshire*

### Ingoldmells
### ❀ Hardy's Animal Farm
Grays Farm, Anchor Lane
Tel: (01754) 872267
See rare breeds and commercial farm animals with access to a pig breeding unit, rabbits, guinea pigs and wildfowl. There is an adventure playground, farm museum and working shires. *Open 22 Mar-5 Oct, daily, 1000-1800; last admission, 1700. £2.50/£1.75/£1.75. (M8/9)*

### Ingoldmells
### ❀ Magical World of Fantasy Island
Sea Lane  Tel: (01754) 872030
Britain's first fully themed indoor family resort with an array of themed rides. Standing hand-in-hand with leisure, shopping, entertainment and outdoor funfair attractions. *Open 6 Mar-25 Apr, Sat, Sun, from 1000; 2-11 Apr, daily from 1000; 1 May-31 Oct, daily, from 1000; 7 Nov-26 Dec, daily, from 1000; closed 25 Dec. (M8/9)*

### Long Sutton
### ❀ Butterfly and Wildlife Park
Tel: (01406) 363833
One of Britain's largest walk-through butterfly houses with exotic butterflies, an insectarium, gift shop, gardens, adventure playground, pet's corner and picnic areas. *Open 30 Mar-31 Oct, daily, 1000-1700. £4.20/£2.90/£3.90. (K15) See page 40 for more information.*

### Mablethorpe
### Mablethorpe Animal Gardens Nature Centre and Seal Trust
North End  Tel: (01507) 473346
A wildlife sanctuary in gardens and natural dunes with the emphasis on Lincolnshire wildlife, past and present, the Seal Trust Wildlife Hospital and 70 species of animals. *Open 29 Mar-24 Oct, daily, 1000-1700. £3.50/£1.50/£2.50. (L6/7)*

### Rand
### Rand Farm Park
White House Farm  Tel: (01673) 858904
An open farm park offering a wide variety of traditional farm animals to touch, see and enjoy. There is also a tearoom, adventure playground, farm shop and soft play area. *Open 1 Jan-30 Mar, daily, 1000-1600; 31 Mar-31 Oct, daily, 1000-1800; 1 Nov-30 Mar, daily, 1000-1600; closed 25, 26 Dec. £2.95/£2.50/£2.50. (G7)*

### Saxilby
### ❀ Bransby Home of Rest for Horses
Bransby  Tel: (01427) 788464
A rest home for 200 rescued horses, ponies and donkeys in over 100 acres with 2 large farmyards, stabling and a gift shop. *Open all year, daily, 0900-1600. (D8)*

### Skegness
### Skegness Model Village
South Parade  Tel: (01754) 762262
A miniature village set amongst 0.5 acres of gardens. It includes a working model fairground and a working garden railway. The village is illuminated during main season. *Open 2 Apr-31 Oct, daily, 1100-2100. £1.50/£1.10/£1.25. (M9)*

### Skegness
### ❀ Skegness Natureland Seal Sanctuary
North Parade, The Promenade
Tel: (01754) 764345
A collection of performing seals, baby seals, penguins, an aquarium, crocodiles, snakes, terrapins, scorpions, tropical birds and butterflies during May to October. *Open all year, daily, 1000-1700; winter, 1000-1600; closed 25, 26 Dec, 1 Jan. Please contact for details of admission prices. (M9)*

*Butterfly and Wildlife Park, Long Sutton, Lincolnshire*

### Weston
### Baytree Owl Centre, Baytree Nursery
Tel: (01406) 371907
A landscaped area with owls from around the world. Flying displays will take place in the new indoor arena between March and October. There is also a creepy crawly house. *Open all year, daily, summer, 0930-1730; winter, 0930-1600; closed 25, 26 Dec, 1 Jan. £2.50/£2.00/£2.00. (I/J14/15)*

### Weston
### Fun Farm
High Road  Tel: (01406) 373444
Children's indoor play experience, restaurant and shop. Pre-school craft and play sessions. *Open daily, 1000-1800; closed 25, 26 Dec, 1 Jan. Child £1.99. (I/J14/15)*

Put on your "sensible" shoes and come out and about in Cambridgeshire and Lincolnshire. With a Blue Badge Guide to lead you, take to the city streets to see the sights and hear the tales, the legends and the history behind those facades.

Or take to the footpaths - there are plenty to choose from. If you should walk the 86 miles of the Nene Way, somewhere along the route, in the region of Peterborough, you'll come to the "Dog in a Doublet" sluice. Do send us a postcard - it sounds fascinating!

Some say the only way to travel in this area is by bike. The students of Cambridge certainly do so, as do many of the local folk - always a good sign that it's true. The Hull to Harwich cycle route lingers through Lincolnshire - making the most of the gentle hills and woodlands of the Wolds.

If you choose to explore the waterways, you can hire a narrowboat. Or go sailing on Grafham Water. Maybe you'll try your skill at punting in Cambridge - or if you really don't want to risk a wetting, hire a chauffeur to do the work.

## Nature Reserves

## Cambridgeshire

### Brampton Wood
Huntingdon
1 mile W of the A1 and
2 miles E of Grafham. (CWT, SSSI).
Brampton Wood supports a wide variety of plants and animals. Well-known for butterflies, birds and insects. *(H21/22)*

### Dunhams Wood
March   Tel: (01354) 652134
Take the B1099 from March to Downham Market.
A 4.5-acre, newly-created wood in the middle of arable fenland containing an increasingly important arboretum. There are sculptures and a miniature railway in the wood. *Open 30, 31 Mar, 4, 5, 25, 26 May, 27 Jul, Sun, Mon, 1400-1700; 3-30 Aug, Sun, 1400-1700. Admission £1.00/50p/£1.00. (L18)*

### Fowlmere Nature Reserve
Fowlmere  Tel: (01763) 208978
Manor Farm, High Street
An 86-acre nature reserve incorporating a nature trail and 4 bird-watching hides. Attractions include unspoilt wetland scenery and birdlife including the kingfisher. *Open at any reasonable time. £1.00/50p/£1.00. (K25)*

### Gamlingay Wood
Gamlingay
Take the B1040 towards Waresley.
(CWT).
Ancient ash and maple wood. Habitat for mosses, liverworts, fungi and insects. *(I24)*

### ⊛ Ouse Washes
March
B1093 to Manea. (CWT,RSPB, SSSI).
445 acres managed by the Wildlife Trust. A prime site for birds and dragonflies. Observation hides, information centre and toilets. *(L19)*

### Waresley and Gransden Wood
B1046 towards Great Gransden. (CWT).
Ancient woodland with ash and oak. Bluebell, primrose and wood anemone flower under the birch on the drier acidic greens and exposed in the small valley. *(I24)*

### ⊛ Wicken Fen
Tel: (01353) 720274
Off the A1123. (NT).
The last remaining undrained portion of the Fen levels of East Anglia, rich in plant and invertebrate life and good for birds. Also a working windpump and restored Fen cottage. *Open all year, daily, centre, 0900-1700; Fen cottage, 5 Apr-25 Oct, Sun, 1400-1700; closed 25 Dec. Reserve and Cottage £3.50/£1.75/£3.50. (M22)*

### ⊛ Wildfowl and Wetlands Trust
Tel: (01353) 860711
Welney Centre, Welney  Off the A1101
A wetland nature reserve of 1800 acres attracting large numbers of ducks and swans in winter, waders in spring and summer plus a range of wild plants, butterflies and insects. *Open all year, daily 1000-1700; closed 25 Dec. £3.00/£1.80/£2.40. (B11)*

## Lincolnshire

### Chambers Farm Wood
Apley  Tel: (01623) 822447
On the B1202, south of Wragby.
A forest nature reserve within an area of ancient woodland which is mainly hardwoods, especially the small-leaved lime. Visitor facilities at weekends. *(G8)*

### Collyweston Quarries Nature Reserve
Stamford
A43 south from Stamford.
Limestone grassland and a Site of Special Scientific Interest. Old Roman quarry now supporting rare plants, including a number of orchid species. *(E/F17)*

### Gibraltar Point National Nature Reserve and Visitor Centre
Skegness Tel: (01754) 762677
Off the A52, 3 miles south of Skegness.
Nature reserve with 1500 acres of habitat including sand dunes, salt marsh, sandy shores and freshwater marsh. There is also a visitor and residential centre. *Open Nature Reserve, all year, daily, dawn-dusk; Visitor Centre, 4 Jan-26 Apr, Sat, Sun, Bank Hol Mon, 1030-1300; 1400-1700; 1 May-30 Sep, daily, 1030-1300, 1400-1700; 4 Oct-27 Dec, Sat, Sun, 1030-1300, 1400-1700. (M10)*

*Wildfowl and Wetlands Trust, Welney, Cambs*

### Naturalists' Organisations & Other Abbreviations used in this section

CWT: The Wildlife Trust for Cambridgeshire, 3b Langford Arch, London Road, Sawston, Cambridge CB4 4EE. Tel: (01223) 712400.

NT: The National Trust, Blickling, Norwich, Norfolk NR11 6NF. Tel: (01263) 733471.

RSPB: Royal Society for the Protection of Birds, HQ: The Lodge, Sandy, Beds, SG19 2DL. Tel: (01767) 680541. East Anglia Regional Office, Stalham House, 65 Thorpe Road, Norwich NR1 1UD. Tel: (01603) 661662.

SSSI: Site of Special Scientific Interest

## Country Walks

# Cambridgeshire

### The Clopton Way

9 miles from the Cambridgeshire-Bedfordshire border to Wimpole, where it connects with the Wimpole Way. To the west, the Clopton Way connects with the Greensand Ridge Walk in Bedfordshire. *Leaflet 40p available from Cambridgeshire County Council.*

### Fen Rivers Way

17-mile walk between Cambridge and Ely. The path follows well drained floodbanks with stunning views across a Fenland landscape rich in wildlife. The route is served by excellent public transport. *A pack containing a route guide with helpful local information is available from Cambridgeshire County Council, price £2.00.*

### Grafham Water Circular Ride

A circular ride of 13 miles around the reservoir. Route includes ancient woodlands, medieval granges and excellent views across the water. *Leaflet 30p from Cambridgeshire County Council.*

### Nene Way

Stretches 86 miles from Badby, Northamptonshire, near Daventry, to the Dog in a Doublet sluice, Cambridgeshire. *Details of the 10 mile section from Wansford to Peterborough available from Peterborough City Council. Tel: (01733) 63141.*

### Ouse Valley Way

Long distance river valley walk along the Great Ouse from Eaton Socon to Earith. Total length 26 miles. *Information pack available from Huntingdon Tourist Information Centre, 50p.*

### The Roman Road

15 miles, connects Cambridge with the Icknield Way and can be used by walkers, equestrian and off-road cyclists. Part of a Roman road dubbed via Devana in the 18th century. The route is shown on ordnance survey maps, or talk to the Countryside Access officers at Cambridgeshire County Council. *In addition, two leaflets describe short circular walks from the Roman Road.*

### Three Shires Way

This long distance bridle way runs for 37 miles from the village of Tathall End in Buckinghamshire to Grafham Water in Cambridgeshire. Walkers and cyclists are also welcome to use this fascinating route. *Free leaflet giving details from Cambridgeshire County Council.*

### Wimpole Way

13 miles through woodlands and fields from Cambridge to Wimpole Hall, where it meets the Clopton Way which continues westward into Bedfordshire and the Greensand Ridge Walk. *Leaflet 40p from Cambridgeshire County Council.*

For more information of routes in the Cambridgeshire area, contact:
Cambridgeshire County Council, Environment and Transport, Shire Hall, Castle Hill, Cambridge, CB3 0AP. Telephone: (01223) 717445.

# Lincolnshire

### The Viking Way

147 miles from the banks of the Humber to the shores of Rutland Water. Crossing the Lincolnshire Wolds and apart from the Cathedral City of Lincoln its course is almost entirely through countryside, quiet villages and small market towns. *Guidebook £5.95 inc p&p Lincolnshire Tourism.*

### Bridle Routes

A pack of thirteen bridle routes covering the County which can be used by horseriders, walkers and mountain bikes. *Bridle Route Pack £4.70 inc p&p Lincolnshire Tourism.*

### The Gingerbread Way

25 mile circular route around the villages of Grantham. *70p Lincolnshire Tourism.*

### The Nev Cole Way

57 mile route following the bank of the River Humber from Burton on Stather to Nettleton. *£2.00 Lincolnshire Tourism.*

### Circular Countryside and Conservation Walks

*The Wolds £4.50, Lincoln and District £4.20, Kesteven and the Fens £3.50 Lincolnshire Tourism.*

For more information of routes in the Lincolnshire area, contact:
Lincolnshire County Council, County Offices, 64 Newland, Lincoln, LN1 1YL. Telephone: (01522) 552809.

*Viking Way, Lincolnshire Wolds*

*Baysgarth, Barton, Lincolnshire*

## Country Parks

# Cambridgeshire

### Ferry Meadows Country Park

Nene Park, 2 miles W of Peterborough city centre off the A605.
Lakes, meadows and woods with walks, nature reserve, picnic and play areas, boating, fishing, miniature railway, visitor centre, cafe and caravan club site. Water sports centre with board, dinghy sailing and cycle hire. Two pay and play golf courses and pitch and putt. *(G18/19)*

### ⊛ Grafham Water

Tel: (01480) 812154
1 mile W of A1 and Buckden roundabout
Man-made reservoir which offers cycle hire, bird-watching, windsurfing, sailing, trout fishing, children's play area, natural trails and wildlife garden. Picnic sites, restaurant, cafe, toilets and visitor centre. *Parking £1.00 per car weekdays, £2.00 per car weekend and Bank Hols. Coaches free, must pre-book. (G/H22)*

### Wandlebury Country Park and Nature Reserve

Tel: (01223) 243830
Off the A1307, south of Cambridge
An Iron Age ring ditch, woodlands, footpaths, walks, wildlife and public footpaths to a Roman road and picnic areas. *Open all year, daily, dawn-dusk. (L24)*

# Lincolnshire

### ⊛ Hartsholme Country Park

Tel: (01522) 686264
South west of the city, signposted from the A46 Lincoln bypass
A 40-hectare country park comprising woodland, lakes and open grassland with a visitor centre and ranger service. *Open all year, daily, dawn-dusk. (D/E8/9)*

### Normanby Hall Country Park

Tel: (01724) 720588
Four miles north of Scunthorpe, off the B1430
Gardens, parkland, nature trails and deer woods in 350 acres with ornamental and wild birds, a well-stocked gift shop, a Regency Hall, farming museum and a walled Victorian garden. *Open all year, daily, 0900-1700 (1600 in winter), (2100 in summer). Admission £2.00/£1.50. (D2)*

### ⊛ Skegness Water Leisure Park

Tel: (0500) 821963
On the A52, 2.5 miles north of Skegness
A water leisure park with facilities for cable-tow water-skiing and coarse fishing, a new narrow-gauge railway, touring caravans, tent park and a children's playground. *Open 1 Mar-24 Nov, daily 0900-1730. (M9)*

### Snipe Dales Country Park

Horncastle. Off the B1195.
A nature reserve and wooded area in a total of 220 acres. *Open all year, daily, dawn-dusk. (I8/9)*

### Tallington Lakes

Tel: (01778) 347000
On the A16 between Market Deeping and Stamford
Lakes with windsurfing, water-skiing, adventure playground, beach, picnic area, jet skiing, a dry ski slope, fishing, canoeing and sailing; also a bar, restaurant and snack bar. *Open all year, daily, dawn-dusk. Admission per vehicle: £3.00. (G16/17)*

### ⊛ Tattershall Park Country Club

Tel: (01526) 343193
Take the A153 from Sleaford towards Skegness
A club house with 2 bars, function room, restaurant, snooker room, gym and sauna. Activities include jet-skiing, water-skiing and horse-riding. *Open all year, daily, 0900-dusk. (H10)*

### Whisby Nature Park

Thorpe-on-the-Hill Tel: (01522) 500676
On the A46 at the southern end of Lincoln bypass
A park with 300 acres of lakes, ponds, woodland, scrub and grassland containing a wide range of habitats supporting an abundance of wildlife with a visitor centre. *Open at any reasonable time. (D9)*

*Fenland Landscape*

## On the Water

### Holidays Afloat on Cruisers, Narrow Boats and Yachts

### Cambridgeshire

#### ⊛ Fox Boats
10 Marina Drive, March
Tel: (01354) 652770
9 narrow boats, short break/weekly hire. 28.5 miles of Fenland Waterway, stretching from the River Nene, to the River Ouse, which offers possible cruises to nearby Ely, Bedford, Cambridge, Peterborough, Oundle and Northampton. *(K18)*

### Lincolnshire

#### Cathedral City Cruises
Lincoln  Tel: (01522) 546853.
Enjoy a relaxing cruise and see Lincoln and its surrounding area from the enclosed comfort of the MV "City of Lincoln" daily scheduled trips. Ideal for the Party with a difference at affordable prices. *Open 2 Apr-30 Sep, daily, from 1100. (E8)*

*Saxilby, Lincolnshire*

## Sport for all

### Golf Courses

### Cambridgeshire

#### ⊛ Hemingford Abbots Golf Club
Fairways Lodge  Tel: (01480) 495000
Nine hole with new tee positions on the second nine. New water features. Bar and food in Club-house. Come and play our first class greens. *Pay and play fees, weekdays £7.50/£11.50 (9/18 holes), weekends £10.50/£17.00 (9/18 holes). (I22)*

#### Malton Golf
Malton Lane, Meldreth, Royston
Tel: (01763) 262200
Described as the best new course in the area and designed in consultation with Bruce Critchley, BBC Commentator and Walker Cup Player. 18 holes set amongst 230 acres of beautiful countryside, surrounded by woodlands and wetlands. *Open to all on a pay and play basis. Driving range, clubhouse. Open: please contact for details. Weekdays: £10, Weekends: £12. (J/K25)*

#### ⊛ St. Neots Golf Club
Crosshall Road  Tel: (01480) 472363
Attractive tight tree-lined parkland course with water hazards and exceptional greens. Friendly welcome. Par 69. *Handicap certificate required. (H23)*

#### ⊛ Thorpe Wood Golf Course
Nene Parkway, Peterborough
Tel: (01733) 267701
18-hole pay-as-you-play parkland course. No restrictions. *Telephone bookings 7 days in advance. (H12)*

### Outdoor Activities

#### ⊛ Grafham Water
Huntingdon  Tel: (01480) 810521
Sailing, windsurfing, mountain biking, canoeing, archery, ropes courses and orienteering. *Brochures available for a range of courses and holidays for adults and young people. (G/H22)*

### Racing
**Market Rasen Racecourse**
Lincolnshire
Tel: (01673) 843434 *(G6)*

**Skegness Stadium and Swaffham Raceway**
Lincolnshire
Tel: (01754) 762544 *(M9)*

### Specialist Holidays and Activities

#### ⊛ Cambridge Pursuits
Cambridgeshire
Tel: (01223) 502134.
Guided tours of Cambridge by foot, punt and bike. *Weekend packages available. Cambridge Pursuits, 91 Garden Walk, Cambridge, CB4 3EW. (K/L23/24)*

Lincolnshire is known for excellent sausages, and also for fish. The port of Grimsby is one of the biggest fish markets in the country, and there are traditional smoke houses too, working with methods handed down from generation to generation. From the Fens come freshwater fish including eel and perch. Also from the Fens, from the rich growing country around Wisbech comes soft fruit - raspberries, strawberries, black and red currants, and gooseberries. Pick your own or buy them fresh from roadside stalls or farm shops.

The growing conditions of these counties are perfect for grain too, and the East of England produces one third of England's total output to prove it.

The many windmills dotted along the horizon worked hard in days gone by to grind the corn. The process of stone grinding generates hardly any heat, and consequently the nutritional value and flavour of flour produced by windmills still working today, is much greater than in flour produced by modern milling techniques.

Most Lincolnshire bakers have a secret. It is their recipe for Lincolnshire Plum Bread. Which gives you a wonderful excuse to keep on testing until you find the one who makes your favourite combination of spiciness and fruitiness.

Growing conditions and the more-than-average sunshine of this region provide just the right climate for grapes, and these are grown to produce excellent wine at Chilford Hall Vineyard.

Just one thing we don't produce - despite the village name of Stilton, we don't make Stilton cheese. But what we do do with it is roll it. Down hills. Yes - every Spring the Stilton Cheese Rolling Festival takes place. I'm not pulling your leg - come and see!

## Restaurants

### Cambridgeshire

### Cambridge
### ⊛ Arundel House Hotel
Chesterton Road, Cambridge CB4 3AN
Tel: (01223) 367701  Fax: (01223) 367721
Elegant, privately owned, 105 bedroom C19th Victorian terrace hotel beautifully located overlooking the River Cam and open parkland, only a few minutes walk from the historic city centre and famous University colleges. The hotel is well known for its friendly relaxed atmosphere and has a reputation for providing some of the best food in the area, at very modest prices, in its award winning restaurant. The hotel's magnificent Victorian style conservatory, which overlooks an attractive walled garden adjacent to the bar, offers an alternative menu throughout the day, including cream teas with additional seating outside. The hotel facilities also include a large car park. *(K/L23/24)*

### Cambridge
### Cambridge Garden House Moat House
Granta Place, Mill Lane,
Cambridge CB2 1RT
Tel: (01223) 259988
In the heart of historic Cambridge the Garden House Hotel offers 117 recently refurbished superior, en suite bedrooms, six conference and meeting rooms, a bar and lounge and an AA Rosette award-winning restaurant offering delicious modern cuisine. This hotel is situated on the banks of the River Cam with its own private garden. Private car parking is available and full leisure facilities in our Club Moativation. *(K/L23/24)*

### Cambridge
### ⊛ Galleria Restaurant
33 Bridge Street, Cambridge
Tel: (01223) 362054  Fax: (01233) 301623
Boasting a reputation of being the oldest French Restaurant in Cambridge. Enjoy the only City riverside balcony. Cooking to traditional French recipes: excellent food with very reasonable prices. The unique design of the restaurant creates a relaxed environment. *Open: Mon-Sat 1100-2300; Sun 1100-2230. Lunch prices between £2.95 - £5.95. Dinner, three courses with house wine £15.00 per person. (K/L23/24)*

*River Cam, Cambridge*

### Cambridge
#### ☸ Hobbs Pavilion Restaurant
Park Terrace
Tel: (01223) 367480
E-mail: hill.hobbs@dial.pipex.com
Full menus on Internet at
http://www.touristnetuk.com/em/hobbs
A selection of savoury and sweet pancakes filled with fascinating combinations from Bumper Vegetarian (cheese, spinach, basil, tomatoes) to Hobbs Special Steak with mashed potatoes. Full range of first courses from the blackboard. More traditional main courses come from the Char Grill - Dover Sole (£12.95), Duck Breast (£9.95), Chicken Breast (£8.50). Selection of wines served by the bottle or glass. A good place to take children. Seats 60. *Open: 1200-1415 lunch, 1900-2145 dinner. Closed Sun, Mon, Bank Holidays, mid Aug-mid Sept. Average price: £14.50 dinner with coffee, per head. 100% non-smoking. (K/L23/24)*

*Hemingford Abbots, Cambridgeshire*

### Cambridge
#### ☸ Panos
Hills Road
Tel: (01223) 212958
Elegant professional standards, close to Botanic Gardens with easy access to the railway station and historic centre. The cuisine has its own special interest and originality, offering a variety of Greek and French dishes - even a traditional 'Mezze' as a first course. Desserts, all home-made, include Crêpe Suzette and Baklava. Turkish coffee and Cappuccino are offered. The expertly chosen range of wines is very reasonably priced. The lunch menu varied, imaginative and attractively competitive at £12.50 for 2 courses. Daily "special" always available. *Restaurant open Mon-Fri lunch and dinner, Sat dinner, Sun closed. 2 course lunch £12.50, 3 course dinner £15.95. (L23/24)*

### Duxford
#### ☸ Duxford Lodge Hotel
Ickleton Road, Duxford CB2 4RU
Tel: (01223) 836444
Beautiful gardens, village setting, close to Duxford Air Museum, just south of Cambridge. This attractive hotel has much going for it. Beautifully maintained public rooms and delightful bedrooms provide a relaxed informal atmosphere. Modern french cooking in 'Le Paradis' restaurant has strong Provencal touches in dishes such as a superlative Tuna and Tomato tart, lovely pan fried turbot with olive oil, garlic, thyme and lemon and a tart tatin the way I like it, heavy on the caramelization with great custard sauce. Cheerful enthusiastic service. *Closed Saturday lunch. Lunch/Dinner prices from £9.95 (2 courses). (L25)*

### Ely
#### ☸ The Old Fire Engine House
25 Saint Mary's Street, Ely CB7 4ER
Tel: (01353) 662582
The Old Fire Engine House is a restaurant and Gallery, which has been owned and run by the same family since 1968. An 18th century brickbuilding close to Ely Cathedral, it has a large walled garden, friendly staff and an informal atmosphere. The cooking is based on local ingredients and classic English dishes form the mainstay of the menus. There is an extensive wine list and afternoon teas are also served. Art Gallery features monthly exhibitions of work by local and national artists. *Open for coffee, lunch, tea and dinner - telephone for details. (M20)*

*Cambridgeshire ● Lincolnshire*

St Ives, Cambridgeshire

### Madingley
### ❀ Three Horseshoes
(2m NW Cambridge)
Tel: (01954) 210221

Just outside Cambridge, this enchanting thatched village inn is one of the busiest quality restaurants in East Anglia. Richards Stokes' creative cooking has a clear Mediterranean bias, but concentrates on maximising the flavour of the best possible ingredients, whatever they may be. The pretty conservatory and the informal bar area both provide a relaxed atmosphere. Also on offer are superb wines (national winner of 1994 Italian wine list of the year award) and three real ales in perfect condition. *Open: daily. Average prices: lunch & dinner à la carte £19.00, bar food from £3.95. (K23)*

### Huntingdon
### ❀ The Old Bridge Hotel
Tel: (01480) 52681

The ultimate 'country hotel in a town'. The lounges extend into a really splendid conservatory with attractive and comfortable cane chairs and tables amidst lush green plants in great tubs. Here one can enjoy exceptional brasserie style food, with a lavish buffet, also available at lunchtime. Also a top-class, panelled restaurant with a wine list regularly named as one of the finest in the UK. Enjoy tea, coffee and drinks any time of day in the comfortable lounge and bar or outside on the patio. *Open: daily. Average prices: 3 course restaurant meal £17.50. Brasserie meals from £3.95. (I21/22)*

### Keyston
### ❀ The Pheasant Inn
(off A14 Between
Huntingdon & Thrapston)
Tel: (01832) 710241

A delightful thatched village pub, its 17th century interior decorated with farming bygones beneath the old beams. Chef Patron Martin Lee produces a sophisticated menu which is acclaimed in every major national guide. In both the restaurant and the bar area you can enjoy imaginative and interesting dishes, competitively priced and finely presented, with several real ales and over 15 wines by the glass. Should the sun shine, enjoy eating outside overlooking the village green. *Open: daily. Average prices: lunch or dinner à la carte £17.00, bar food from £3.25. (F21)*

### Kimbolton
### ❀ The New Sun Inn
20-22 High Street
Tel: (01480) 860052

16th Century beamed Inn and Restaurant. Real Ales and home made food using local produce. Bar meals £2.00-£6.00. Three-course meal an average of £15.00. Traditional Sunday lunch £5.25. *Open 365 days of the year. House Specials include Garlic Mushrooms with Bacon and Cream, Chocolate Fudge and Walnut Pudding. (G22)*

### Outwell
### ❀ Crown Lodge Hotel
Downham Road, Outwell,
Wisbech PE14 8SE
Tel: (01945) 773391

Situated on the A1101/A1122 Downham Market to Wisbech road on the banks of the Well Creek in the Fenland village of Outwell. Enjoy the choice of a relaxed bar, patio garden setting or the more formal surroundings of the Crown Room. Wherever you choose your meal will be beautifully presented and prepared with pride. Mick Castell, head chef, and his team will combine the freshest and local produce with more exotic ingredients to prepare dishes of flair and imagination that are sure to tempt you. *Open: daily, lunch 10.00am-2pm, dinner 6.30pm-10pm. Prices: bar meals from £3.95, à la carte from £14.95. (L/M17)*

*Cambridgeshire ● Lincolnshire*

*Lincolnshire 'Poacher Cheese'*

## *afternoon teas*

## Cambridgeshire

### Elton
### ⊛ Bressingham Plant Centre Tea Room
Bressingham Plant Centre,
Elton Hall, Elton, Peterborough
Tel: (01832) 280058

8 miles west of Peterborough on A605. Enjoy tasty lunchtime delights and tempting tea-time treats in the peaceful Plant Centre setting, with over 5,000 varieties of colourful garden plants. *Open: Daily including Sunday, 0900-1730 except Christmas Day/Boxing Day. See also entry for Bressingham Plant Centre under Nurseries & Garden Centres page 38, and Elton Hall under Historic Houses page 25. (G18/19)*

### Ely
### ⊛ Steeplegate
16/18 High Street
Tel: (01353) 664731

Proprietor: Mr J S Ambrose  Seats: 40 Home-made cakes, scones and fresh cream teas served in historic building backing onto cathedral. Medieval vault on view. Craft goods also sold. Small groups welcome. *Open: Daily except Sun. (M20)*

### St Ives
### ⊛ Connies Traditional Tea Rooms and Riverbank Restaurant
4 The Quay, St Ives, PE17 4AR
Tel: (01480) 498199

Proprietor: Connie Stevens. Seats: 86 inside, 16 in courtyard  Overlooking the river and 15th century bridge chapel. Connies's exudes an old world charm where lovingly prepared home-made food is served courteously. With emphasis on presentation and quality, we aim to make your visit pleasurable. Home-baking. Full meals. Cream teas. Licensed. Four rooms, three with open fires in winter Courtyard. *Open: All year, 7 days a week. (J21/22)*

## *regional produce*

## Cambridgeshire

### Linton
### Chilford Hall Vineyard
Clifford Hundred Ltd., Balsham Road
Linton, Cambridge CB1 6LE
Tel: (01223) 892641

Taste and buy award winning wines from the largest vineyard in Cambridgeshire. See the grapes growing in the eighteen acre vineyard, learn how English wine is made and appreciate the subtle difference between each of the Chilford quality wines. Also on sale, a range of local specialities-browse and buy! *Open from Easter - 31 Oct. Group visits by arrangement throughout the year. Vineyard tours £4.50 per person or £3.75 for groups of over 15. Free tastings and souvenir glass. Take the A11/1307 then just follow -'Chilford Hall Vineyard' signs. Telephone for group bookings. (M25)*

## Lincolnshire

### Waddingham
### Brandy Wharf Cider Centre
Waddingham,
Gainsborough DN21 9RW
Tel: (01652) 678364

Hidden in the sprawling Ancholme valley on the B1205 Caistor-Gainsborough road is Brandy Wharf, 5 miles east of the main A15. Here we have a 4 acre riverside orchard complete with a unique cider tavern offering over 60 various ciders including up to 15 on draught, plus fruit wines. Meals are available daily (except Tues lunchtimes) ranging from a satisfying sandwich to specialities Scrumpy Cider Sausage. You need to see our full menu to appreciate the choice. Also museum, festivals, events. Leaflet. *Open: daily, 1200-1500, 1900-2300 (Sundays 2230). (E5)*

### Wainfleet
### George Bateman & Son Ltd
Salem Bridge Brewery, Wainfleet
Tel: (01754) 880317

An attractive family brewery where the true art of brewing has not been lost by time. Using raw materials from the UK, Bateman's Beers have won numerous awards. Evening and weekend visits available by prior appointment. *Evening visits: £10.00 per head (inc. tour of the brewery, beer sampling and supper). (L10)*

In an area so distinct and evocative as the Fens, an area where for generations people have made a living from skills such as willow basket making or reed harvesting and wode milling, it's hardly surprising that this continues to be a place where creativity flourishes. In your travels you'll come across many galleries and craft studios.

## Cambridgeshire

steeplegate

### Ely
🌣 **Steeplegate**
16-18 High Street, Ely
Tel: (01353) 664731
Unusual gifts of good taste in Craft Gallery beside the cathedral. Tearoom. We sell woodwork, books, ceramics, jewellery, lace and toys. *Open all year, daily except Sunday, 0900-1730. (M20)*

*Alford Craft Market, Lincolnshire*

## Lincolnshire

### Lincoln
🌣 **Cobb Hall Centre**
St Paul's Lane, Bailgate,
Lincoln LN1 3AX
Tel: (01522) 534627
Complex of small retail units: crafts, antiques, garden shop, patio plants, pots and landscape design. Ladies' aerobic and fitness wear, hairdresser and stylist, tea room. Situated between two car parks in tourist area, adjacent to Castle. *(E8)*

*A day out at Lincoln Castle*

### Cromwell Country
- follow in the footsteps of the great Lord Protector.
**Starting point:** Huntingdon, Cambs *(I21)*
**Mileage:** 21m
**Morning** - visit the *Cromwell Museum* with its artefacts and portraits, then take the A1123 to the riverside town of *St. Ives*, with its unusual bridge chapel and statue of Cromwell in the Market Square.
**Afternoon** - continue along the A1123 to Stretham (about 12m), then turn left onto the A10 to *Ely*. Visit the magnificent *Cathedral and Oliver Cromwell's House*. Try on the medieval hats and watch out for his ghost!

### Time Travel East
- jump aboard our time machine, for a journey through the centuries.
**Starting point:** Peterborough, Cambs *(H18)*
**Mileage:** 15m
**Morning** - start the day in the Bronze Age with the prehistoric excavations at *Flag Fen*, then its into Norman times at the beautiful *Peterborough Cathedral*, where the tomb of Catherine of Aragon can be seen.
**Afternoon** - take a Victorian-style steam train ride aboard the *Nene Valley Railway*, then take the A47/A1 north to end the day in *Stamford*, described as 'the best stone town in England' with its Georgian streets and lanes. If there's time, a visit can be made to the immense Elizabethan *Burghley House*.

### Royalty & Religion
- re-live the characters and drama of Lincolnshire's rich and turbulent past.
**Tour 1: Starting Point:** Lincoln, Lincs *(E8)*
**Mileage:** 30m
**Morning** - spend the morning in the beautiful city of *Lincoln*. Visit the *Cathedral*, wander down Steep Hill (and back up again!) and see one of the three original Magna Carta documents at the *Norman Castle*.
**Afternoon** - take the A57/A156 to *Gainsborough*, and visit the *Old Hall*, where Henry VIII banqueted. Take the A631 to Beckingham, where you turn right onto the A161 to *Epworth*. Visit the *Old Rectory*, home of John and Charles Wesley, the founders of Methodism.

### Milling Mayhem
- enjoy a windy day out amongst some of Britain's best-kept windmills
**Starting point:** Sleaford, Lincs *(F12)*
**Mileage:** 23m
**Morning** - take the A17 to Heckington, and visit the magnificent *Windmill*, the only surviving one of its type in Britain with eight sails. Continue on the A17 to Swineshead Bridge, then take the A1121/A52 to Boston.
**Afternoon** - climb the seven-floored *Maud Foster Windmill* and enjoy home-made cakes made with freshly ground flour. End the day by taking the A16 north for 5m to the *Sibsey Trader Windmill*, built in 1877.

### Tennyson Country
- discover the rolling Lincolnshire Wolds, inspiration for one of England's greatest poets.
**Starting point:** Louth , Lincs *(J6)*
**Mileage:** 23m
**Morning** - this Georgian town is where Tennyson was briefly educated, and his Poems by 'Two Brothers' was published in 1827. Take the A153 south for 4m, then turn left onto the scenic 'Bluestone Ridge' road. Follow the road for 4m, pass the viewpoint then turn right to Tetford. Follow signs to *Somersby*, where Tennyson was born at the rectory in 1809. Visit the church with its mementoes.
**Afternoon** - remain on the unclassified road for 0.5m, then turn right to Hagworthingham. At the junction with the A158, turn left. After 8m, visit *Gunby Hall*, Tennyson's haunt of `ancient peace'.

*Woodmans Cottage, Tennyson Country, Lincolnshire*

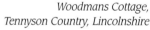

*Cambridgeshire ● Lincolnshire*

*Burghley House, Stamford, Lincolnshire*

## Aviation Heritage

- trace the story of British aviation, at historic airfields and museums

**Tour 1:**

**Starting point:** Coningsby , Lincs *(H/I10)*

**Mileage:** varied (depending on tour taken)

**Morning** - visit the historic planes of the *Battle of Britain Memorial Flight*. Then take the B1192 to Woodhall Spa, to see the *Dambusters Memorial* and the Squadron bar at the *Petwood House Hotel*.

**Afternoon** - spend the rest of the day exploring the *North Kesteven Airfield Trail*, including the *Metheringham Visitor Centre* and the *RAF College at Cranwell*, home of the Red Arrows aerobatic team.

**Tour 2: Starting point:**
Cambridge, Cambs *(K/L23/24)*

**Mileage:** 11m

**Morning** - take a walking tour of the city, including the *Eagle pub* where you visit the historic Air Force bar.

**Afternoon** - leave the city on the A1303 to visit the *American Cemetery & Memorial*. Retrace your steps to junction 13 of the M11 and follow this south to junction 10. Spend the rest of the day at Europe's top aviation museum, the *Imperial War Museum at Duxford*, with over 140 historic aircraft to see.

## Birds & Bees

- wander amongst the nectar-rich countryside and wildlife of the east.

**Tour 1:**

**Starting point:** Long Sutton , Lincs *(K15)*

**Mileage:** 23m

**Morning** - let exotic butterflies land in your hands at *The Butterfly & Wildlife Park*, then take the A1101 south to *Wisbech*. Take a tour of the *Elgood's Brewery* and enjoy a pint in the adjacent garden.

**Afternoon** - visit the wonderful *Peckover House*, with its orangery and fernery. Then take the A1101 (via Outwell) to the *Welney Wildfowl & Wetlands Trust*, which attracts large numbers of ducks and swans.

**Tour 2: Starting point:** Brigg, Lincs *(E/F3/4)*

**Mileage:** 17m

**Morning** - leave Brigg on the A18/B1206 to the butterfly and falconry displays at *Elsham Hall Country Park*.

**Afternoon** - take the B1206/B1204 north to South Ferriby. At the junction with the A1077, turn left and enjoy the views over the Humber Estuary. After 5.5m, turn right onto the B1430 and follow signs to *Normanby Hall Country Park*, with its Regency mansion and excellent Victorian walled garden.

*Springfields Gardens, Spalding, Lincolnshire*

### Bloomin' Beautiful

- enjoy the spectacular colours and delicate fragrances of some of England's finest gardens.

**Tour 1: Starting point:** Spalding, Lincs *(I15)*
**Mileage:** 3m
**Morning** - take the road north to Pinchbeck (the old A16) to visit *The Spalding Bulb Museum*, where you can learn about the industry. Then visit the steamy *Tropical Forest*, before returning to Spalding.
**Afternoon** - visit the colourful gardens of *Ayscoughfee Hall, Museum and Garden*, then end the day at the famous bulb showground of *Springfields*, with its Daffodils, Hyacinths and Tulips.

**Tour 2: Starting point:**
Cambridge, Cambs *(K/L23/24)*
**Mileage:** 5m
**Morning** - start the day in *Cambridge*, visit the famous Botanic Garden and try your hand at punting.
**Afternoon** - leave Cambridge on the A1303 towards Newmarket. At the junction with the A14, take the B1102 towards Burwell, following the signs to the 17th century *Anglesey Abbey, Gardens & Lode Mill*.

**Tour 3:**
**Starting point:** Grantham, Lincs *(D13)*
**Mileage:**      Harlaxton & Belton 6.5m
                  Harlaxton & Grimsthorpe 17m
**Morning** - leave Grantham on the A607 to the classic re-created *Harlaxton Manor Gardens*.
**Afternoon** - two choices, either visit the magnificent Belton House, by returning on the A607 to Grantham and onto the village of Belton. OR head to the wildflowers and vegetables of *Grimsthorpe Castle*, by taking the A607 to the A1 junction. Follow this south for 7m to the roundabout with the A151, turn left and head to Grimsthorpe.

*Anglesey Abbey, Cambridgeshire*

### A Fishy Something!

- seaside fun and games for all the family on the Lincolnshire coast

**Tour 1:**
**Starting point:** Skegness, Lincs *(M9)*
**Mileage:** 4m
**Morning** - enjoy the seaside attractions of Skegness, one of Britain's best family resorts. Meet the friendly seals at Natureland, take a donkey ride on the beach and watch out for the "Jolly Fisherman" character!
**Afternoon** - head north along the A52 to Ingoldmells, and end the day amongst the tropical attractions of Fantasy Island. Don't miss a ride on Europe's largest looping roller coaster (opening early 1999).

**Tour 2: Starting point:** Grimsby, Lincs *(I3)*
**Mileage:** 3m
**Morning** - experience the sights and smells of Grimsby's great fishing industry at the award-winning heritage centre. Then enjoy some of Britain's best fish and chips.
**Afternoon** - head south to the seaside town of Cleethorpes, where more fish can be seen at the Deep Sea Experience, or alternatively become a giant lugworm at the Discovery Centre. End the day on the stomach-churning Boomerang ride at Pleasure Island.

*A fun day out at Skegness, Lincolnshire*

*Cambridgeshire* ● *Lincolnshire*

# *Norfolk & Suffolk*

Norfolk and Suffolk well deserve their popularity and it's not surprising that so many of us love these counties. The pace is gentle here, so take time to get to know the area. Explore quiet lanes and unspoilt villages. Take to the water and discover the *Norfolk Broads*. Stand back and admire the wide skies and landscape of *Constable Country*. Meander along the coast and enjoy seaside towns and spacious beaches ...

*Our coastline* Let me come with you and show you around. We'll discover the coastline together, beginning at the seaside town of *Hunstanton*, near *King's Lynn*. Unlike any other seaside town in the East of England, *Hunstanton* faces West, towards the Wash. It is famous for its cliffs, striped red and white, made from layers of red carrstone and white chalk. It was built as a sea bathing resort in 1846 and still retains much of its original Victorian elegance.

*Seals and steam trains* Moving eastwards the coastline becomes salt marsh, ideal habitat for many seabirds. There is much undisturbed space around here, scattered with bird reserves. Nelson was born here, and as you travel you will notice pub names and other reminders of Norfolk's famous son. *Holkham* beach is a paradise of wide open sand backed by dunes and pine

trees, and nearby *Wells-next-the-Sea* has the most fascinating array of beach huts of all shapes and sizes, many built high up on stilts. From *Wells*, there's a miniature steam railway which takes you inland through farmland and poppy fields to *Little Walsingham*, a religious centre which drew pilgrims in the middle ages as it still does today. Many of the religious buildings can still be seen. *Blakeney* is famous for its seals. Take a boat to *Scolt Head* to see them basking on the rocks. Just inland is *Holt*, a small attractive town with many houses made of flint, a building material much used in this area. From *Holt*, the North Norfolk Steam Railway will take you to *Sheringham*. Both *Sheringham* and nearby *Cromer* grew up around the fishing industry and it's not hard to imagine the hard work and bustle on the beach every time the catch came in. At *Cromer* the fishing boats still work off the beach and you can buy freshly caught crabs straight from the fishermen. There is safe bathing here from sandy beaches. Small seaside towns such as *Mundesley* and *Happisburgh* are dotted along the coast east of *Cromer*, and inland is the market town of *North Walsham*.

*Fun of the fair* Next we reach bright, lively *Great Yarmouth* with all the fun of the fair and more besides. Here are wonderful wide, sandy beaches and the impressive Marine Parade with colourful gardens and almost every

imaginable holiday attraction and amenity. Here are all-weather sports and entertainments, as well as an interesting

*continued*

## contents

*Below: Cavendish, Suffolk*
*Left: Norwich, Norfolk*

historical quayside and numerous museums and other places of interest.

Over the border in Suffolk is *Lowestoft*, Britain's most easterly town, which successfully combines the roles of holiday resort and modern fishing and commercial port. Here are the seaside pleasures of clean, sandy beaches, indoor and outdoor sports, and also, turning inland, you will find *Oulton Broad*, a fine stretch of water which is part of the Broads National Park. You can explore the water by cruiser, sailing boat or rowing boat. There are indoor and outdoor sports, a family theme park, museums, events and festivals.

### Keeping with tradition

*Southwold* and *Walberswick*, linked by a ferry over the river are two very attractive and individualist seaside towns. Visit either, and you may begin to wonder if you are back in the 1940s or '50s, or even whether the rest of the world really exists. So resistant are they to change that when a young lady recently proposed to sell ice cream from a barrow on *Southwold*'s promenade, there was an uproar of disapproval from the townsfolk. Perhaps it is this very resistance

to change which makes these towns so special. Helped, certainly by some excellent restaurants and the good beer brewed here.

Parts of this coastline, battered by weather and the might of the North Sea, are

### Ghostly bells toll under the sea

gradually being eroded into the sea. A visit to *Dunwich* Museum will bring home the reality. A series of photographs shows the church, once standing near the cliff edge, gradually disappear over the years bit by bit until only a part of the wall is left, and finally nothing but a gravestone remains. Stand on the cliff today and they say you can hear the church bells tolling under the sea. Much of the coastline is an undisturbed home for birds and wildlife, and at *Minsmere* Bird Reserve the habitat is managed

*Southwold, Suffolk*

carefully to encourage the huge variety of birds, including the avocet, which choose this as their annual breeding place.

Avocets nest at *Orford Ness* too, a ten mile long shingle spit of land which the National Trust has opened up to visitors. Cut off from the sea by this shingle spit is the attractive village of *Orford* and from the castle keep is a grand view of brick and timber cottages and marshes beyond.

The holiday village of *Thorpeness* was a "dream" creation as a sanctuary for children

### Beware the crocodile!

and a place to while away long hours in fascination and safety. The lake is a paradise. Moor your hired boat to explore the island homes of the characters from Peter Pan - but beware the crocodile doesn't catch you! On the horizon is "The House in the Clouds", the most fantastic of dwelling places which began life as a water tower in disguise.

Now we reach the little town of *Aldeburgh*, where the fishing boats may be seen drawn up on the beach, and the fish and chips are the best in the world. The famous Aldeburgh Festival was begun here by

Benjamin Britten and Peter Pears in 1948 and it has developed now into a year round programme of music and arts shared between Aldeburgh and Snape Maltings Concert Hall. Finally *Felixstowe*, a popular family resort, magnificent when its floral displays are in full bloom, though sometimes these flower creations can be a bit cheeky - recently a pink floral dinosaur was known occasionally to squirt onlookers with water!

Let me take you inland now, to explore villages, towns and countryside. Just inland from *Aldeburgh* and *Felixstowe*, on the banks

### Inland landscapes

of the River Deben is the quiet, Georgian town of *Woodbridge*. Its tide mill on the quay, with boats moored close by, is a favourite view for photographers. Close by, the town of *Framlingham* is of interest particularly for its bizarre castle, whose ruined walls are topped by Tudor brick chimneys. Between these towns and the coast is a landscape of river estuaries and heathland, with the forest playgrounds of *Rendlesham* and *Tunstall* where there is safe off road cycling as well as good walking country. For more

*Framlingham Castle, Suffolk*

forest playground, head for *Thetford Forest* where there are miles of forest trails to explore. At the heart of the forest, at *Santon Downham*, there are waymarked trails, a maze and much more.

On the edge of the forest is *Thetford*, a market town which has been thriving since before the Norman Conquest, and many traces of its past remain, from the Iron Age ramparts surrounding the Norman Castle mound, to the priory ruins and fine buildings of the town centre.

A favourite drive of mine is the tree-lined route through the forest from Thetford towards *King's Lynn*, but first I want to take you east, to the Waveney Valley.

The River Waveney forms the natural boundary between Norfolk and Suffolk.

### Wilds and wetlands along the Waveney

This gentle countryside is an area of grazing land and marshes, providing a quiet habitat for wetland birds and plants and a safe haven for otters, some of which have been reared at the Otter Trust at *Bungay* and released into the wild. Dotted along the valley are several attractive market towns. *Bungay* is one of these, also *Beccles*. Many visitors see *Beccles* from the river which is wide here and navigable, but after mooring your boat to stop for a drink in one of the riverside pubs it is worth looking further to discover the heart of this interesting town. Up river is *Harleston*, a favourite spot for artists, and *Diss*, a thriving market town whose older part centres around its market place and its mere, a large lake which is a haven for ducks.

Just south of the river is *Eye*, a small 18th century market town. Climb to the top of the castle mound for an excellent view of the town and surrounding countryside.

*continued*

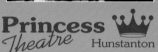

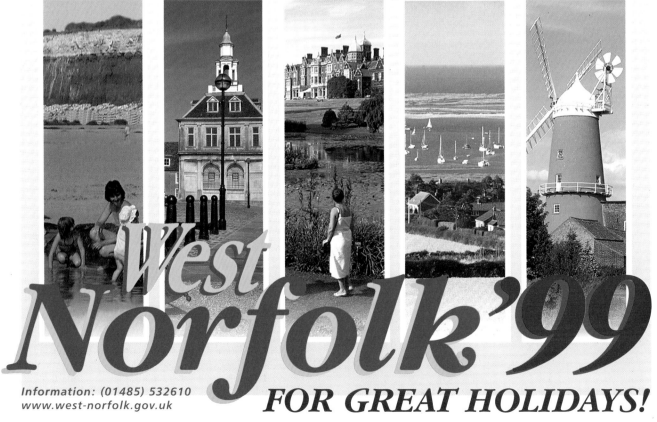
*Norfolk ● Suffolk*

## Market towns

The market place at the heart of *Wymondham* is dominated by the ancient timber framed octagonal Market Cross. The town's impressive Abbey has two tall towers which appear against the skyline from whichever way you approach. Inside are ranks of arches and windows soaring upto the beautiful hammerbeam roof. *Swaffham's* market place is triangular, and so extensive that it gives the town an air of expansive tranquillity, transformed every Saturday by the famous open air market and public auction. Around the market place are fine Georgian buildings.

## Afloat on the Broads

The best way to see the Broads is at a gentle pace from a boat. You'll be travelling through so timeless and natural a place that it's hard to believe that this landscape is man made.

In the middle ages when *Norwich* was the third largest city in England, Broadland was one of the most densely populated parts of the country. In need of fuel, people turned to the peaty marshes around the rivers, and excavated huge pits - by hand. As the sea level rose, the peat diggings started to flood and today these are the shallow lakes we know as the *Broads*.

The adjoining villages of *Wroxham* and *Hoveton* are known as the "capital of the Broads" and most visits start from a boatyard here. At *Ranworth*, stop and visit the church to see the wonderful views from its tower. *Potter Heigham* is known for its medieval bridge, and the holiday village of *Horning* stretches a mile along the river.

*Ranworth Broad, Norfolk*

Some of Britain's rarest wildlife can be found here. If you're here in spring, listen out for the odd "booming" sound of the bittern. This bird nests among the reeds and sounds like a muffled fog horn!

## Newmarket, home of Horseracing

Get to *Newmarket* in the early morning and you will see the racehorses out training on the gallops - a fine sight to watch. This has been the home of horseracing ever since James I's Scottish nobles introduced racing to England. You can gain a fascinating insight into the way horses are bred and trained, raced and cared for by visiting the National Stud and the National Horseracing Museum.

## Seeking favour in the next life

Wend your way south east of *Newmarket*, picking a route which takes you through *Clare* and *Cavendish*, two of my favourite places, and a foretaste of what is to come. Soon you will reach Suffolk's wool towns, a group of villages and towns which grew in the 14th and 15th centuries thanks to the trade in wool. *Lavenham* and *Hadleigh* were among the most prosperous towns in England at the time, and have many fine medieval buildings as evidence of this wealth. *Lavenham's* half timbered Guildhall and Little Hall are both open to visitors. The villages of *Kersey* and *Lindsey* have wool connections too.

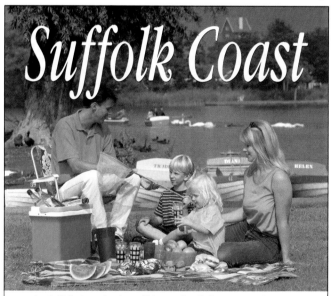

*Norfolk ● Suffolk*

*Long Melford* also prospered and has one of the most magnificent churches in the country, built by wealthy traders hoping to find favour in the next life. It also has two fine Tudor mansions and a multitude of antique shops.

*Willy Lott's Cottage, Flatford*

Nearby *Sudbury* prospered with the weaving and silk industries, but it is most famous as

## Artists' Inspiration

the birthplace of its talented son, Thomas Gainsborough. And now, simply follow the course of the River Stour through countryside so lovely that it will come as no surprise that this is the river valley which brought inspiration to that other famous artist, John Constable. *Stoke-by-Nayland*, *East Bergholt*, *Dedham* and *Flatford* have all been settings for his paintings, and all are most attractive places.

However much we would like to linger in the countryside, we can't leave Norfolk and

## Fine city, fine towns

Suffolk without a visit to the larger towns. We have four to visit - *Norwich*, *King's Lynn*, *Ipswich* and *Bury St Edmunds*. *Norwich* has so much to see. At the heart of the city is the Norman Castle, described as "the most ambitious secular building of its generation anywhere in Europe". It is surrounded by the Castle Green Park, and stands proudly over the discreetly designed Castle Mall shopping centre. *Norwich* has one of England's finest Norman Cathedrals as well as the striking Catholic Cathedral. It has the most complete medieval street pattern in England with 1,500 historic buildings including the fine guildhall, within its walled centre. The market place is busy and colourful and the many fine museums shed further insight into the history of this interesting city. And for a more restful view of this fine city, take a walk along the river, or even a boat trip through the city and nearby countryside.

The Old Custom House is a landmark on the quay at *King's Lynn*. Medïeval streets run from the town centre down to the quays, and merchants' houses with their private warehouses are a reminder of the wealth of the town. It has two guildhalls, both still in use, one as an Arts Centre, the other the place to visit to hear and see the "Tales of the Old Gaol House".

In the middle of *Ipswich* is Christchurch Mansion. You can look around this Tudor Mansion which is set in beautiful parkland, and contains a fine collection of paintings by Suffolk artists Gainsborough and Constable. The Ancient House is heavily decorated with pargeting - its design depicting the four continents (the fifth not having been discovered at the time it was made). It's the finest example of pargeting in the whole of England. *Ipswich* has 12 medieval churches, and its Victorian brewery is still producing good beer.

*Bury St Edmunds* is the only town in Britain to have a cathedral left uncompleted - but not for much longer! *Bury's* biggest project for the Millennium is to finish the job and build a tower worthy of the rest of the building. Close to the cathedral are the dramatic ruins of the medieval abbey set in the Abbey Gardens where Bury's gardeners show off their skills with stunning floral displays, the showpiece of a town decorated with flowers at every possible opportunity. There is plenty of intriguing architecture including Moyse's Hall Museum, the oldest house in the town, and the Georgian Manor House Museum.

*The smallest pub in Britain, 'The Nutshell', Bury St Edmunds, Suffolk*

# Tourist Information Centres

With so much to see and do in this area, it's impossible for us to mention all of the places you can visit. You will find Tourist Information Centres (TICs) throughout Norfolk and Suffolk, with plenty of information on all the things that you can do and the places you can visit. TICs can book accommodation for you, in their own area, or further afield using the 'Book A Bed Ahead Scheme'. They can be the ideal place to purchase locally made crafts or gifts, as well as books covering a wide range of local interests. A list of the TICs in this area can be found below, together with a map reference to help you locate them.

\* Not open all year.

## Norfolk

**Aylsham**, Bure Valley Railway Station, Norwich Road, Tel: (01263) 733903 (K6/7)
**Cromer**, Bus Station, Prince of Wales Road, Tel: (01263) 512497 (L4/5)
**Diss**, Meres Mouth, Mere Street, Tel: (01379) 650523 (JI3)
\* **Fakenham**, Red Lion House, Market Place, Tel: (01328) 851981 (G/H6)
\* **Great Yarmouth**, Marine Parade, Tel: (01493) 842195/846345 (P9)
\* **Hoveton**, Station Road, Tel: (01603) 782281 (M8)
**Hunstanton**, Town Hall, The Green, Tel: (01485) 532610 (D5)
**King's Lynn**, The Old Gaol House, Saturday Market Place, Tel: (01553) 763044 (C7/8)
\* **Mundesley**, 2a Station Road, Tel: (01263) 721070 (M5)
**Norwich**, The Guildhall, Gaol Hill, Tel: (01603) 666071 (L9)
\* **Sheringham**, Station Approach, Tel: (01263) 824329 (K4)
\* **Wells-next-the-Sea**, Staithe Street, Tel: (01328) 710885 (G/H4)

## Suffolk

\* **Aldeburgh**, The Cinema, High Street, Tel: (01728) 453637 (O16)
\* **Beccles**, The Quay, Fen Lane, Tel: (01502) 713196 (N/O12)
**Bury St Edmunds**, 6 Angel Hill, Tel: (01284) 764667 (F/G15)
**Felixstowe**, Leisure Centre, Undercliff

Road West, Tel: (01394) 276770 (M19)
**Ipswich**, St Stephens Church, St Stephens Lane, Tel: (01473) 258070 (K18)
\* **Lavenham**, Lady Street, Tel: (01787) 248207 (G17)
**Lowestoft**, East Point Pavilion, Royal Plain, Tel: (01502) 523000/523057 (P11)
**Newmarket**, Palace House, Palace Street, Tel: (01638) 667200 (D15)
\* **Southwold**, Town Hall, Market Place, Tel: (01502) 724729 (P13/14)
**Stowmarket**, Wilkes Way, Tel: (01449) 676800 (I16)
**Sudbury**, Town Hall, Market Hill, Tel: (01787) 881320 (G18)
**Woodbridge**, Station Buildings, Tel: (01394) 382240 (L17)

## Blue Badge Guides:

There are also experts available to help you explore some of our towns and cities. These Registered Blue Badge Guides have all attended a training course sponsored by the East of England Tourist Board. Below are some of the tours offered by these Guides - you can obtain further information by contacting the appropriate Tourist Information Centre, unless otherwise indicated. Some Blue Badge Guides have a further qualification to take individuals or groups around the region for half day, full day or longer tours if required.

## Norfolk

### King's Lynn
**Regular Town Tours:** Individuals may join the tours, which leave the Tales of the Old Gaolhouse, May-Jul, Wed, Sat, 1400. Aug, Sep, daily except Tue and Thu, 1400. Sun, 1430.

**Group Tours:** Guided tours can be arranged for groups by contacting the King's Lynn Town Guides on Tel: (01553) 765714.

### Norwich
**Regular City Tours:** Historic Norwich walking tours lasting 1.5 hours leave from the Tourist Information Centre in the Guildhall at 1430 from Apr-Oct. Sun only Jun-Sep at 1100.

**Evening Tours:** Themed tours depart at 1900 from outside the Guildhall, up to twice weekly during Jun-Sep, lasting 1.5 hours.

**Group Tours:** Guides are available at any time for private groups on a variety of themes. Each tour lasts about 1.5 hours, one guide can escort up to twenty people. Guides for City Coach Tours are also arranged, lasting approximately, 1.25 hours.

**Day or Half Day Groups Coach Tours:**
Regional Guides are available for tours of Norfolk and East Anglia. Assistance with itineraries. Please contact the Tourist Information Centre for a leaflet giving further details on the above tours. Tel: (01603) 666071. Fax: (01603) 765389.

## Suffolk

### Ipswich
**Regular Town Tours:** Individuals may join the tours, lasting approximately 90 minutes, leaving from the Tourist Information Centre. May-Sep, Tue, Thu, 1415.

**Group Tours:** Tours can be arranged for groups all year. Please give at least one weeks notice.

### Bury St Edmunds
**Regular Town Tours:** Tours with Blue Badge Guides, lasting 1.5 hours, leave from the Tourist Information Centre. Tickets can be purchased in advance or on the day. Tours run daily in the summer, except Sat; contact for times. Also available special themed evening walks during August. Tel: (01284) 764667.

**Historical Tours:** Tours of the Abbey Ruins with Medieval monk Brother Jocelin, and of the Great Churchyard with Victorian grave digger, William Hunter. Tickets can be purchased in advance or on the day. Tours on Saturdays throughout the summer. Tel: (01284) 764667.

**Tours for Groups:** Guides can be arranged for groups at any time if enough notice is given. Special themes also available. Tel: (01284) 764667.

**St Edmundsbury Cathedral:** New for 1999 - Informative and fun tours of the cathedral. £2.00/50p/£2.00. Tel: (01284) 754933.

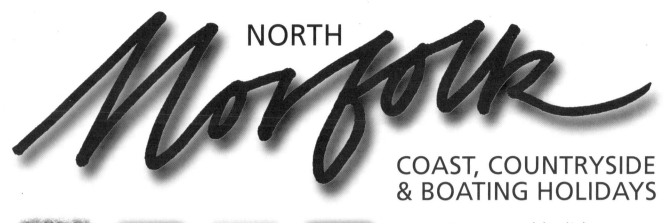

*Norwich Tourist Information Centre, Norfolk (see page 61)*

*Norfolk* ● *Suffolk*

### Sandringham
#### ⚜ Sandringham
Tel: (01553) 772675

The country retreat of HM The Queen. A delightful house and 60 acres of grounds and lakes. There is also a museum of royal vehicles and royal memorabilia. *Open House 1 Apr-20 Jul, 5 Aug-3 Oct, daily, 1100-1645; Grounds, 1 Apr-24 Jul, 5 Aug-3 Oct, daily, 1030-1700. £5.00/£3.00/£4.00. (D/E 6/7)*

### Thetford
#### ⚜ Euston Hall
Euston Estate Office
Tel: (01842) 766366

Hall housing paintings by Van Dyck, Lely and Stubbs with pleasure grounds designed by John Evelyn and 'Capability Brown' and the 17thC church of St Genevieve. *Open 3 Jun-30 Sep, Thu, 1430-1700; 27 Jun, 5 Sep, Sun, 1430-1700. Please contact for details. See page 66 for more information. (G13)*

### Thetford
#### ⚜ Thetford Warren Lodge
Tel: (01604) 730320

The ruins of a small 2-storey medieval gamekeeper's lodge which can only be viewed from the outside. *Open at any reasonable time. (F/G13)*

### Wells-next-the-Sea
#### ⚜ Holkham Hall
Tel: (01328) 710227

A classic 18thC Palladian-style mansion. Part of a great agricultural estate and a living treasure house of artistic and architectural history along with a bygones collection. *Open 4, 5 Apr, 2, 3 May, Sun, Bank Hol Mon, 1130-1700; 30 May-30 Sep, Sun-Thu, 1300-1700. Hall and Museum closed 18 Jul for Holkham Country Fair. £6.00/£3.00/£6.00. See below for further information. (G4)*

## Suffolk

### Flatford
#### ⚜ Bridge Cottage
East Bergolt Tel: (01206) 298260

A 16thC building with a tea garden, shop and a Constable exhibition set in a part of the Dedham Vale with many walks. *Open 3 Mar-30 Apr, Wed-Sun, 1100-1730; 1 May-30 Sep, daily, 1000-1730; 1 Oct-28 Nov, Wed-Sun, 1100-1530; 1-19 Dec, Wed-Sun, 1100-1530; closed 2-5 Apr. (J19)*

*Sandringham, Norfolk*
*(by gracious permission of HM The Queen)*

### Hadleigh
#### Guildhall
Market Place Tel: (01473) 823884

A medieval timber-framed complex, Grade I Listed (with a Victorian addition) dating from 14th-15thC. *Open 6 Jun-26 Sep, Thu, Sun, 1400-1700. £1.50/free/£1.00. (I18)*

### Haughley
#### Haughley Park
Tel: (01359) 240701

A Jacobean manor-house with gardens and woods set in parkland. *Open 2, 9 May, Sun, 1430-1730; 4 May-28 Sep, Tue, 1430-1730. £2.00/£1.00/£2.00. (I15/16)*

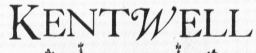

### Ickworth
### ⊛ Ickworth House Park and Gardens
Tel: (01284) 735270

An extraordinary oval house with flanking wings, begun in 1795. Fine paintings, a beautiful collection of Georgian silver, an Italian garden and 'Capability Brown' park walks. *Please contact for details of opening times. £5.20/£2.20/£5.50. (F16)*

### Lavenham
### ⊛ Lavenham Guildhall of Corpus Christi
Market Place   Tel: (01787) 247646

An impressive timber-framed building dating from the 1520s. Originally the hall of the Guild of Corpus Christi, now a local museum with information on the medieval wool trade. *Open 27 Mar-31 Oct, daily, 1100-1700; closed 2 Apr. £2.80/free/£2.80. (G/H17)*

*Otley Hall, Otley, Suffolk*

### Lavenham
### ⊛ Little Hall
Market Place  Tel: (01787) 247179

A 15thC hall house with a crown-post roof which contains the Gayer-Anderson collection of furniture, pictures, sculpture and ceramics. There is also a small walled garden. *Open 30 Mar-2 Nov, Wed, Thu, Sat, Sun, 1400-1730; last admission 1700; Bank Hol Mons, 1030-1730; last admission 1700. £1.50/50p/£1.50. (G/H17)*

### Long Melford
### ⊛ Kentwell Hall
Tel: (01787) 310207

A mellow redbrick Tudor manor surrounded by a moat, this family home has been interestingly restored with Tudor costume displays, a 16thC house and mosaic Tudor rose maze. *Please contact for details of opening times and prices. See page 65 for more information. (G17/18)*

### Long Melford
### ⊛ Melford Hall
Tel: (01787) 880286

A turreted brick Tudor mansion with 18thC and Regency interiors. A collection of Chinese porcelain, gardens and a walk in the grounds. Dogs must be on leads. *Open 3-25 Apr, Sat, Sun, Bank Hol Mon, 1400-1730; 1 May-30 Sep Wed-Sun, Bank Hol Mon, 1400-1730; 2-31 Oct, Sat, Sun, 1400-1730; last admission 1700. £4.20/£2.10/£4.20 . (G18)*

### Otley
### ⊛ Otley Hall
Hall Lane  Tel: (01473) 890264

A 15thC moated medieval hall, rich in architecture and family history, set in 10 acres of garden including a canal, mount, nuttery, herbacious and rose garden. *Open 4, 5 Apr, 2, 3, 30, 31 May, 29, 30 Aug, Sun, Bank Hol Mon, 1230-1800; Gardens 12 Apr-20 Sep, Mon,1400-1700. £4.00/£2.50/£4.00. (K/L 16/17)*

### Somerleyton
### ⊛ Somerleyton Hall and Gardens
Tel: (01502) 730224

An Anglo Italian-style building with state rooms, a maze, a garden with azaleas and rhododendrons, a miniature railway, shop and refreshment room for light luncheons and teas. *Open 4 Apr-27 Jun, Thu, Sun, Bank Hol Mon, 1230-1730; 1 Jul-31 Aug, Tue-Thu, Sun, Bank Hol Mon, 1230-1730; 2-26 Sep, Thu, Sun, 1230-1730. Please contact for details of admission prices. (O/P11)*

### Wingfield
### ⊛ Wingfield Old College
Tel: (01379) 384888

This delightful medieval house with walled gardens offers a unique arts and heritage experience. Exhibits of contemporary art and the newly opened College Yard Visitor Centre. *Open 3 Apr-26 Sep, Sun, Bank Hols, 1400-1800. £2.80/£1.00/£2.20. (L13/14)*

# *Ancient Monuments*

## Norfolk

### Baconsthorpe
#### ⊛ Baconsthorpe Castle
A 15thC part-moated, semi-fortified house. The remains include the inner and outer gatehouse and the curtain wall. Baconsthorpe Post Office sells guide books and postcards. *Open all year, daily, 1000-1600. (J5)*

### Binham
#### ⊛ Binham Priory
Tel: (01604) 230320
Extensive remains of an early 12thC Benedictine priory. The original nave of the church is still used as the parish church. *Open at any reasonable time. (H5)*

### Castle Acre
#### Castle Acre Castle
The remains of a Norman manor-house which became a castle with earthworks, set by the side of a village. *Open at any reasonable time. (F8)*

### Castle Acre
#### ⊛ Castle Acre Priory
Stocks Green
Tel: (01760) 755161
The impressive ruins of a Cluniac priory built by William de Warenne in about 1090 with a church and decorated 12thC west front and 16thC gatehouse and a prior's lodgings. *Open 1 Jan-21 Mar, Wed-Sun, 1000-1600; 22 Mar-31 Oct, daily, 1000-1800/1800 or dusk in Oct; 3 Nov-31 Dec, Wed-Sun, 1000-1600; closed 24-26 Dec. £2.95/£1.50/£2.20. (F8)*

### Castle Rising
#### ⊛ Castle Rising Castle
Tel: (01553) 631330
Castle Rising Castle is a fine example of a Norman castle. The rectangular keep, one of the largest, was built around 1140 by William D'Albini to celebrate his marriage. *Open 1 Jan-21 Mar, Wed-Sun, 1000-1300, 1400-1600; 22 Mar-31 Oct, daily, 1000-1800/1800 or dusk in Oct; 3 Nov-31 Dec, Wed-Sun, 1000-1300, 1400-1600; closed 24-26 Dec. £2.30/£1.20/£1.70. (D7)*

### Great Yarmouth
#### ⊛ Burgh Castle Church Farm
Burgh Castle
The remains of a 3rdC Roman fort overlooking the River Waveney. The monument can only be approached on foot. There is information and a tearoom available from Easter to October. *Open at any reasonable time. (P9)*

### Great Yarmouth
#### ⊛ Caister Roman Site
The remains of a Roman commercial port which was possibly a fort. The footings of walls and buildings are seen all along the main street. *Open at any reasonable time. (P9)*

### Great Yarmouth
#### ⊛ North West Tower
North Quay Tel: (01493) 332095
Medieval tower which was originally part of the town walls. Has an exhibition about trading wherries. The traditional cargo craft used on the Broads and information centre. *Open 1 Jul-30 Sep, daily, 1000-1545. (P9)*

### Lynford
#### ⊛ Grimes Graves
The Exhibition Building
Tel: (01842) 810656
Remarkable Neolithic flint mines Four thousand years old and first excavated in the 1870s with over 300 pits and shafts; one open to the public, and a 30ft deep, 7 radiating gallery. *Open 3 Jan-21 Mar, Wed-Sun, 1000-1300, 1400-1600; 22 Mar-31 Oct, daily, 1000-1300, 1400-1800/1800 or dusk in Oct; 3 Nov- 29 Dec, Wed-Sun, 1000-1300, 1400-1600; closed 24-26 Dec. £1.75/90p/£1.30. (F12)*

### Ludham
#### Saint Benets Abbey
(Parish of Horning), Ludham
The ruins of a monastery founded in 1020 AD by King Canute. A gatehouse with interesting carvings, 18thC windmill tower and a perimeter wall around the 34 acres with fishponds. *Open at any reasonable time. (N8)*

*Castle Rising Castle, Norfolk*

*Historical re-enactment, Castle Acre, Norfolk*

### New Buckenham
**New Buckenham Castle**
Tel: (01953) 860374
A Norman motte-and-bailey castle and chapel keep, said to be the largest in diameter in England. *Open all year, daily, Mon-Sat, 0800-1800; closed 2,5 Apr, 25, 26 Dec, 1 Jan. £1.50/50p/50p. (J12)*

### North Elmham
**North Elmham Chapel**
High Street
The remains of a Norman chapel, later converted into a house and enclosed by earthworks. *Open at any reasonable time. (H/I7)*

### Norwich
**⊛ Norwich Cathedral**
The Close
Tel: (01603) 764385
A Norman cathedral from 1096 with 14thC roof bosses depicting bible scenes from Adam and Eve to the Day of Judgement, cloisters, cathedral close, shop and restaurant. *Open 1 Jan-14 May, daily, 0730-1800; 15 May-30 Sep, daily, 0730-1900; 1 Oct-31 Dec, daily 0730-1800. (L9)*

### Norwich
**Roman Catholic Cathedral of St John The Baptist**
Unthank Road
Tel: (01603) 624615
A fine example of a 19thC Gothic-style building. *Open all year, daily, 0800-1600. (L9)*

### Norwich
**Saint Peter Mancroft Church**
Haymarket
Tel: (01603) 610443
A church with a Norman foundation (1075). The present church consecrated in 1455, a font (1463), Flemish tapestry (1573), an east window with medieval glass, Thomas Browne memorial. *Open all year, Mon-Fri, 0930-1630; Sat, 1000-1230; closed 25 Dec, 1 Jan, Bank Hol Mon. (L9)*

### Thetford
**Thetford Priory**
Tel: (01604) 730320
The 14thC gatehouse is the best preserved part of this Cluniac priory, built in 1103. The extensive remains include a plan of the cloisters. *Open at any reasonable time. (G12/13)*

### Walsingham
**Shrine of our Lady of Walsingham**
Holt Road
Tel: (01328) 820266
A pilgrimage church containing the Holy House, standing in extensive grounds. *Open all year, daily, dawn-dusk. (H5)*

### Weeting
**⊛ Weeting Castle**
Tel: (01604) 730320
The ruins of an early medieval manor-house within a shallow rectangular moat. *Open at any reasonable time. (E12)*

## Suffolk

### Bungay
**Bungay Castle**
Tel: (01986) 893148
The remains of an original Norman castle with Saxon mounds. The castle is in the centre of a fine market town. *Open any reasonable time; gatehouse tower and keep by key from nearby premises (stated on notice board), Mon-Sat, 0900-1700; Sun, 1000-1400. Please contact for details. (M12)*

### Bury St Edmunds
**⊛ Bury St Edmunds Abbey**
The remains of a Benedictine abbey in beautifully kept gardens. The 2 great gateways (one being 14thC) are the best preserved buildings. There is also a visitor's centre. *Open all year, Mon-Fri, 0730-dusk; Sat, Sun, Bank Hol Mon, 0900-dusk; for opening hours of visitors centre, please telephone (01284) 763110. (F/G15)*

### Bury St Edmunds
**Saint Edmundsbury Cathedral**
The Cathedral Office, Angel Hill
Tel: (01284) 754933
A 16thC nave which was St James church but was made a cathedral in 1914. The east end was added post-war and completed in late-1960. The north side was built in 1990. *Please contact for details of opening times. (F/G15)*

*Leiston Abbey, Suffolk*

## Landguard Fort, Felixstowe
Tel: (01394) 277767
Situated at Landguard Point on the estuary of the River Orwell, Landguard Fort was originally built in 1744 with 1875 modifications and additions in 1890, 1901 and 1914. Considerable renovations were made to this Georgian/Victorian Fort during 1997-1998 which is open to the public on Sundays and Public Bank Holidays from May to September. The Fort is also open every Wednesday from 1pm to 5pm during the same period and there are guided tours of the Magazines, Lamp Passages and Casemates.

*Norfolk ● Suffolk*

## Clare
### Clare Castle Country Park
Malting Lane
Tel: (01787) 277491
A small country park incorporating the remains of a castle and a Victorian railway station in a 30-acre site fronting onto the River Stour. *Open all year, daily, dawn-dusk. (E18)*

## Eye
### Eye Castle
Castle Street
Tel: (01449) 676800
A Norman motte-and-bailey with medieval walls and a Victorian folly. The Castle has always had close associations with royalty since the Norman conquest. *Open 2 Apr-31 Oct, daily, 0900-1900/dusk. (K14)*

## Felixstowe
### ⊛ Landguard Fort
A fort of 18th, 19th and 20thC construction, an ancient monument. A 1744 fort with 1875 modifications and additions in 1890, 1901 and 1914. *Open 5 May-29 Aug, Wed, 1300-1700; Sun, 1030-1700; 5-26 Sep, Sun, 1030-1700. £2.00/£1.50/£1.00. (M19) See page 68 for futher details.*

## Framlingham
### ⊛ Framlingham Castle
Tel: (01728) 724189
A castle with 12thC curtain walls, 13 towers, Tudor-brick chimneys and a wall walk, built by the Bigod family, the Earls of Norfolk. The home of Mary Tudor in 1553. *Open 1 Jan-21 Mar, daily, 1000-1600; 22 Mar-31 Oct, daily, 1000-1800/1800 or dusk in Oct; 1 Nov-31 Dec, daily, 1000-1600; closed 24-26 Dec. £2.95/£1.50/£2.20. (M15)*

## Herringfleet
### ⊛ Saint Olave's Priory
Priory remains with an early 14thC undercroft and a brick vaulted ceiling. See also the nearby windmill. *Open at any reasonable time, for key telephone (01493) 488609. (O11)*

## Leiston
### ⊛ Leiston Abbey
The remains of a 14thC abbey for premonstratensian canons including the transepts of the church and a range of cloisters and a restored chapel. *Open at any reasonable time. (O15/16)*

## Lindsey
### Saint James's Chapel
Tel: (01604) 730320
A small 13thC medieval chapel once attached to the nearby castle. *Open all year, daily, 1000-1600. (H18)*

*Orford Castle, Suffolk*

## Orford
### ⊛ Orford Castle
Tel: (01394) 450472
A 90-ft high keep with views across the River Alde to Orford Ness, built by Henry II for coastal defence in the 12thC with a local topographical display and sculpture. *Open 1 Jan-21 Mar, Wed-Sun, 1000-1300, 1400-1600; 22 Mar-31 Oct, daily, 1000-1800/dusk in Oct; 3 Nov-31 Dec, Wed-Sun, 1000-1300, 1400-1600. £2.30/£1.20/£1.70. (N/O17)*

## Walpole
### Walpole Old Chapel
Halesworth Road
A unique religious building of the 17thC; this country's earliest surviving building of Congregational form. A property of the Historic Chapels trust. *Open 1 May-11 Sep, Thu, Sat, 1100-1600. Realistic contributions are very welcome. (N14)*

## West Stow
### ⊛ West Stow Country Park and Anglo-Saxon Village
The Visitor Centre, Icklingham Road
Tel: (01284) 728718
Reconstructions of 6 pagan Anglo-Saxon buildings with a 7th in the process of reconstruction and an information point with displays of excavation plans and other information. *Open all year, daily, 1000-1700; last admission 1600; closed 24-26 Dec. £3.50/£2.50/£2.50. (F14)*

## Woodbridge
### Sutton Hoo Burial Site
Sutton Hoo
An Anglo-saxon royal burial site. Sutton Hoo is a group of low grassy burial mounds overlooking the River Deben in south east Suffolk. *Open 3 Apr-31 Oct, Sat, Sun, Bank Hol Mon; guided tours, 1400, 1500. £2.00/£1.00/£2.00. (M18)*

# museums & heritage Centres

## Norfolk

### Burston

**Burston Strike School**

Tel: (01379) 741565

A building erected to house a school for scholars of the strike. An interpretative exhibit of artefacts, documents and photographs. *Open all year, daily, dawn-dusk. (J/K 12/13)*

### Cockley Cley

**Iceni Village and Museums**

Tel: (01760) 724588

An Iceni tribal village reconstruction, believed to be on the original site. Medieval cottage/forge with museum, Saxon church c630 AD, carriage, vintage engine and farm museum. *Open 2 Apr, 1030-1730; 11 Apr-31 Oct, daily, 1100-1730. £3.30/£1.80/£2.30. (F9/10)*

### Cromer

**Cromer Lifeboat Museum and Lifeboat**

The Pier and Gangway  Tel: (01263) 512503

Models, pictures and photographs. The lifeboat 'Ruby and Arthur Read II' is a new Tyne-class lifeboat and can be viewed at the lifeboat house and sometimes at the museum. *Open 1 Mar-31 Oct, daily, 1000-1600. (L4/5)*

### Cromer

**⊛ Cromer Museum**

East Cottages, Tucker Street

Tel: (01263) 513543

A late-Victorian fisherman's cottage with displays of local history (fishing, bathing resort), geology, natural history and archaeology. *Open all year, Mon-Sat, 1000-1700; Sun, 1400-1700; closed Mon, 1300-1400; 1, 2 Apr, 24-27 Dec, 1 Jan. £1.20/60p/70p. (L4/5)*

### Dereham

**Hobbies Museum of Fretwork and Craft Centre**

34-36 Swaffham Road

Tel: (01362) 692985

A museum of fretwork machines dating back to 1900 with magazines and hobbies weeklies from 1895 and samples of old fretwork designs. *Open 1 Apr-27 Aug, Mon-Fri, 1000-1200, 1400-1600. (H/I 8/9)*

### Dickleburgh

**100th Bomb Group Memorial Museum**

Common Road  Tel: (01379) 740708

A museum housed in an original World War II control tower with other buildings, showing the history of the 100th Bomb Group plus 8th Air Force exhibits and a visitor's centre. *Open 6 Feb-25 Apr, Sat, Sun, Bank Hol Mon, 1000-1630; 2 May-26 Sep, Wed, Sat, Sun, Bank Hol Mon, 1000-1700; 3 Oct-28 Nov, Sat, Sun, 1000-1630. (K13)*

### Diss

**Diss Museum**

Market Place  Tel: (01379) 650618

Housed in the historic Shambles building, award-winning Diss Museum provides visitors with a variety of changing displays on local history and prehistory. *Open all year, Wed, Thu, 1400-1600; Fri, Sat, 1030-1630; closed 10 Apr, 25 Dec-5 Jan. (J13)*

### Erpingham

**Alby Bottle Museum, Alby Craft Centre**

Cromer Road  Tel: (01263) 761327

The only bottle museum in East Anglia with over 3,000 Norfolk bottles, flagons and bottles for ginger beer, poisons and mineral water plus many bottle-related items. *Open 31 Mar-19 Dec, Tue-Sun, 1000-1700. 30p/10p/30p. (K/L6)*

### Erpingham

**Alby Lace Museum and Study Centre/Stitches and Lace**

Alby Craft Centre, Cromer Road

Tel: (01263) 768002

Lace exhibits aged up to 300 years old. Hand-made bobbin lace and sometimes needle lace are demonstrated. Small ready-made items and large pieces to commission. *Open 17 Jan-14 Mar, Sun, 1000-1300, 1400-1700; 17 Mar-19 Dec, Tue-Fri, Sun, Bank Hol Mon, 1000-1300, 1400-1700. (K6)*

*Cromer Museum, Norfolk*

### Fakenham

**Fakenham Museum of Gas and Local History**

Hempton Road  Tel: (01328) 863150

A complete small-town gasworks with a local history section and displays of working gas meters and working exhausters. *For 1999 undergoing restoration work, please contact for details of opening times. £1.50/25p/£1.00. (G/H6)*

### Glandford

**Shell Museum and Saint Martins Church**

Tel: (01263) 740081

The museum has exhibits of shells, fossils, pottery, objects of local history, church carvings, a stained-glass window and clock. *Open 2 Mar-30 Oct, Tue-Sat, Bank Hol Mon, 1000-1230, 1400-1630. £1.50/50p/£1.00. (I5)*

### Great Yarmouth

**⊛ Elizabethan House Museum**

4 South Quay  Tel: (01493) 855746

A 16thC merchant's house displaying rooms as though still lived in by families in the past. Includes Victorian kitchen/scullery, tudor bedroom and conspiracy room. *Please contact for details of opening times. £1.90/90p/£1.40. (P9)*

### Great Yarmouth

**⊛ Maritime Museum**

Marine Parade  Tel: (01493) 842267

The maritime history of Norfolk with herring fishery, a large collection of ship models, World War II and home-front exhibitions. *Please contact for details of opening times and prices. (P9)*

### Great Yarmouth

**⊛ Old Merchant's House**

Row III House and Greyfriars Cloisters

South Quay  Tel: (01493) 857900

Typical 17thC town houses, one with splendid plaster ceilings containing local original architectural and domestic fittings salvaged from other 'Row' houses. *Open 22 Mar-31 Oct, daily, 1000-1700. £1.75/90p/ £1.30. (P9)*

### Great Yarmouth

**⊛ Tolhouse Museum**

Tolhouse Street  Tel: (01493) 858900

One of the oldest municipal buildings in England, once the town's courthouse and gaol. Prison cells can still be seen with displays illustrating the long history of the town. *Please contact for details of opening times. (P9)*

### Gressenhall
#### ◉ Norfolk Rural Life Museum
Beech House  Tel: (01362) 860563
A former workhouse illustrating the history of Norfolk over the last 200 years. Union Farm is a working 1920s farm with traditional breeds of livestock, also crafts and exhibits. *Open 28 Mar-31 Oct, Mon-Sat, 1000-1700; Sun, 1200-1730. £3.70/£1.60/£2.70. (H8)*

### Harleston
#### Harleston Museum
King Georges Hall, Broad Street
A museum housing an exhibition of items of historical interest relating to Harleston and the district. *Open 5 May-29 Sep, Wed, 1000-1200, 1400-1600; Sat, 1000-1200. (L12/13)*

### Holt
#### ◉ Picturecraft of Holt
23 Lees Courtyard, Off Bull Street
Tel: (01263) 711040
The main art gallery exhibits 19 artists' work which change every 3 weeks with picture-framing specialists and an artists' material centre. *Open all year, Mon-Wed, Fri-Sat, 0900-1700; Thu, 0900-1300; closed 25 Dec, 1 Jan. (J5)*

### Hunstanton
#### Le Strange Old Barns
Antiques, Arts and Craft Centre,
Golf Course Road  Tel: (01485) 533402
Antiques, arts and craft centre in a lovely location, 200 yards from the beach. *Open 1 Jan-25 May, daily, 1000-1700; 26 May-26 Oct, daily, 1000-1800; 27 Oct-31 Dec, daily, 1000-1700; closed 25 Dec. (D5)*

### King's Lynn
#### Guildhall of St George
27 King Street  Tel: (01553) 774725
A regional arts centre, the medieval Guildhall now houses a theatre with a regular programme of daytime and evening events: film, concerts, galleries and annual arts festival. *Open all year, Mon-Sat, 1000-1700; closed Bank Hol Mon, 25 Dec. (C/D 7/8)*

### King's Lynn
#### ◉ Lynn Museum
Market Street  Tel: (01553) 775001
Housed in a Victorian church. Lynn Museum has displays on natural history, archaeology and local history. *Open all year, Tue-Sat, 1000-1700; closed on Bank Hols. 80p / 40p / 50p. (C/D 7/8)*

### King's Lynn
#### ◉ The Old Gaol House
The Old Gaol House,
Saturday Market Place
Tel: (01553) 763044
A personal stereo tour of the Old Gaol House tells the true stories of Lynn's infamous murderers, highwaymen and even witches. *Open 2 Jan-28 Mar, Fri-Tue, 1000-1615; 1 Apr-30 Oct, daily, 1000-1115; 1 Nov-28 Dec, Fri-Tue, 1000-1625; closed 25, 26 Dec, 1 Jan. £2.20/£1.60/£1.60. (C/D 7/8)*

### King's Lynn
#### ◉ Town House
#### Museum of Lynn Life
46 Queen Street  Tel: (01553) 773450
The past comes to life in this newly-opened museum with historic room displays including costumes, toys, a working Victorian kitchen and a 1950s living room. *Open 2 Jan-30 Apr, Mon-Sat, 1000-1600; 1 May-30 Sep, Mon-Sat, 1000-1700; 1 Oct-31 Dec, Mon-Sat, 1000-1600; closed Bank Hols. £1.20/60p/70p. (C/D 7/8)*

### King's Lynn
#### ◉ True's Yard Heritage Centre
3-5 North Street  Tel: (01553) 770479
Two fully-restored fisherman's cottages with research facilities for tracing ancestry in King's Lynn. There is a museum, gift shop and tearoom. *Open all year, daily, 0930-1600; closed 25 Dec. £1.90/£1.00/£1.50. (C/D 7/8)*

### Litcham
#### Litcham Village Museum
'Fourways'  Tel: (01328) 701383
A local village museum and underground lime kiln. The Museum houses local artifacts from Roman times to date and a local photograph collection with 1000 photographs. *Open 2 Apr-3 Oct, Sat, Sun, Bank Hols, 1400-1700. (G8)*

### Little Dunham
#### Dunham Museum
Tel: (01760) 723073
An exhibition building showing collections of old working tools, bygones and machinery. There is a leathersmith and shoemakers. *Open 1 Apr-31 Aug, Sun-Thu, 1100-1500. 50p per car. (G8/9)*

### Little Walsingham
#### ◉ Shirehall Museum
#### and Abbey Grounds
Common Place  Tel: (01328) 820510
A Georgian country courthouse, local museum and Tourist Information Centre. Ruins of the Augustinian abbey, peaceful gardens, woodland walks set in approximately 7 acres. Museum, abbey grounds and Tourist Information Centre. *Open 2 Apr-30 Sep, Mon-Sat, 1000-1630. 75p/40p/40p. (H5)*

### Ludham
#### Toad Hole Cottage Museum
How Hill  Tel: (01692) 678763
An 18thC building with 5 small rooms plus a Broads information area. A cottage museum giving the impression of the home and working life of a family on the marshes. *Open 29 May-31 May, daily, 1100-1700; 1 Jun-30 Sep, daily, 1000-1800; 1-31 Oct, daily, 1100-1700. (N8)*

*Ancient House Museum, Thetford, Norfolk*

## Norwich Castle Museum

The ancient Norman keep of Norwich Castle dominates the city. Once a royal palace, it now houses a magnificent regional collection of art, archaeology and natural history, including the bones of the prehistoric West Runton elephant and our roaring tiger, much loved by younger visitors. Discover the Castle's darker secrets with a tour of the battlements and dungeon. A café, gift shop and lively events programme are available.
*Please telephone to check opening times after September 1999 as the Castle will be closing for re-development.*

**Open: Mon to Sat 10am to 5.00pm**
 **Sun. 2.0pm to 5.00pm**
**Further Information:**
**Tel (01603) 493654**

Norfolk Museums Service
A Joint service of the
County & District Councils

### Norwich
### ⊛ Bridewell Museum
Bridewell Alley  Tel: (01603) 667228

A museum with displays illustrating local industry during the past 200 years with a recreated 1920s pharmacy and a 1930s pawnbroker's shop. There are also temporary exhibits. *Open 1 Apr-30 Sep, Tue-Sat, 1000-1700. £1.30/60p/90p. (K/L9)*

### Norwich
### ⊛ Castle Museum
Castle Hill  Tel: (01603) 223624

A large collection of art including an important collection by Norwich School artists, archaeology, natural history, temporary exhibitions, a 12thC castle keep and tour. *Open all year, Mon-Sat, 1000-1700; closed 2 Apr, 23-27 Dec. (K/L9)*

### Norwich
### ⊛ Inspire Hands-On-Science Centre
St Michael's Church, Coslany Street  Tel: (01603) 612612

Inspire is a hands-on science centre housed in a medieval church. Suitable for all ages, it allows everyone to explore and discover the wonders of science for themselves. *Open all year, Tue-Sun, 1000-1730; closed 24 Dec-1 Jan. £3.00/£2.50/£2.50. (K/L9)*

### Norwich
### ⊛ Mustard Shop
3 Bridewell Alley  Tel: (01603) 627889

A decorated 19thC-style shop which houses a museum with a series of displays illustrating the history of Colman's Mustard. *Open all year, Mon-Sat, 0930-1700; closed Bank Hols, 25, 26 Dec, 1 Jan. (L9)*

### Norwich
### The Norwich Gallery
Norwich School of Art and Design, St Georges Street  Tel: (01603) 610561

Gallery showing temporary exhibitions of contemporary art, design and crafts. *Open all year, Mon-Sat, 1000-1700; closed 2-6 Apr, 17 Dec-8 Jan. (K/L9)*

### Norwich
### ⊛ Royal Norfolk Regimental Museum
Shirehall, Market Avenue  Tel: (01603) 223649

A museum with displays about the county regiment from 1685, linked to the castle by a prisoners' tunnel and a reconstructed World War I communication trench. *Open all year, Mon-Sat, 1000-1700; Sun, 1400-1700; closed 2 Apr, 23-26 Dec, 1 Jan. £1.30/60p/90p. (K/L9)*

*Castle Museum, Norwich, Norfolk*

### Norwich
### ⊛ Sainsbury Centre for Visual Arts
University of East Anglia  Tel: (01603) 456060

Housing the Sainsbury collection of works by Picasso, Bacon and Henry Moore alongside many other objects of pottery and art. Also a cafe and an art bookshop with activities monthly *Open all year, Tue-Sun, 1100-1700; closed 23 Dec-4 Jan. £2.00/£1.00/£1.00. (K/L9)*

*The Mustard Shop, Norwich, Norfolk*

*Norfolk ● Suffolk*

*Moot Hall, Aldeburgh, Suffolk*

### Norwich
#### ⊛ Saint Peter
#### Hungate Church Museum
Princes Street  Tel: (01603) 667231
A 15thC church with a fine hammerbeam roof, Norwich painted glass, displays on how the church affects lives and a brass rubbing centre with a wide range of replica brasses. *Open 1 Apr-30 Sep, Mon-Sat, 1000-1700. (K/L9)*

### Potter Heigham
#### The Museum of the Broads
The Broads Haven
Displays of tools from the traditional Broads industries and many Broads boats. *Open 2 Apr-31 Oct, daily, 1200-1600. £2.00/£1.00/£1.50. (O8)*

### Sheringham
#### Sheringham Museum
Station Road  Tel: (01263) 822895
A local history museum housing all things to do with the social history and life of the town plus lifeboat history and a new art gallery. *Open 2-3 Apr, 1 May-31 Oct, Tue-Sat, 1030-1630; Sun, 1400-1630; 6 Nov-12 Dec, Sat, 1000-1600; Sun, 1400-1630; 15-24 Dec, Tue-Sat, 1030-1630; Sun, 1400-1630. £1.00/50p/50p. (F9)*

### Swaffham
#### Swaffham Museum
Town Hall, London Street
Tel: (01760) 721230
An 18thC building, formerly a brewer's home. Small social history museum for Swaffham and the surrounding villages. Annual exhibitions plus displays from Stone Age to 20thC. *Open 29 Mar-23 Oct, Tue-Sat, 1100-1600. 50p/free/50p. (F9)*

### Thetford
#### ⊛ Ancient House Museum
White Hart Street  Tel: (01842) 752599
A museum of Thetford and Breckland life in a remarkable early-Tudor house. Displays on local history, flint, archaeology and natural history. *Open 2 Jan-29 May, Mon-Sat, 1000-1230, 1300-1700; 30 May-29 Aug, Mon-Sat, 1000-1230, 1300-1700; Sun, 1400-1700; 30 Aug-31 Dec, Mon-Sat, 1000-1230, 1300-1700; closed 2 Apr, 24-27 Dec. 80p/40p/50p. (G12/13)*

### Thetford
#### ⊛ Charles Burrell Museum
Minstergate  Tel: (01842) 751166
The Charles Burrell Steam Museum draws together an impressive collection of exhibits to tell the story of Charles Burrell and Son (1770-1932). *Open 6 Mar -31 Oct, Sat, 1000-1700; Sun, 1400-1700, Bank Hol Mon, 1000-1700. £1.25/70p/70p. (G12/13)*

### Wells-next-the-Sea
#### Wells Maritime Museum
Old Lifeboat House, The Quay
Tel: (01328) 711646
The maritime history of Wells, housed in the old lifeboat house. *Open 2 Apr-25 Jul, Tue-Fri, 1400-1700; Sat, Sun, 1000-1300, 1400-1700; 26 Jul-1 Sep, daily, 1000-1300, 1400-1700, 1800-2000, 2 Sep-24 Oct, Tue-Fri, 1400-1700; Sat, Sun, 1000-1300, 1400-1700. 75p/25p/75p. (G/H4)*

### Wymondham
#### Wymondham Heritage Museum
Bridewell, Norwich Road
Tel: (01953) 600205
The museum, established in 1984, has exhibits of local origin. Some displays are generally changed annually or bianually. *Open 1 Mar-30 Nov, Mon-Sat, 1000-1600; Sun, 1400-1600. £1.75/50p/£1.25. (J10)*

## Suffolk

### Aldeburgh
#### Moot Hall and Museum
A 16thC Listed ancient building with a museum displaying items of local interest such as photographs and artefacts depicting life in Aldeburgh. *Open 3 Apr-31 May, Sat, Sun, Bank Hol Mon, 1430-1700; 1-30 Jun, daily, 1430-1700; 1 Jul-30 Aug, daily, 1030-1230, 1430-1700; 1-30 Sep, Sat, Sun, 1430-1700. 50p/free/50p. (O16)*

### Beccles
#### Beccles and District Museum
Leman House, Ballygate
Tel: (01502) 715722
A Grade I Listed building concerning printing, Waveney, agricultural costumes, cultural and domestic items. Also a model of the town in 1841 and a natural history diorama. *Open 1 Apr-31 Oct, Tue-Sun, Bank Hol Mon, 1430-1700. (N/O11/12)*

### Brandon
#### ⊛ Brandon Heritage Centre
George Street  Tel: (01842) 813707
The centre gives details of the flint, fur and forestry industries in the Brandon area, together with a local interest section housed in the former fire station premises. *Open 3 Apr-31 May, Sat, Bank Hol Mon, 1030-1700; Sun, 1400-1700; 3 Jun-29 Aug, Thu, Sat, 1030-1700; Sun, 1400-1700; 4 Sep-31 Oct, Sat, 1030-1700; Sun, 1400-1700. 50p/40p/40p. (E/F12)*

### Bungay
#### Bungay Museum
Waveney District Council Office, Broad Street  Tel: (01986) 892176
The museum consists of 2 small rooms upstairs which are inter-connecting. These contain showcases of general items from Norman to Victorian periods. *Open all year, Mon-Fri, 0900-1300, 1400-1600; closed Bank Hol Mon, 24-31 Dec. 50p/free/30p. (M12)*

### Bungay
#### ⊛ Saint Peter's Brewery and Visitor Centre
St Peter's Hall, St Peter
Tel: (01986) 782322
A small brewery in the grounds of a 13thC hall with a 17thC barn containing the visitor centre. *Open 28 Mar-30 Sep, daily, 1100-1800. £5.00/50p/£1.00. (M12)*

### Bury St Edmunds
#### Abbey Visitor Centre
Samson's Tower, Abbey Precinct
Tel: (01284) 763110
The Abbey Visitor Centre is housed in Samson's Tower which is part of the west front of the now ruined Abbey of St Edmund. *Open 1 Apr-31 Oct, daily, 1000-1700; closed 2 Apr. (F/G15/16)*

*Norfolk ● Suffolk*

*Moyse's Hall Museum, Bury St Edmunds*

### Bury St Edmunds
**Bury St Edmunds Art Gallery**
Cornhill  Tel: (01284) 762081
Housed at Market Cross, Robert Adam's only public building in Eastern England, originally designed as a playhouse. The upper floor is now used for changing exhibitions. *Open all year, Tue-Sat, 1030-1700. 50p/30p/30p. (F/G15/16)*

### Bury St Edmunds
**⊛ Manor House**
5 Honey Hill  Tel: (01284) 757076
A collection of clocks, watches, costumes and textiles with fine and decorative arts of national importance in a magnificent 18thC building. *Open all year, Tue-Sun, Bank Hol Mon, 1000-1700; closed 2 Apr, 25, 26 Dec. £2.70/£1.75/£1.75  (F/G15/16)*

### Bury St Edmunds
**⊛ Moyse's Hall Museum**
*HOUSE MAY BE CLOSED IN 1999*
Cornhill  Tel: (01284) 757488
A Norman domestic building containing local history and the archaeology of West Suffolk with relics of the Maria Marten 'Red Barn Murder' along with temporary exhibitions. *Please contact for details, house may close during 1999 for renovation. £1.50/95p/95p. (F/G15/16)*

### Cavendish
**Sue Ryder Foundation Museum**
Sue Ryder Foundation Headquarters
Tel: (01787) 280252
Displays showing the reason for establishing the Sue Ryder Foundation and its work. Past, present and future. *Open all year, daily, 1000-1730; closed 25 Dec. 80p/40p/40p. (F18)*

### Dunwich
**⊛ Dunwich Museum**
St James's Street  Tel: (01728) 648796
A museum showing the history of Dunwich from Roman times, chronicling its disappearance into the sea and local wildlife. *Open 6-28 Mar, Sat, Sun, 1400-1630: 1 Apr-30 Sep, daily, 1130-1630; 1-31 Oct, daily 1200-1600. (O14)*

### Felixstowe
**Felixstowe Museum**
Landguard Point, Viewpoint Road
Tel: (01394) 276748
The museum is housed in the Ravelin block adjacent to Landguard Fort. There are 12 rooms covering history of the Fort. *Opening for 1999, a model room. Open 2-25 Apr, Sun, Bank Hols 1400-1700; 5 May-29 Sep, Wed, Sun, 1400-1700; Bank Hol Mon and Sun, 1400-1700. £1.00/50p/£1.00. (M19)*

### Flatford
**Granary Museum**
The Granary, East Bergholt
Tel: (01206) 298111
A collection of bicycles, cameras, various old tools and domestic implements. *Open all year, daily, 1000-1900. 30p/free/30p. (J19)*

### Framlingham
**Lanman Museum**
Framlingham Castle
Tel: (01728) 724189
A museum with rural exhibits relating to everyday life in Framlingham and the surrounding area including paintings and photographs. *Open 10 Apr-30 Sep, Tue-Sun, 1100-1330, 1400-1630; Mon, 1400-1630. 40p/20p/20p. (L/M15)*

### Halesworth
**Halesworth and District Museum**
The Almshouses, Steeple End
Tel: (01986) 873030
A museum housed in the 19thC railway station building. Displays of local geology and archaeology including fossils, prehistoric flints and medieval finds from excavations. *Open 1 May-30 Sep, Tue, Wed, 1030-1230, 1400-1600; Thu, Sat, 1030-1230; Bank Hol Mon, 1400-1600. (N13/14)*

### Haverhill
**Haverhill and District Local History Centre**
Town Hall, High Street
Tel: (01440) 714962
A collection of over 2000 items relating to Haverhill and district. There is also a vast collection of photographs. *Open all year, Tue, 1900-2100; Wed, Thu, 1400-1600; Fri, 1400-1600, 1900-2100, Sat, 1030-1530; closed 2, 4 Apr. (D18)*

### Ipswich
**⊛ Christchurch Mansion**
Christchurch Park  Tel: (01473) 253246
A fine Tudor mansion built between 1548/50, collection of furniture, panelling, ceramics, clocks and paintings from the 16th-19thC. Art exhibitions in Wolsey Art Gallery. *Open 2 Apr-31 Dec, Tue-Sat, 1000-1700; Sun, 1430-1630; closed 24, 25, 26 Dec, 1 Jan. (K18)*

### Ipswich
**⊛ Ipswich Museum and Gallery**
High Street  Tel: (01473) 213761
Displays of Roman Suffolk, Suffolk wildlife, Suffolk and world geology, the Ogilvie bird gallery, 'Peoples of the World' and 'Anglo-Saxons come to Ipswich displays. *Open all year, Tue-Sat, 1000-1700; closed 2 Apr, 24-26 Dec, 1 Jan. (K18)*

### Ipswich
**The John Russell Gallery**
4-6 Wherry Lane  Tel: (01473) 212051
Eighteenth-century wharf in the oldest and most historic part of the docklands of Ipswich. *Open all year, Mon-Sat, 0930-1700; closed Bank Hol Mon, 2, 5 Apr, 24 Dec-11 Jan. (K18)*

### Ipswich
**⊛ Tolly Cobbold Brewery and the Brewery Tap**
Cliff Road  Tel: (01473) 231723
Taste the malt and smell the hops on a fully-guided tour of this magnificent Victorian brewery. Also visit the new brewhouse and bottlers' room and then visit the Brewery Tap. *Open 1 Jun-30 Sep, daily at 1200. £3.90/£3.90/£3.90. (K18)*

### Kentford
**Animal Health Trust Visitor Centre**
Lanwades Park  Tel: (01638) 751000
The John MacDougall Visitors' Centre gives an insight into the veterinary work of the Animal Health Trust charity. Coffee shop serves light refreshments and tours available. *Open all year, Mon-Fri, 0900-1700; closed Bank Hols. (E/F15)*

### Laxfield
**Laxfield and District Museum**
The Guildhall, High Street
The museum is housed in the early 16thC guildhall opposite church in the centre of Laxfield. Displays relate to the domestic and working life of the village in the 19th/20thC. *Open 15 May-26 Sep, Sat, Sun, Bank Hol Mon, 1400-1700. (M14)*

*Christchurch Mansion, Ipswich, Suffolk*

### Leiston
**Long Shop Museum**
Main Street  Tel: (01728) 832189
An award-winning museum with 3 exhibition halls full of items from our glorious age of steam. *Open 4 Apr-1 Nov, Mon-Sat, 1000-1700; Sun, 1100-1700. £2.50/75p/£2.00. (O15/16)*

### Lowestoft
**Lowestoft Museum**
Broad House, Nicholas Everitt Park
Tel: (01502) 511457
A museum housing displays on local history, Lowestoft porcelain, fossils, flint implements, medieval artefacts from local sites and domestic history. *Please contact for details of opening times. (P11)*

### Lowestoft
**Royal Naval Patrol Service Association Museum**
Sparrows Nest  Tel: (01502) 586250
A museum with photographs of models of World War II officers and crews, minesweepers and anti-submarine vessels. *Open 10 May-15 Oct, Mon, 1000-1400; Tue-Fri, 1000-1200, 1400-1630; Sun, 1400-1630. (P11)*

### Mildenhall
**Mildenhall and District Museum**
6 King Street  Tel: (01638) 716970
A local voluntary museum housed in early 19thC cottages with modern extensions. Exhibitions on RAF Mildenhall, Fenland and Breckland including local archaeology and local history. *Open 3 Mar-23 Dec, Wed, Thu, Sat, Sun, 1430-1630; Fri, 1100-1630. (E14)*

### Newmarket
**⊛ National Horse-Racing Museum and Tours**
99 High Street  Tel: (01638) 667333
A museum displaying the development of horse-racing. A display of sporting art includes loans from the Tate gallery. Also a 'hands-on' gallery. *Open 2 Mar-30 Jun, Tue-Sun and Bank Hol Mon, 1000-1700; 1 Jul-31 Aug, daily, 1000-1700; 1 Sep-1 Nov, Tue-Sun, 1000-1700. £3.50/£1.50/£2.50. (C/D15/16)*

### Orford
**Dunwich Underwater Exploration Exhibition**
The Orford Craft Shop
Tel: (01394) 450678
Exhibits show progress in the underwater exploration of the former city and underwater studies off the Suffolk coast. *Open all year, daily, 1100-1700; closed 25, 26 Dec. 50p/50p/50p. (N/O17)*

### Shotley Gate
**HMS Ganges Association Museum**
Unit 4 and 5, Shotley Marina
The history of HMS Ganges contained in a 2-roomed museum with photographs, artifacts and documentation. *Open all year, Sat, Sun, 1100-1700; Bank Hol Mons, 1100-1700. (L19)*

### Sizewell
**⊛ Sizewell Visitors Centre**
Sizewell B Power Station
Tel: (01728) 653890
A visitor centre giving details about all aspects of electricity generation. *Open 2 Apr-29 Oct, Mon-Fri, 1000-1600; please phone for Sat, Sun, Bank Hol opening. (O15/16)*

### Snape
**⊛ Snape Maltings Riverside Centre**
Tel: (01728) 688303
A 19thC maltings on the banks of the River Alde with shops, galleries, restaurants, river trips, painting and craft courses in the summer and a world-famous concert hall. *Open all year, daily, 1000-1700; closed 25, 26 Dec. (N16)*

### Southwold
**Southwold Lifeboat Museum**
Gun Hill  Tel: (01502) 722422
A museum with RNLI models, photographs of lifeboats and relics from old boats. *Open 31 May-30 Sep, daily, 1430-1630. (O/P13/14)*

### Southwold
**Southwold Museum**
Bartholomew Green
Tel: (01502) 722437
Museum housing local history, archaeology, natural history, exhibits relating to Southwold railway and The Battle of Sole Bay and domestic bygones. *Open 2 Apr-31 Jul, daily, 1430-1630; 1-31 Aug, daily, 1100-1230; 1 Sep-31 Oct, daily, 1430-1630. (O/P13/14)*

### Southwold
**Southwold Sailors' Reading Room**
East Cliff
A building of character where retired seamen have a social club and reading room. There are maritime exhibits and local history. *Open all year, daily, 0900-1700; closed 25 Dec. (O/P13/14)*

### Stowmarket
**Museum of East Anglian Life**
Tel: (01449) 612229
East Anglia's open-air museum, set in 70 acres of Suffolk countryside. Museum displays and special events to interest visitors of all ages. *Please contact for details of opening times. £4.00/£2.35/£3.40. (I/J16)*

### Sudbury
**⊛ Gainsborough's House**
46 Gainsborough Street
Tel: (01787) 372958
The birthplace of Thomas Gainsborough. An elegant townhouse with paintings by Gainsborough, a garden, print workshop and a programme of temporary exhibitions. *Open 2 Jan-31 Mar, Tue-Sat, 1000-1600; Sun, 1400-1600; 1-9, 11 Apr-31 Oct, Tue-Sat, 1000-1700; Sun, Bank Hol Mon, 1400-1700; 1 Nov-31 Dec, Tue-Sat, 1000-1600; Sun, 1400-1600; closed 24 Dec-1 Jan. £3.00/£1.50/£2.50. (G18)*

### Woodbridge
**Suffolk Horse Museum**
The Market Hill  Tel: (01394) 380643
An indoor exhibition about the Suffolk Punch breed of heavy horse. *Open 5 Apr-30 Sep, daily, 1400-1700. £1.50/£1.00/£1.00. (L/M17)*

### Woodbridge
**Woodbridge Museum**
5a Market Hill  Tel: (01394) 380502
A museum with exhibits on Sutton Hoo and Burrow Hill. Exhibits reflect the life of Woodbridge and its people. *Open 3 Apr-31 Oct, Thu-Sat, 1000-1600; Sun, Bank Hols, 1430-1630; daily, except Wed during summer school holidays. £1.00/30p/£1.00. (L/M17)*

### Woolpit
**Woolpit and District Museum**
The Institute  Tel: (01359) 240822
A 17thC timber-framed building with one permanent display of brickmaking and other displays, changing yearly, depicting the life of a Suffolk village. *Open 28 Mar-26 Sep, Sat, Sun, Bank Hol Mon, 1430-1700. (H15/16)*

*Sizewell Visitors Centre, Suffolk*

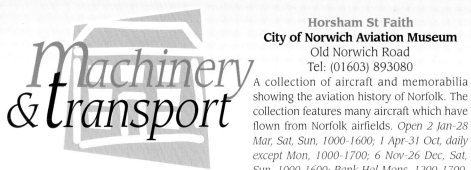

# machinery & transport

## Norfolk

### Aylsham
#### ❀ Bure Valley Railway
Aylsham Station, Norwich Road
Tel: (01263) 733858

A 15-inch narrow-gauge steam railway covering 9 miles of track from Wroxham in the heart of the Norfolk Broads to Aylsham which is a bustling market town. *Open 28 Mar-30 Apr, daily, 1015-1515; 2 May-29 Jun, Sun-Thu, 1015-1515; 1 Jul-31 Aug, daily, 1015-1515; please contact for details of opening during Sep and Oct. (K6/7)*

### Bressingham
#### ❀ Bressingham Steam Museum and Gardens
Tel: (01379) 687386

Steam rides through 5 miles of woodland. Six acres of the Island Beds plant centre. Mainline locomotives, the Victorian Gallopers and over 50 steam engines. *Open 31 Mar-2 Nov, daily 1030-1730. Please contact for details of opening times. (I/J13)*

### Dickleburgh
#### 100th Bomb Group Memorial Museum
See entry in Museums section.

### Forncett St Mary
#### Forncett Industrial Steam Museum
Low Road
Tel: (01508) 488277

A unique collection of large industrial steam engines including one that used to open Tower Bridge. Seven engines can be seen working on steam days. *Open 2 May, 6 Jun, 4 Jul, 1 Aug, 4 Sep, 3 Oct, 7 Nov, 1100-1700. £3.50/free/£3.00. (K11)*

### Horsham St Faith
#### City of Norwich Aviation Museum
Old Norwich Road
Tel: (01603) 893080

A collection of aircraft and memorabilia showing the aviation history of Norfolk. The collection features many aircraft which have flown from Norfolk airfields. *Open 2 Jan-28 Mar, Sat, Sun, 1000-1600; 1 Apr-31 Oct, daily except Mon, 1000-1700; 6 Nov-26 Dec, Sat, Sun, 1000-1600; Bank Hol Mons, 1200-1700. £2.50/£1.50/£1.50. (L8)*

### North Walsham
#### Norfolk Motor Cycle Museum
Railway Yard
Tel: (01692) 406266

A museum displaying a wide collection of motor cycles dating from 1920 to 1960. *Open 2 Jan-31 Mar, Mon-Sat, 1000-1630; 1 Apr-31 Oct, daily, 1000-1630; 1 Nov-31 Dec, Mon-Sat, 1000-1630; closed 24, 25 Dec, 1 Jan. £2.00/£1.00/£1.50. (L/M6)*

### Reepham
#### ❀ Reepham Station Cycle Hire
Station Road
Tel: (01603) 871187

Traffic-free cycle hire along the 26-mile Marriott's Way, formerly a railway route. Also pine furniture, gifts, teas, giant outdoor draughts and illustrations of bygone shopping. *Open all year, daily, 1000-1700; closed 24 Dec-2 Jan. (J7)*

### Thetford
#### ❀ Charles Burrell Museum
See entry in Museums section.

### Thursford
#### ❀ Thursford Collection
Thursford Green
Tel: (01328) 878477

Musical evenings some Tuesdays from mid-July to the end of September. A live musical show with 9 mechanical organs and a Wurlitzer show starring Robert Wolfe daily during April and October. *Open 2 Apr-24 Oct, daily, 1200-1700. £4.50/£2.00/£4.20. (H6)*

*Thursford Collection, Norfolk*

### Wells-next-the-Sea
#### Wells Walsingham Railway
Stiffkey Road
Tel: (01328) 710631

Four miles of railway; the longest 10.25-inch railway in the world with a new steam locomotive 'Norfolk Hero' now in service, the largest of its kind ever built. *Please contact for details of opening times. £5.00/£3.50/£5.00. (G/H4)*

### West Walton
#### Fenland and West Norfolk Aviation Museum
Bambers Garden Centre, Old Lynn Road
Tel: (01945) 585946

Museum with Vampire T11 and Lightning aircraft, uniforms, aero engines, aircraft components, artefacts, memorabilia, radio equipment, souvenirs, models and a replica Spitfire. *Open 1 Mar-31 Oct, 1000-1600. Sat, Sun, Bank Hols. Apr-Sep 0930-1700 £1.50/75p/75p. (A8/9)*

*Bressingham Steam Museum & Gardens, Norfolk*

### Weybourne
**⊛ Muckleburgh Collection**
Weybourne Old Military Camp
Tel: (01263) 588210

Collection of over 136 military vehicles and heavy equipment used by the allied armies during and since World War II including fighting tanks, armoured cars and artillery. *Open 14 Feb-28 Nov, daily, 1000-1700. £4.00/£2.00/£3.00. (J4)*

### Wroxham
**Barton House Railway**
Hartwell Road, The Avenue
Tel: (01603) 782470

A 3.5-gauge miniature steam passenger railway and a 7.25-gauge steam and battery-electric railway. Full-size M and GN accessories including signals and signal boxes. *Open 18 Apr, 16 May, 20 Jun, 18 Jul, 15 Aug, 19 Sep, 17 Oct, Sun, 1430-1730. 40p/20p/40p. (M8)*

## Suffolk

### Carlton Colville
**East Anglia Transport Museum**
Chapel Road
Tel: (01502) 518459

A working museum with one of the widest ranges of street transport vehicles on display and in action. Developing street scene and a 2-ft gauge railway. *Open 2 Apr-29 Sep, Sun, Bank Hol Mon, 1100-1730; Wed, Sat, 1400-1700;19 Jul-31 Aug, Mon, Tue, Thu, Fri, 1400-1700; last admission 1 hour before closing. £4.00/£2.00/£2.00. (P11/12)*

*Mechanical Music Museum and Bygones Trust, Cotton, Suffolk*

### Cotton
**Mechanical Music Museum and Bygones Trust**
Blacksmith Road
Tel: (01449) 613876

A selection of fairground organs and pipe organs, street pianos, music boxes, polyphons and many other musical items. *Open 6 Jun-26 Sep, Sun, 1430-1730; 3 Oct, Sun, 1000-1700. £3.00/£1.00/£3.00. (J15)*

### East Bergholt
**Granary Museum**
See entry in Museums section.

### Flixton
**Norfolk and Suffolk Aviation Museum**
East Anglia's Aviation Heritage Centre
The Street
Tel: (01986) 896644

A museum with 30 aircraft on display together with a large indoor display of smaller items connected with the history of aviation. Donations are encouraged. *Open 4 Apr-24 Oct, Tue, Sun and Bank Hol Mons, 1000-1700; school holidays, Tue-Thu, 1000-1700. (M12)*

### Ipswich
**Ipswich Transport Museum**
Old Trolleybus Depot, Cobham Road
Tel: (01473) 715666

The museum features over 90 vehicles built or operated in and around Ipswich, together with other associated displays and small exhibits. *Open 4 Apr-28 Nov, Sun, Bank Hol Mon, 1300-1630; 3-28 Aug, Mon-Fri, 1300-1630. £2.25/£1.25/£1.75. (K18)*

### Lowestoft
**Lydia Eva Steam Drifter/Mincarlo Trawler**
Yacht Basin, Lowestoft Harbour
Tel: (01603) 782758

The Lydia Eva is the last surviving steam drifter built at King's Lynn. Mincarlo was launced in 1930. The last side-fishing trawler to be built and engined in Lowestoft in 1962. *Open 2 Apr-31 Oct, daily, 1000-1630; please phone Great Yarmouth Tourist Information Centre on 01493 842195 or Lowestoft Tourist Information Centre on 01502 523000 to confirm details. (P11)*

### Oulton Broad
**ISCA Maritime Museum**
Caldecott Road
Tel: (01502) 585606

Worldwide collection of ethnic, manpowered and sailing boats. Some of the craft displayed are extinct in their country of origin. *Open 2 Jan-31 Mar, daily, 1000-1600; 1 Apr-30 Sep, daily, 1000-1800; 1 Oct-24 Dec, daily, 1000-1600; last admission 1 hour before closing. £3.50/£2.00/£2.50. (P11)*

### Parham
**390th Bomb Group Memorial Air Museum**
Parham Airfield
Tel: (01728) 621373

A museum housed in the original control tower with a refreshment and sales hut and an archive building. *Open 7 Mar-30 May, Sun, Bank Hol Mon, 1100-1800; 9 Jun-25 Aug, Wed, 1100-1800; 29 Aug-24 Oct, Sun, 1100-1800. (M16)*

### Stowmarket
**Museum of East Anglian Life**
See entry in Museums section.

### Wetheringsett
**Mid-Suffolk Light Railway Museum**
Brockford Station
Tel: (01449) 766899

A re-created mid-Suffolk light railway station with exhibits relating to Mid-Suffolk Light Railway and restoration of the station and trackwork on part of the original route. *Open 4 Apr-26 Sep, Sun, Bank Hol Mon, 1100-1700. £1.00/50p/£1.00. (J15)*

*Billingford Windmill, Norfolk*

## Norfolk

### Acle
**Stracey Arms Drainage Mill**
Stracey Arms
An exhibition of photos and the history of drainage mills in Broadland. A restored drainage mill with access by 2 ladders to the cap showing the brakewheel and gears. *Open 10 Apr-30 Sep, daily, 0900-2000. £1.00/50p/£1.00. (O9)*

### Billingford
**Billingford Windmill**
Tel: (01379) 740414
A restored cornmill with all internal machinery intact, in addition to the wind-driven machinery. *Open all year, daily, 1100-1500, 1900-2100 on summer nights. 70p/30p/70p (K13)*

### Cley-next-the-Sea
**Cley Mill**
Tel: (01263) 740209
A towermill used as a flourmill until 1918 and converted to a guesthouse in 1983. Built in the early 1700s, it is an outstanding example of a preserved mill with sails. *Open 28 Mar-1 Oct, daily, 1400-1700. £1.50/75p/75p. (I4)*

### Denver
**Denver Windmill**
A fully-restored windmill and all its internal machinery with a splendid Blackstone oil engine. The latter undergoing refurbishment. *Open 3 Apr-29 Sep, Wed, Sat, 1000-1600; Sun, 1400-1600; Bank Hol Mons, 1000-1600. (C10)*

### Dereham
**Dereham Windmill**
Cherry Lane, Norwich Road
Tel: (01842) 752599
A brick towermill, built in 1836 and restored in 1984-87. It is now complete with cap, fantail and sails and some machinery intact. Also a permanent exhibition on windmills. *Open 14-May-12 Sep, Thu-Sun 1200-1500 please telephone Thetford Tourist Information Centre for confirmation on (01842) 752599. (H/18/9)*

### Great Bircham
**Bircham Mill**
Tel: (01485) 578393
A Norfolk cornmill with working machinery and a small working bakery museum. There are also tearooms, ponies and cycle hire. *Open 28 Mar-30 Sep, Wed, Sun, 1000-1700. £2.50/£1.00/£2.00. (E6)*

### Halvergate Marsh
**Berney Arms Windmill**
c/o 8 Manor Road, Great Yarmouth
Tel: (01604) 730320
A most splendid and the highest remaining Norfolk marshmill in working order with 7 floors. Built in the late 19thC by millwrights Stolworthy and situated on Halvergate Marsh. *Open 22 Mar-30 Sep, daily, 0900-1300, 1400-1700. £1.30/70p/£1.00. (O9/10)*

### Horsey
**Horsey Windpump**
Tel: (01493) 393904
This windmill is 4 storeys high and the gallery affords splendid views across the marshes. *Open 27 Mar-30 Sep, daily, 1100-1700. £1.20/60p/£1.20. (O7)*

### Letheringsett
**Letheringsett Watermill**
Riverside Road   Tel: (01263) 713153
An historic working watermill with an iron water wheel and main gearing restored with an additional vintage Ruston Hornsby oil engine. Flour, animal and pet feed are for sale. *Please contact for details of opening times. £2.00/£1.50/£2.00. (I/J5)*

### Sculthorpe
**Sculthorpe Mill**
Lynn Road   Tel: (01328) 856161
A Grade II Listed watermill, set within 6 acres of meadow. There are plans to set up a nature trail, working with the Wensum Valley Conservation Trust. Unbridged ford and walk. *Please contact for details of opening times and prices. (G6)*

### Starston
**Starston Windpump**
Tel: (01379) 852393
A restored windpump. *Open at any reasonable time. (L12)*

*Norfolk ● Suffolk*

## Suffolk

### Herringfleet
**Herringfleet Marshmill**
Tel: (01473) 583352
The last surviving smock drainage mill in the Broads area; the last full-size working windmill in the country with 4 common sails and a tailpole. *Open 9 May, 1300-1700; also open for 2 further days in the year, weather permitting. (O11)*

### Holton St Peter
**Holton Saint Peter Postmill**
Mill House   Tel: (01986) 872367
A restored 18thC post windmill with 4 sails and a working fantail. *Open 31 May, 30 Aug, Bank Hol Mon, 1000-1800. (N13)*

### Pakenham
**Pakenham Watermill**
Mill Road, Grimstone End
Tel: (01787) 247179
An 18thC working watermill on a Domesday site with an oil engine. The Mill was restored by the Suffolk Preservation Society and the Suffolk Building Preservation Trust. *Open 2 Apr-29 Sep, Wed, Sat, Sun, Bank Hols, 1400-1730. £2.00/£1.20/£1.75. (H15)*

### Saxtead Green
**◉ Saxtead Green Postmill**
The Mill House. Tel: (01728) 685789
An elegant white windmill, dating from 1776. A fine example of a traditional Suffolk postmill. Climb the stairs to the 'buck' to see the machinery, all in working order. *Open 22 Mar-30 Oct, Mon-Sat, 1000-1300, 1400-1800. £1.75/90p/£1.30. (L15)*

### Stanton
**Stanton Postmill**
Mill Farm, Upthorpe Road
Tel: (01359) 250622
A postmill dating from 1751. In working order with an exhibition of postmills in the United Kingdom and other local mills. *Open 4, 5 Apr, 2, 3, 30, 31 May, 1100-1900; 4 Jul-26 Sep, Sun, 1100-1900. £1.50/20p/£1.50. (H14)*

### Thelnetham
**Thelnetham Windmill**
Mill Road. Tel: (01359) 250622
A tower windmill, built in 1819 with 4 very large patent sails driving 2 pairs of millstones. In full working order with flour available for sale. *Open 4, 5 Apr, 2, 3, 30, 31 May, Sun, Bank Hol Mon, 1100-1900; 4 Jul-26 Sep, Sun, 1100-1900. £1.25/25p/£1.25. (I13)*

### Thorpeness
**Thorpeness Windmill**
Tel: (01394) 384948
A working windmill housing displays on the Suffolk Coast and Heaths and Thorpeness village as well as mill information. *Please contact for details of opening times and prices. (O16)*

### Woodbridge
**◉ Buttrums Mill**
Burkitt Road   Tel: (01394) 382045
A fine 6-storey towermill which is now fully restored with sails and machinery. There is also a display on history and machinery. *Open 1 May-26 Sep, Sat, Sun, Bank Hol Mon, 1400-1800. £1.00/25p/£1.00. (L/M17)*

### Woodbridge
**Woodbridge Tidemill**
Tidemill Quay   Tel: (01473) 626618
A completely restored 18thC tidalmill. The machinery works at varying times, subject to tides. *Please contact for details of opening times. £1.00/50p/£1.00. (L/M17)*

*Woodbridge Tide Mill, Suffolk*

Wild gardens, formal gardens, specialist gardens ... Norfolk and Suffolk have something to excite you, whatever your taste.

Nowhere else will you find anything quite like Norfolk Lavender. The National Collection of Lavenders is here, and many varieties can be seen and purchased. If you visit Norfolk in early summer, you are likely to see whole fields of purple lavender, being cultivated for a range of lavender products.

In contrast, in the south of Norfolk you may see fields of roses. Peter Beales Roses has a world famous collection of over 1100 different varieties of roses, many rare and some found nowhere other than here.

There are two outstanding gardens at Bressingham, and a Plant Centre to inspire. Adrian Bloom's garden uses conifers and heathers as the basis for striking displays throughout the year. Alan Bloom's 70 years of gardening expertise is very evident in the wonderful planting combinations of perennials shown off in island beds.

Fairhaven Garden Trust is a delightful woodland and water garden on the Norfolk Broads. It is a tranquil place of natural beauty with an unusual combination of cultivated and wild flowers. Candelabra primulas flourish in the damp ground near the waterways which are spanned by small bridges.

By contrast, Helmingham Hall Gardens are more formal, set in and around the moated house. The main walled garden has gorgeous, wide herbaceous borders, and flower tunnels intersect an immaculate kitchen garden.

And then there's Wyken Hall. The garden is fine - the food is excellent!

# Gardens & Vineyards

## Norfolk

### Attleborough
### ❀ Peter Beales Roses
London Road   Tel: (01953) 454707
A large display garden featuring the majority of our world famous collection of classic roses. Mainly old-fashioned and those rare and of historic value. *Open 5-30 Jan, Mon-Sat, 0900-1630; 1 Feb-9 Apr, Mon-Sat, 0900-1630; Sun, 1000-1600; 2-5 Apr, Fri-Mon, 1000-1600; 14 Apr-23 Dec, Mon-Sat, 0900-1630; Sun, Bank Hol Mon, 1000-1600. (I11)*

### Blickling
### ❀ Blickling Hall
See entry in Historic Houses section.

### Dereham
### Norfolk Herbs
Dereham  Tel: (01362) 860812
Specialist growers of culinary, medicinal and aromatic herb plants. Herb shop and hand thrown garden terracotta. Display garden and plant sales area. Herbal advice and information; garden design. *Open 3 Feb-31 Mar, Wed-Sat, 0900-1700; 1 Apr-31 Jul, daily, 0900-1800; 1-31 Aug, Tue-Sun, 0900-1800; 1 Sep-23 Dec, Wed-Sat, 0900-1700. (C10)*

### Downham Market
### ❀ The Collectors World
### of Eric St John-Foti
See entry in Historic Houses section.

### East Harling
### ❀ Harling Vineyard
Eastfield House, Church Road
Tel: (01953) 717341
Vineyards with a tasting room, shop, toilets, car park, gardens and grounds. *Open shop, all year, daily, 1030-1800; Tastings, 2 Apr-31 Oct, daily, 1030-1800; closed 25 Dec. £2.50/free/£2.50. (H/I12)*

*Fairhaven Garden Trust, South Walsham, Norfolk*

*Peter Beales Roses, Attleborough, Norfolk*

### Erpingham
**Alby Crafts Gardens**
Cromer Road   Tel: (01263) 761226
Four acres of garden with a bee garden and ponds beside the craft centre. *Open 27 Mar-31 Oct, Tue-Sun, Bank Hol Mon, 1000-1700. £1.50/£1.50. (K6)*

### Grimston
**⊛ Congham Hall Herb Garden**
Lynn Road   Tel: (01485) 600250
Garden with over 650 varieties of herbs in formal beds with wild flowers and a potager garden. Over 250 varieties of herbs for sale in pots. *Open 4 Apr-26 Sep, Sun-Fri, 1400-1600. (E7)*

### Heacham
**⊛ Norfolk Lavender Limited**
Caley Mill   Tel: (01485) 570384
Lavender is distilled from the flowers and the oil made into a wide range of gifts. There is a slide show when the distillery is not working. *Open all year, daily, 1000-1700; closed 25, 26 Dec, 1 Jan. (D5)*

### Houghton
**⊛ Houghton Hall**
See entry in Historic Houses section.

*Norfolk Lavender, Norfolk*

### Neatishead
**Willow Farm Flowers**
Cangate   Tel: (01603) 783588
One of the largest displays of dried, silk and parchment flowers in the region situated in a magnificent 300-year-old thatched barn in the heart of the Norfolk Broads. *Open 1 Feb-23 Dec, Tue-Sat, 1000-1600; Sun, 1400-1600; Bank Hol Mon, 1000-1600. (M7)*

### Norwich
**⊛ Dragon Hall**
See entry in Historic Houses section.

### Norwich
**⊛ Mannington Gardens and Countryside**
Mannington Hall   Tel: (01263) 584175
Gardens with a lake, moat, woodland and an outstanding rose collection. There is also a Saxon church with Victorian follies, countryside walks and trails with guide booklets. *Please contact for details of opening times. £3.00/free/£2.50. (K6)*

### Norwich
**Plantation Garden**
4 Earlham Road
A rare surviving example of a private Victorian town garden, created between 1856-1897 in a former medieval chalk quarry and undergoing restoration by volunteers. *Open mid Apr-25 Oct, Sun, 1400-1700. £1.00/free/£1.00. (L9)*

### Oxborough
**⊛ Oxburgh Hall**
See entry in Historic Houses section.

### Raveningham
**Raveningham Gardens**
The Stables   Tel: (01508) 548480
Extensive gardens surrounding an elegant Georgian house provide the setting for many rare, variegated and unusual plants and shrubs with sculptures, parkland and a church. *Open 4-5 Apr, Sun, Bank Hol Mon, 1400-1730; 9 May-25 Jul, Sun, 1400-1730. £2.00/free/£1.00. (N11)*

### Roughton
**⊛ Felbrigg Hall**
See entry in Historic Houses section.

### Sandringham
**⊛ Sandringham**
See entry in Historic Houses section.

### South Walsham
**⊛ Fairhaven Garden Trust**
School Road Tel: (01603) 270449
One hundred and seventy acres of woodland and water gardens including a private inner broad and separate bird sanctuary. Primulas, azaleas and rhododendrons are on display. *Open Apr-31 Oct, Tue-Sun, Bank Hols, 1100-1730. £3.00/£1.00/£2.70. (M/N8)*

### Thetford
**⊛ Euston Hall**
See entry in Historic Houses section.

### Wells-next-the-Sea
**⊛ Holkham Hall**
See entry in Historic Houses section.

### Wroxham
**⊛ Hoveton Hall Gardens**
Tel: (01603) 782798
Approximately 10 acres of gardens in a woodland setting with a large walled herbaceous garden and a Victorian kitchen garden. There are also woodland and lakeside walks. *Open Easter Sunday - mid Sept, Wed, Fri, Sun and Bank Hol Mons, 1100-1730. (M8)*

*Giffords Hall Vineyard and Sweet Pea Centre, Hartest, Suffolk*

## Suffolk

### Ashbocking
**James White Cider and
Apple Juice Co.**
White's Fruit Farm, Helmingham Road
Tel: (01473) 890202
Cider making, apple juice production and bottling on view along with a Downie produce farm shop selling apple juice and ciders produced on site. Free tastings are also given. *Open Shop all year, daily, 1000-1700; Production Mon-Fri, 1000-1700; closed 25, 26 Dec. (K17)*

### Boxford
**⊛ The Heraldic Garden and
Lady Hilda Memorial Arboretum**
Boxford House   Tel: (01787) 210208
A selection of fauna and flora found in heraldry which form the examples used in audio-peripatetic (hearing and strolling) presentations. *Please contact for details of opening times. £4.00/£2.50/£3.50. (H18/19)*

### Bruisyard
**⊛ Bruisyard Vineyard
and Herb Centre**
Church Road. Tel: (01728) 638281
A 10-acre vineyard showing summer work and maintenance of the vines, a tour of the winery and herb garden. A video show and display of wine making is also provided. *Open 16 Jan-24 Dec, daily, 1030-1700. £3.50/£2.00/£3.00. (M15)*

### Cavendish
**Cavendish Manor Vineyards**
Nether Hall   Tel: (01787) 280221
A vineyard with a period manor-house, museum, art gallery and shop. *Open all year, daily, 1100-1600; closed 25-31 Dec. £2.50/free/£2.50. (F18)*

### East Bergholt
**⊛ East Bergholt Place Garden**
East Bergholt Place
Tel: (01206) 299224
The Place Garden was laid out at the turn of the century and covers 15 acres with fine trees, shrubs, rhododendrons, camellias and magnolias. *Open 1 Mar-30 Sep, daily, 1000-1700; closed 4 Apr. £2.00/free/£2.00. (J19)*

### Flatford
**⊛ Bridge Cottage**
See entry in Historic Houses section.

### Framlingham
**⊛ Shawsgate Vineyard**
Badingham Road   Tel: (01728) 724060
An attractive 15-acre vineyard with a modern, well-equipped winery, vineyard walk, guided tours, wine tasting all day, a picnic area, children's play area and shop open all year. *Open 1 Feb-24 Dec, daily, 1030-1700; please phone for weekend opening during winter. £3.25/free/£2.75. (L/M15)*

### Hadleigh
**Guildhall**
See entry in Historic Houses section.

### Hartest
**⊛ Giffords Hall Vineyard
and Sweet Pea Centre**
Tel: (01284) 830464
A 33-acre small country living with vines, a winery, rare breeds of sheep, pigs, free-range chickens, a rose garden, wild flower meadows and a sweet pea centre. *Open 2 Apr-31 Oct, daily, 1100-1800. £3.00/free/£2.90. (G17)*

### Haughley
**Haughley Park**
See entry in Historic Houses section.

### Helmingham
**⊛ Helmingham Hall Gardens**
Estate Office   Tel: (01473) 890363
A moated and walled garden with many rare roses and possibly the best kitchen garden in Britain. Also highland cattle and safari rides in the park to view the red and fallow deer. *Open 25 Apr-5 Sep, Sun, 1400-1800. £3.50/£2.00/£3.00. (K16)*

### Ickworth
**⊛ Ickworth House,
Park and Gardens**
See entry in Historic Houses section.

### Lamarsh
**Paradise Centre**
Twinstead Road   Tel: (01787) 269449
Five acres of garden with 3 ponds and paddocks with unusual pets. Unusual plants for sale and a picnic play area. *Open 28 Mar-24 Oct, Sat, Sun, Bank Hol Mon, 1000-1700. £1.50/£1.00/£1.00. (G19)*

### Lavenham
**⊛ Lavenham Guildhall of
Corpus Christi**
See entry in Historic Houses section.

### Lavenham
**⊛ Little Hall**
See entry in Historic Houses section.

### Long Melford
**⊛ Kentwell Hall**
See entry in Historic Houses section.

### Long Melford
**⊛ Melford Hall**
See entry in Historic Houses section.

### Otley
**⊛ Otley Hall**
See entry in Historic Houses section.

### Somerleyton
**⊛ Somerleyton Hall and Gardens**
See entry in Historic Houses section.

### Stanton
**Wyken Hall Gardens
and Wyken Vineyards**
Tel: (01359) 250287
Seven acres of vines, 4 acres of garden, an Elizabethan manor-house and 16thC barn. There is a spectacular woodland walk through ancient woodland to the vineyard. *Open 4 Feb-24 Dec, Thu-Sun, Bank Hol Mon, 1000-1800. £2.50/free/£1.50. (H14)*

### Stoke-by-Clare
**Boyton Vineyard**
Hill Farm, Boyton End
Tel: (01440) 761893
A vineyard with vines growing in the gardens of a Listed period farmhouse. Tours of the vineyard are followed by a talk and wine tasting. *Open 1 Apr-31 Oct, daily, 1030-1800. (E18)*

### Wingfield
**⊛ Wingfield Old College**
See entry in Historic Houses section.

*Helmingham Hall Gardens, Suffolk*

# Nurseries & Garden Centres

## Norfolk

### Attleborough
### ❀ Peter Beales Roses
Peter Beales Roses, London Road,
Attleborough, NR17 1AY
Tel: (01953) 454707
Fax: (01953) 456845
E-mail: Sales@classicroses.co.uk

A large and world famous collection of roses featuring over 1100 rare, unusual and beautiful varieties of which 250 are unique. The National Collection of Rosa Species is held here. Browse through 2.5 acres of container roses available in the summer months, or order for winter delivery. Experts are always on hand for advice or help in the selection of new varieties. *Open Mon-Fri. 0900-1700, Sat. 0900-1630, Sun. 1000-1600. Catalogue available on request (I11)*

### Bressingham
### ❀ Bressingham Plant Centre
Bressingham, Diss, Norfolk
Tel: (01379) 687464/688133

3 miles west of Diss on A1066. Unique 2 acre Plant Centre adjacent to world famous Bressingham Gardens. A 'Mecca' for plant lovers with a superb range of over 5,000 varieties. 2,000 varieties of perennials include 200 plants introduced by founder Alan Bloom MBE, VMH. Inspiring plant displays, events, plus Pavilion Tea Room for light refreshments. Enjoy the choice, quality, service and value which have made Bressingham a byword for excellence.
*Open: Daily including Sun, 0900-1730 except Christmas Day/Boxing Day.*
See also entry for Bressingham Steam Museum and Gardens under Machinery & Transport on page 76 and The Pavilion Tea Room under Afternoon Teas on page 102. *(J13)*

### Gressenhall
### ❀ Norfolk Herbs
Blackberry Farm, Dillington,
Nr Gressenhall, Dereham NR19 2QD
Tel: (01362) 860812

(approx 1 mile north of Dereham on the B1110, turn left on bend at end of golf course and we are approx. 1.5 miles on right). Norfolk's specialist Herb Farm, in a beautiful wooded valley renowned for its wildlife. Visitors may browse through a vast array of aromatic, culinary and medicinal herb plants and learn all about growing and using herbs. *Open Apr-Jul, daily, Aug, Tue-Sun, 0900-1800; Sep-Mar, Wed-Sat, 0900-1700. Closed Dec 24-Jan 31. For group visits or visiting outside of these hours, please telephone for an appointment. (H8)*

### Heacham
### ❀ Norfolk Lavender Ltd.
Caley Mill, Heacham, Norfolk (on A149)
Tel: (01485) 570384
Fax: (01485) 571176

The Fragrant Plant Meadow and new Conservatory offer a wide selection of scented plants to add to our lavenders, herb plants and cottage garden collection. Also Tours (May-Sep) - Learn about the harvest and ancient distillation process. Countryside Gift Shop stocks the full range of Norfolk Lavender's famous fragrant products with a wide choice of other gifts to suit all pockets. Miller's Cottage Tearoom - Specialising in locally baked cakes, scones, cream teas and light lunches. The National Collection of Lavenders. *FREE ADMISSION.*
*Open daily 1000-1700 (closed Dec 25, 26 and Jan 1). (D5)*

### King's Lynn
### ❀ The African Violet Centre
Terrington St Clement,
King's Lynn, Norfolk
Tel: (01553) 828374

Beside the A17, 5 miles from King's Lynn. Wide variety of gold medal winning African Violets on show. Cultural advice given. Good selection of African Violets and other seasonal plants for sale. Attractive nursery shop and tearoom for light refreshments. Ample parking, coach parties welcomed. Talk and demonstration to parties, by appointment. The all weather attraction with free admission! *Open daily 1000-1700. Closed Christmas/New Year. (B7)*

### Norwich
### ❀ Notcutts Garden Centres
Daniels Road (Ring Road),
Norwich, Norfolk.  Tel: (01603) 453155

Ipswich Road, Woodbridge, Suffolk
Woodbridge  Tel: (01394) 445400

Notcutts Garden Centres are wonderlands for gardeners. Over 2000 varieties of guaranteed hardy plants. No need to be a specialist. There's plenty of help on hand. Why not spend some time wandering at leisure. There's so much to see - display borders, pools, furniture, stoneware, books, gift ideas and pot plants, plus lots of tips on how to improve your garden. Whatever your interests, there's plenty for you at Notcutts.
Also at
Ardleigh Tel: (01206) 230271
Peterborough Tel: (01733) 234600
St.Albans Tel: (01727) 853224
*Norwich (L9), Woodbridge (L/M17)*

### Taverham
### ❀ Taverham Garden Centre
Fir Covert Road, Taverham, Norwich
Tel: (01603) 860522

Taverham Garden Centre is set in 15 acres of beautiful countryside, 7 miles from Norwich on the A1067 Norwich/Fakenham road. We offer a riot of colour all year round. Acres of greenhouses packed with beautiful flowers and pot plants, grown to the highest standards. There's an unrivalled choice of plants, shrubs, trees; an extensive range of bulbs and seeds; attractive garden furniture and ornaments, terracotta pots, planters, paving slabs, pools and conservatories. Plus dried and silk flowers, books, pet food, coffee bar, craft complex. Fully trained staff. Disabled facilities, coach parties welcome. Parking for 1000 cars. *Open Mon-Sat, 0900-1730. Sun, 1000-1730. (K8)*

### Wenhaston
### Wootten's of Wenhaston
Wootten's Plants, Blackheath,
Wenhaston, Suffolk IP19 9HD
Tel: (01502) 478258.

1.5 miles off A12 south of Blythburgh
A beautifully laid out nursery with superbly grown herbaceous plants, many of them rare. An extraordinary range of plants thumping with health. Masses of salvias, a huge collection of Barnhaven primulas, at least 10 different sorts of foxgloves and more than 40 irises. More than 80 kinds of old fashioned scented leaf pelargoniums. "To get there, I spent seven hours in the car driving through a monumental cloud burst. It was worth it" Anna Pavord, The Independent. *Open daily 0930-1700. (N/O14)*

### Westleton
### ❀ Fisk's Clematis Nursery
Westleton, nr Saxmundham,
Suffolk IP17 3AJ
Tel: Westleton (01728) 648263

Midway between Aldeburgh and Southwold on the B1125 Many varieties of clematis in flower, on walls, pergola and in greenhouses. We have specialised in growing clematis since 1950. Plants on sale and advice available. *Open Mon-Fri, 0900-1700 Sat and Sun in summer 1000-1300, 1400-1700. (O15)*

### Reymerston
### ❀ Thorncroft Clematis Nursery
The Lings, Reymerston, Norwich,
Norfolk  NR9 4QG
Tel: (01953) 850407

On B1135 exactly halfway between Wymondham and Dereham.
Come and visit our nursery and garden in the 'heart' of the Norfolk countryside where these beautiful, versatile climbers can be seen growing in a natural setting. Our nursery stocks over 200 beautiful, and unusual varieties. Delivery arranged all-year round for our quality plants. Send 5 x 2nd class stamps for catalogue. *Open 1 Mar-31 Oct, 1000-1630 Closed Wednesdays. (Visits Nov-Feb by appointment). (I9/10)*

# Suffolk

### East Bergholt
### ❀ The Place For Plants
East Bergholt Place Garden,
Suffolk  CO7 6UP
Tel: (01206) 299224

Plant Centre and Garden for Specialist and Popular Plants. 2 miles East of the A12 on the B1070 Manningtree Road, on the edge of East Bergholt.
A plant centre has been set up in the Victorian walled garden at East Bergholt Place, selling an excellent range of unusual and popular plants including shrubs, trees, climbers, herbaceous plants, ferns, grasses, etc. *The 15 acre garden and arboretum is also open during the Spring and Summer. Plant Centre open daily, 1000-1700. Garden open - Please see entry in Gardens and Vineyards section on page 82. (J19)*

### Woodbridge
### ❀ Notcutts Garden Centres
See entry under Norwich, Norfolk

*'Poppies', Nayland, Suffolk*

There are family activities by the score throughout this Guide, so no child need worry about where to take the parents next holiday.

If it's excitement you're seeking, Pleasure Beach can provide bags of it, with more rides and attractions than you could possibly take in in one visit. There's a rollercoaster, log flume and the ominous "Terminator", among others.

On your visits to farm attractions, look out for three breeds particularly special to Suffolk. The Red Poll cow, Suffolk Punch and Suffolk Sheep are known as the "Suffolk Trinity".

Look out for snow leopards, squirrel monkeys, crocodiles and reindeer! Not exactly natives to these parts, but we have them here, and they are fascinating to watch.

Did you know we have dinosaurs here too? Don't believe me? Just outside Norwich is their lair - go and check them out!

*Country Fair at Holkham Hall, Norfolk*

## Norfolk

### Attleborough
**Kool Kidz**
34-35 Haverscroft Industrial Estate, New Road   Tel: (01953) 457333
Indoor activity centre including large soft play area, educational equipment, cafe bar, satellite TV and refreshments. Birthday parties available and free parking. *Open all year, daily, 1000-1900; closed 25, 26 Dec, 1 Jan. Child £2.95. (I11)*

### Banham
**⊛ Banham Zoo**
The Grove  Tel: (01953) 887771
See conservation in action at East Anglia's premier zoological gardens. Our aim is to provide a great day out amongst some of the world's rare and endangered species. *Open all year, daily, 1000-dusk; closed 25, 26 Dec. Please contact for details of admission prices. (J12)*

### Cromer
**Funstop**
Exchange House, Louden Road
Tel: (01263) 514976
A children's indoor adventure centre with a giant slide, ball pond, tubes, scrambling nets, a special under-4's area, a super snack bar and lots more. *Open 2 Jan-26 Apr, Fri-Sun, daily during school hol, 1000-1800; 1 May-30 Sep, daily, 1000-1800; 2 Oct-26 Dec, Fri-Sun, Daily during school hol, 1000-1800; closed 25, 26 Dec. Child from £1.65. (L4/5)*

### Downham Market
**Hillside Animal Sanctuary**
Bridge Farm  Tel: (01603) 891227
Visit our rescued farm animals. Information centre and gift shop. *Open 4 Apr-31 Oct, Sun, 1300-1700. £1.50/£1.00/£1.00. (C10)*

### Fleggburgh
**⊛ The Village**
Burgh St Margaret  Tel: (01493) 369770
Over 35 acres of working crafts, railway, animals, live steam, bygone memorabilia, live shows, a traditional fairground, adventure play area and Compton-Christie organ. *Open 29 Mar-31 Oct, daily, 1000-1700. £5.95/£3.95/£5.45. (O8)*

### Filby
**⊛ Thrigby Hall Wildlife Gardens**
Tel: (01493) 369477
A wide selection of Asian mammals, birds, reptiles, tigers, crocodiles and storks. A 250-year-old landscaped garden with play area and willow pattern gardens. *Open all year, daily, 1000-1730. £5.50/£3.20/£4.50. (O8/9)*

### Frettenham
**Redwings Horse Sanctuary**
Hill Top Farm, Hall Lane
Tel: (01603) 737432
A sanctuary where visitors are able to meet the rescued horses, ponies and donkeys. There are stalls, craft shops, bric-a-brac, refreshments and a 'vegeburger' bar. *Please contact for details of opening times. (L8)*

### Great Ellingham
**⊛ The Tropical Butterfly Gardens and Bird Park**
Long Street Nursery
Tel: (01953) 453175
Tropical butterfly gardens with 2400 sq ft of landscaped gardens containing hundreds of tropical butterflies and plants as well as falconry displays, tearooms and shops. *Open 23 Mar-2 Nov, Mon-Sat, 0900-1730; Sun, 1000-1730. £2.75/£1.70/£2.50. (I11)*

*Banham Zoo, Norfolk*

### Great Witchingham
**Norfolk Wildlife Trust: Broads Wildlife Centre**
Tel: (01603) 872274
A large collection of British and European wildlife in 40 acres of parkland with a pet's corner, play areas, model farm and clear-water carp pool. *Open 1 Apr-31 Oct, daily, 1030-1800. £4.00/£2.50/£3.50. (J7)*

### Great Yarmouth
**The Mint**
31 Marine Parade  Tel: (01493) 842968
Family entertainment centre including 'Quasar' the live action laser game. *Open all year, daily, 0900-2300. £1.99/£1.99/£1.99. (P9)*

### Great Yarmouth
**Norfolk Rare Breeds Centre**
Decoy Farm House,
Ormesby St Michael
Tel: (01493) 732990
Rare breeds of domestic farm animals: cattle, sheep, pigs, goats, poultry, donkeys, heavy horses and rabbits, a shop and farm museum and children's play area. *Open 10 Jan-21 Mar, Sun, 1100-1600; 28 Mar-31 Oct, daily except Sat, 1100-1700; 7 Nov-26 Dec, Sun 1100-1600. £3.00/£2.00/£2.50. (O/P8)*

### Great Yarmouth
**☸ Pleasure Beach**
South Beach Parade
Tel: (01493) 844585
Rollercoaster, Terminator, log flume, Flipper, monorail, breakdance, galloping horses, caterpillar, go-karts, ghost train, fun house, sheer terror show and live entertainment. *Open 2-5 Apr, 1030-1000; 15 May-15 Sep, daily, from 1030. (P9)*

### Great Yarmouth
**Sea-Life Centre**
Marine Parade  Tel: (01493) 330631
Walk through the underwater tropical reef shark tank, a sand tank with ray fish and British sharks plus 25 themed displays depicting British marine life and local settings. *Open all year, daily, from 1000; closed 25 Dec. Please contact for details of winter opening times. £5.50/£3.95/£3.95. (P9)*

*Sea-Life Centre, Great Yarmouth, Norfolk*

*Pettitts Animal Adventure Park, Reedham, Norfolk*

### Great Yarmouth
**Treasure World**
11-12 Marine Parade
Tel: (01493) 330444
An animatronic experience on diving, treasure and the history of diving with moving audiovisual exhibits and a restaurant. *Open 1 Apr-30 Sep, daily, 1030-2200. £2.45/£1.45/£1.45. (P9)*

### Hunstanton
**Jungle Wonderland
C H S Amusements**
1st Floor Pier Entertainment Centre,
The Green  Tel: (01485) 535505
An adventure playground catering for children aged 2-12 with a soft play area, a giant ball pool, Kenny the Croc slide, many more safe play items and a 96-seater diner. *Open 1 Jan-28 Mar, Fri-Sun, daily during school hols, 1000-1800; 1 Apr-31 Oct, daily, 1000-1800; 5 Nov-24 Dec, Fri-Sun, daily during school hols, 1000-1800; closed 25, 26 Dec. From £2.50. (D5)*

### Hunstanton
**Sea-Life Centre**
Southern Promenade
Tel: (01485) 533576
See a world which experienced divers see. See and touch a variety of rock pool creatures. Ocean tunnel. Also a seal rehabilitation centre for unwell or abandoned seals. *Open all year, daily, from 1000; closed 25 Dec. £4.95/£3.75/£4.45. (D5)*

### Larling
**International League for the
Protection of Horses Norfolk Office**
Overa House Farm  Tel: (01953) 498682
On view are stables and paddocks with the horses, ponies and donkeys which are looked after by the International League for the Protection of Horses (ILPH). *Open all year, Sat, Sun, 1100-1600; some facilities may not be open in winter. (H/I12)*

### Lenwade
**☸ The Dinosaur Adventure Park**
Weston Estate  Tel: (01603) 870245
Discover the giants from the past as you explore the Dinosaur Trail, venture into the woodland maze and play area. For a family adventure its time you came-n-saurus. *Open 22 Mar-7 Sep, daily, 1000-1700; 11 Sep-31 Oct, Fri, Sat, Sun, 1000-1600. £4.50/£3.50/£4.00. (J8)*

### Poringland
**The Playbarn**
West Green Farm, Shotesham Road
Tel: (01508) 495526
Children's indoor and outdoor play centre. Designed for under 7's. Large barn and clay lump courtyard, beach barn, children's farm, riding school and small animal house. *Open all year, Mon-Fri, 0930-1530; Sun, 1000-1700; closed 25, 26 Dec, 1 Jan. Child £3.00. (L/M10)*

### Reedham
**☸ Pettitt's Animal Adventure Park**
Camphill  Tel: (01493) 700094
A children's theme park with rides, shows, animals, craft demonstrations and a junior rollercoaster called the Black Mamba. *Open 28 Mar-29 Oct, daily except Sat except when Bank Hol, 1000-1730. £5.95/£5.50/£4.95. (N/O10)*

### Snettisham
**☸ Park Farm Snettisham**
Tel: (01485) 542425
Providing unique safari tours, a visitor centre, crafts centre, art gallery, tearoom and souvenir shop. Indoor and outdoor activities include farm animals and pets. *Open 1 Feb-1 Apr, daily, 1000-dusk; 2 Apr-1 Nov, daily, 1000-1730; 5 Nov-26 Dec, Fri, Sat, Sun, 1000-dusk. £3.95/£2.75/£3.50. (D5/6)*

### West Runton
**☸ Norfolk Shire Horse Centre**
West Runton Stables
Tel: (01263) 837339
Shire horses are demonstrated working twice daily with native ponies and a bygone collection of horse-drawn machinery. There is also a children's farm. *Open 29 Mar-30 Jun, daily except Sat unless Bank Hol, 1000-1700; 1 Jul-31 Aug, daily, 1000-1700; 1 Sep-31 Oct, daily except Sat, 1000-1700. £4.50/£2.25/£3.00. (K4)*

## Suffolk

### Baylham
**Baylham House Rare Breeds Farm**
Mill Lane   Tel: (01473) 830264
A rare breeds farm, visitor's centre, riverside walk and a Roman site. *Open 30 March-3 Oct, Tue-Sun, Bank Hol Mon and Oct school hols, 1100-1700. £3.00/£1.50/£2.25. (J17)*

### Earsham
**Otter Trust**
Tel: (01986) 893470
A breeding and conservation headquarters with the largest collection of otters in the world. There are also lakes with a collection of waterfowl and deer. *Open 1 Apr-30 Sep, daily, 1030-1800. £4.50/£2.50/£4.00. (M12)*

### Felixstowe
**Manning's Amusement Park**
Sea Road   Tel: (01394) 282370
A traditional amusement park with large rides and attractions, a children's park, a nightclub, sportsbar, quasar arena and Sunday market. *Open 28 Mar-26 Sep, Sat, Sun and School Hols, please phone for further details. (M19/20)*

### Felixstowe
**Quasar**
The Labyrinth, The Amusement Park
Tel: (01394) 282370
Laser shooting with a 30-gun system (15 red and 15 green) in a 2-storey arena. *Please phone for details. (M19/20)*

### Kessingland
**❀ Suffolk Wildlife Park**
Tel: (01502) 740291
African wildlife and animals from around the world, set in 100 acres of Suffolk coastal parkland. There is also a safari road train and a large children's play area. *Please contact for details of opening times. (P12)*

### Lowestoft
**❀ East Point
Pavilion Visitor Centre**
Tel: (01502) 323000
A glass, all-weather Edwardian-style structure with a large indoor play platform called Discoverig, themed on a North sea gas exploration rig. *Open 2 Jan-31 Mar, Sat, Sun, school hols, 1000-1700; 1 Apr-30 Sep, daily, 0930-1730; 2 Oct-31 Dec, Sat, Sun, school hols, 1000-1700; closed 25, 26 Dec, 1 Jan. Child from £1.70. (P11)*

### Lowestoft
**❀ Pleasurewood
Hills Theme Park**
Leisure Way, Corton
Tel: (01502) 586000
Log flume, chairlift, cine 180, 2 railways, pirate ship, fort, Aladdin's cave, parrot, sealion shows, rollercoaster, waveswinger, Eye in the Sky and Star Ride Enterprise. *Please phone for details. £10.95/£9.95/£6.50. (P11/12)*

*'Fudge' baby Kune Kune boar, Baylham House Rare Breeds Farm, Suffolk*

### Newmarket
**❀ National Stud**
Tel: (01638) 663464
A visit to the National Stud consists of a conducted tour which will include top thoroughbred stallions, mares and foals. *By appointment only. £3.50/£2.80/£2.80. (C/D15)*

### Newmarket
**❀ Wildtracks Ltd**
Chippenham Road, Kennett
Tel: (01638) 751918
An adventure park embracing all kinds of activities for children and adults. *Open 3 Jan, 7 Feb, 7 Mar, 4 Apr, 2 May, 6 Jun, 4 Jul, 1 Aug, 5 Sep, 3 Oct, 7 Nov, 5 Dec. £5.00 per vehicle. (C/D15)*

### Rede
**❀ Rede Hall Farm Park**
Rede Hall Farm   Tel: (01284) 850695
A farm park with Suffolk horses, red poll cattle, rare breeds sheep, pigs and other livestock. Children's pet's corner and play area, nature trail, cart rides and gift shop. *Open 1 Apr-30 Sep, daily, 1000-1730. £3.00/£2.00/£2.00. (F16/17)*

### Southwold
**❀ Southwold Pier**
Tel: (01502) 722105
Pier and amusements. *Open 2 Jan-27 Jun, Sat, Sun, from 1000; 1 Jul-31 Aug, daily, from 0900; 4 Sep-26 Dec, Sat, Sun, from 1000. (P13/14)*

*Boating Lake, Felixstowe, Suffolk*

*Redwings Horse Sanctuary, Frettenham, Suffolk*

### Stonham Aspal
**British Birds of Prey and Conservation Centre**
Stonham Barns, Pettaugh Road
Tel: (01449) 711425
An outdoor flying arena featuring frequent demonstrations of birds of prey in flight with many aviaries, an extensive information centre, a shop and activity projects. *Open all year, daily, 1000-1700; flying demonstrations 1 Mar-31 Oct; closed 25, 26 Dec. £3.50/£2.25/£2.50 (K16)*

### Stonham Aspal
**The Nature Centre**
Stonham Barns, Pettaugh Road
Tel: (01449) 711425
A country complex with the accent on conservation of British wildlife plus small woodland and farmyard animals. *Open all year, daily, 1000-1700; closed 25, 26 Dec. £2.50/£1.95/£2.25. (K16)*

### Stowmarket
**Playworld Ocean Adventure**
Mid-Suffolk Leisure Centre,
Gainsborough Road
Tel: (01449) 674980
A children's indoor play area facility for the under 10's with a wide range of inflatables, a jungle hut with scramble net, slides, aerial runway, grand prix cars, bikes and more. *Open all year, daily, 0930-1900; Sat, Sun, 0900-1800; closed 25, 26 Dec, 1 Jan. Child from £2.30. (I16)*

### Wickham Market
**✿ Easton Farm Park**
Easton   Tel: (01728) 746475
A Victorian farm setting for many species of farm animals including rare breeds. There is a modern milking unit, Victorian dairy, Suffolk horses and a green trail. *Open 21 Mar-30 Jun, Tue-Sun, Bank Hol Mon, 1030-1800; 1 Jul-31 Aug, daily, 1030-1800; 1-30 Sep, Tue-Sun, 1030-1800. (M16)*

### Wickham Market
**Valley Farm Camargue Horses**
Valley Farm Riding and Driving Centre
Tel: (01728) 746916
Britain's only herd of breeding Camargue horses as featured on television. Also the white animal collection including Polo, the long-tailed white boxer. *Open all year, daily, 1000-1600. (M16)*

*Norfolk ● Suffolk*

## Countryside

Head out of town, straight for the countryside, and we have collected a grand choice of activities for you to enjoy.

Get afloat, on a cruiser on the Broads, a river tour on the Deben, or simply a rowing boat on the River Stour. All the details are here.

If you prefer to keep your feet on dry land, you'll find a wealth of nature reserves, each one giving an insight into the nature of its own unique part of Norfolk and Suffolk. Not to be missed is Minsmere, famous for its avocets.

Stride out, on a long distance footpath, or just a two mile walk. The slow way is perhaps the best way to really get to know these counties in depth. If you like to travel just a little bit faster, hire a bike. There are plenty of quiet lanes, or if you like to get away from traffic altogether, head for the forests, or for Alton Water where there is not only a cycle trail around the water, but windsurfing, sailing and canoeing on the water too.

*Fun on the beach, Brancaster, Norfolk*

## Nature Reserves

### Norfolk

### The Norfolk Coast

#### ⊛ Blakeney Point
#### National Nature Reserve
Blakeney Tel: (01263) 740480 (NT)
Shingle spit, sand dunes, seals, shop and display in Lifeboat House. *Access for disabled. Hides. Access by boat from Morston or Blakeney. Car park charge. (I4)*

#### ⊛ Cley Marshes
Cley-next-the-Sea Tel: (01263) 740008
Off the A149. (NWT)
A coastal nature reserve, popular with bird-watchers who come to see migrant and wading birds. Visitor centre overlooks the reserve and contains a small display and a shop. Small beach cafe is sited nearby. *Visitor Centre Apr-Dec, Tue-Sun, Bank Hol Mon, 1000-1700; Marshes all year, access by permit available from visitor centre or Watcher's cottage. Admission £3.00 for non-members. (I4)*

#### Holme Bird Observatory Reserve
Holme-next-the-Sea
Tel: (01485) 525406
Off A149.( NOA)
Nature reserve with over 320 species of birds recorded since 1962. One of 18 bird observatories in the UK. Various species of dragonfly and over 50 species of flora. Bird ringing carried out under National Ringing Scheme organised by British Trust for Ornithology. *Open all year, daily, 1000-1700; members, dawn-dusk; Closed 25 Dec. (D4)*

#### Natural Surroundings
Bayfield Tel: (01263) 711091
Off A148, signposted Glandford
Eight acres of demonstration gardens, orchid meadow and woodland walk with a shop, sales area and light refreshments. *Open 9 Jan-28 Mar, Thu-Sun, 1000-1600; 30 Mar-3 Oct, Tue-Sun, 1000-1730; 7 Oct-19 Dec, Thu-Sun, 1000-1600. Admission £1.75/75p/£1.25. (I5)*

#### ⊛ Titchwell Marsh
Tel: (01485) 210779
Off A149, W of Brancaster (RSPB)
On the picturesque Norfolk coast, Titchwell has a visitor centre, shop, nature trails and hides overlooking reedbeds and the beach. *Reserve open at all times, centre open daily, Mar-Nov, 1000-1700, Nov-Mar, 1000-1600; closed 25, 26 Dec. Free, car park charge £2.00, RSPB members free. (D4)*

### Broadland

#### ⊛ Berney Marshes
Great Yarmouth Tel: (01493) 700645
(RSPB)
Bird-watching in a remote area of the Norfolk Broads. No road access. Access by foot along Weaver's Way. Reached by boat from Breydon Marine or Great Yarmouth. *Bookable in advance with the warden: Mr D Barrett. (O9)*

#### ⊛ Norfolk Wildlife Trust:
#### Broads Wildlife Centre
Ranworth Tel: (01603) 270479 (NWT)
A nature trail and conservation centre with displays showing history and wildlife and a gallery with telescopes and binoculars overlooking the Ranworth Broad nature reserve. *Open 1 Apr-31 Oct, daily, 1000-1700. (M8)*

#### ⊛ Hickling Broad
Hickling Tel: (01692) 598276
Follow signs for Hickling off A149
(EN, NWT)
Reserve with a broad, dykes, marshes, fens and woodland with visitor centre and water trail. *Visitor centre 1 Apr-30 Sep, daily, 1000-1700. Reserve all year, daily, 1000-1700. £2.00/free/£2.00. (O7)*

#### Wildlife Water Trail
How Hill, Ludham Tel: (01692) 678763
Broads Authority, A1062
from Wroxham.
Water trail by small electric launch. Trail covers river and dykes through marshes and fens of the How Hill Nature Reserve. Guide describes area, walk to bird hide. *Open 2 Apr-31 May, Sat, Sun, Bank Hols, 1100-1500; 1 Jun-30 Sep, daily, 1000-1700; 3 Oct-31 Oct, Sat, Sun, 1100-1500. £2.50/£1.50/free. (N8)*

#### ⊛ Strumpshaw Fen
Strumpshaw Tel: (01603) 715191
Take A47 to Great Yarmouth,
then to Strumpshaw. (RSPB).
Woodland, wet meadows, fens and reedbeds. Extensive trails, 4 bird-watching hides and a variety of wildlife. £2.50/50p/£1.50. (N9/10)

*Minsmere Bird Reserve, Suffolk*

## Inland Norfolk

### ⊛ East Wretham Heath
Wretham  Tel: (01953) 498339
Off A1075 3 miles NE of Thetford
(NWT)
Grassland heath with some woodland. Pine plantation, meres and associated wildlife. Self-guided nature trail and access to hide. *Open all year, daily, 1000-1700. (G12)*

### ⊛ Foxley Wood
Foxley  Tel: (01603) 625540
6 miles NE East Dereham (NWT)
Largest ancient woodland in the county. 320-acre woodland comprising of coppice, birch areas, glades and an extensive ride network and nature trails. No dogs please. *Open all year, daily 1000-1700. (I7)*

### ⊛ Pensthorpe Waterfowl Park
Tel: (01328) 851465
Pensthorpe, Fakenham
1 mile south east of Fakenham
A world of wild and endangered waterbirds in a 200-acre nature reserve, one of the largest waterfowl collections in the world. Woodland, meadow, lakeside and riverside nature trails. Water gardens. Courtyard gallery and audio-visual centre with wildlife, photographic, painting and craft exhibitions. Heated wildlife observation gallery. Conservation gift shop. Licensed restaurant. Children's adventure playground. Disabled access. *4 Jan-29 Mar, Sat, Sun, 1100-1600; 31 Mar-31 Dec, daily, 1100-1700; closed 25 Dec. £4.50/£2.00/£4.00. (H6)*

## Suffolk

### ⊛ Dunwich Heath
### Coastguard Cottages
Dunwich Heath  Tel: (01728) 648505
1 mile S of Dunwich off A12. (NT)
Remnant of the once extensive sandlings heaths. Walk and access to beach. Observation room, tearoom and shop in Coastguard Cottages. *Please contact for details of opening times. Car park £1.50. (O14/15)*

### ⊛ Havergate Island
Orford  Tel: (01394) 450732
B1078 to Orford. (RSPB)
Britain's largest colony of avocets also breeding terns. Many wading birds in spring and autumn. Short boat crossing by permit in advance from, The Warden Mr J Partridge, 30 Munday's Lane, Orford, IP12 2LX (please enclose SAE). *Open 2 Jan, 6 Feb, 6 Mar, 4 Apr-30 Aug, 1st and 3rd Sat, Sun of each month and every Thu, 4 Sep, 2 Oct, 6 Nov, 4 Dec, 1000-1500. Members £3.00, non members £5.00 payable in advance. (N/O17)*

### ⊛ Minsmere Nature Reserve
Westleton  Tel: (01728) 648281
Well signposted from the A12
through Westleton   (RSPB)
Reserve on the Suffolk coast now has a purpose-built visitor centre with a shop, tearoom and friendly staff. Nature trails, bird-watching, hides and a wealth of wildlife. *Reserve open daily except Tue, 0900-2100 or dusk. Visitor centre, 1 Nov-31 Jan, daily, 0900-1600; 1 Feb-31 Oct, daily, 0900-1700; Tearoom: 1 Nov-31 Jan 1030-1630, 1 Feb-31 Oct 1030-1600 closed 25, 26 Dec. Nature Trails and Hides, £3.50/50p/£2.50. RSPB members free. (O15)*

### Needham Lake and Nature Reserve
Needham Market Tel: (01449) 676800
From the A14 take the B1078
A large man-made lake and nature reserve with picnic and educational facilities on the outskirts of Needham Market with a gravel pathway around the lake. *(J/K17)*

### ⊛ Orford Ness
Orford  Tel: (01394) 450057
B1084 from Woodbridge. (NT)
10-mile-long shingle spit from Aldeburgh in the north to Shingle Street in the south. It is a Grade I SSSI. Experimental military testing site, including atomic weapons testing throughout the 'cold war'. Viewing platforms, displays and exhibits of its nature conservation value and its historical significance. *Open: 8 Apr-31 Oct, Thur-Sat, ferries every 20 mins from 1000-1220; 4 Nov-18 Dec, Thur-Sat. Please telephone for booking. (O17)*

### ⊛ Thornham Walks
Thornham Magna  Tel: (01379) 788345
Off the A140 from Ipswich or Norwich
Twelve miles of walks through parkland, woods, meadow and farmland. *Open all year, daily, 0900-1800. (J14)*

*Pensthorpe Waterfowl Park, Norfolk*

*Cley, Norfolk*

## Country Walks

### Norfolk

#### Angles Way

77 miles between Great Yarmouth and Knettishall Heath. A Norfolk Broads to Suffolk Brecks path along the Waverley Valley. Minor diversions may be in place during 1999. *Norfolk County Council Recreation Path.*

#### Bure Valley Walk

A 9-mile footpath running between Aylsham and Wroxham along the former railway line, beside the narrow-gauge track of the Bure Valley Railway, allowing for a relaxing return journey. *Leaflet free from Broadland District Council, Thorpe Lodge, 1 Yarmouth Road, Thorpe St Andrew, Norwich, NR7 0DU. Tel: (01603) 703223.*

#### Marriot's Way

21-mile footpath, bridle way and cycle route between Norwich and Aylsham along former railway line. *Free leaflet from Norfolk County Council (SAE please).*

#### Nar Valley Way

A 34-mile footpath from King's Lynn to the Rural Life Museum at Gressenhall. *Free leaflet from Norfolk County Council (SAE please).*

#### Peddars Way and Norfolk Coast Path

Official long-distance footpath of 93 miles, between Knettishall Heath and Holme, then along the coast to Cromer. Through heath and Breckland woods and varied coastal scenery. *Leaflet available from Norfolk County Council.*

#### Wash Coast Path

A 10-mile route between Sutton Bridge Lighthouse and West Lynn giving spectacular views of the salt marshes and the Wash. *Free leaflet from Norfolk County Council (SAE please).*

For more information of routes in the Norfolk area, contact: ⊕ Norfolk County Council, Department of Planning and Transportation, County Hall, Martineau Lane, Norwich, NR1 2SG. Telephone: (01603) 222143.

## Suffolk

#### Constable Trail

A 9-mile walk through the landscape and villages associated with the artist's childhood and life. Four shorter walks available. *Booklet £1.25 inc. postage from Hugh Turner, Croft End, Bures, Suffolk CO8 5JN. Tel: (01787) 227823.*

#### Gipping Valley River Path

Located along the 17-mile long former tow path between Ipswich and Stowmarket alongside the River Gipping. *Free leaflet from Suffolk County Council (SAE please). More detailed leaflet available for 30p from Suffolk County Council or TIC.*

#### Painters Way

28-mile walk along the valley of River Stour, from Sudbury to Manningtree through countryside which inspired Gainsborough, Constable and Munnings. *Booklet £1.25 inc postage from Hugh Turner, (address above).*

#### Stour Valley Path

A 60 mile "regional route" from Newmarket to Cattawade. Follow this waymarked route as it passes through the beautiful Suffolk and Essex countryside along the Stour Valley, including the Dedham Vale Area of outstanding natural beauty. *Laminated route guide with accommodation list from Suffolk County Council, £3.50.*

*River Stour, Sudbury, Suffolk*

### Suffolk Coast and Heath Path

50-mile path through the Suffolk Coast and Heaths. AONB, from Felixstowe to Lowestoft. *Guide available with accommodation advice and information on things to see from Suffolk Coast and Heaths Project. Tel: (01394) 384948.*

### Suffolk Way

A walk of 106 miles crossing distinctive Suffolk countryside from Constable Country at Flatford to Lavenham, continuing to Framlingham and Walberswick, after which it follows the heritage coast to Lowestoft. *Guidebook £2.85 (inc. p&p) from Footpath Guides, Old Hall, East Bergholt, Colchester CO7 6TG.*

### Icknield Way Path

Follows part of the oldest road in Britain for over 120 miles. It connects the ridgeway at Ivinghoe Beacon, Buckinghamshire, with the Peddars Way at Knettishall Heath, Suffolk. *Walker and horse rider routes are available.*

For more information of routes in the Suffolk area, contact: ⊛ Suffolk County Council, Environment and Transport Department, St Edmunds House, County Hall, Ipswich, IP4 1LZ. Telephone: (01473) 583180

## Country Parks

## Norfolk

### ⊛ Fritton Lake Countryworld

Fritton  Tel: (01493) 488208
6 miles SW Great Yarmouth on A143.
250 acres of wood, grassland and formal gardens. 170-acre lake, fishing, rowing, pedalos, launch trips. 9-hole golf, putting, crazy golf. Large adventure playground. Children's farm. Wildfowl reserve. Heavy horses (daily rides). Falconry centre, daily flying displays except Fri. Craft workshop. Cafe and shop. *(O10)*

### ⊛ High Lodge Forest Centre

Visitor Centre in the heart of Thetford Forest  Tel: (01842) 810271
Off the Thetford to Brandon Road, B1107. Forest drive, shop, refreshments, waymarked trails, cycle hire, orienteering, squirrels maze, rope course, playground, picnic areas, forest train, educational visits and events. Forest Office, Santon Downham. *(F12/13)*

### Knettishall Heath Country Park

Knettishall  Tel: (01953) 688265
On the A1066 between
Thetford and Diss.
Park with 375 acres of Breckland heath with access to the River Ouse along walks. Also picnic areas, toilets and the start point for Peddars Way, Angles Way and the Icknield Way. *Open 2 Jan-31 Dec, 0900-dusk; closed 25, 26 Dec. (H13)*

### ⊛ Lynford Arboretum

Tel: (01842) 810271
1 mile E Mundford off A1065.
Over 100 tree species in attractive parkland. Walks around ornamental lake and into the forest. *(F12)*

### ⊛ Pensthorpe Waterfowl Park

See entry in Nature Reserves section.

### ⊛ Sandringham

7 miles NE King's Lynn on A149.
650 acres of wood and heathland. Nature trails and visitor centre. *(D/E6)*

### ⊛ Sheringham Park

Sheringham  Tel: (01263) 823778
Car access off A148 Cromer
to Holt Road. (NT)
Rhododendrons, woodland, spectacular views of park and coastlines. *Car parking charge. (K5)*

### ⊛ Thetford Forest Park

Thetford  Tel: (01842) 810271
On Norfolk/Suffolk border.
50,000 acres of pine forest with heathland and broadland areas. Waymarked walks and trails from over a dozen car parks and picnic sites. Forest Office, Santon Downham. *(F12/13)*

### ⊛ Wolterton Park

Erpingham  Tel: (01263) 584175
From Norwich take A140 to Cromer,
follow brown signs
340 acres of historic parkland with marked trails. Orienteering and adventure playground. Special events programme. Toilets. *Parkland open all year, daily; for hall details please contact. Admission £2.00. (K6)*

*Thetford Forest Park, Norfolk*

## Suffolk

### ⊛ Alton Water

Holbrook Road, Stutton, Ipswich.
Tel: (01473) 328268
B1080 Ipswich to Manningtree.
Water park with walks, nature reserves and picnic areas. Cycle tracks and cycle hire. Water sports centre offering sailing and windsurfing. *Coarse angling, day tickets available. Visitor centre serving snacks. (K19)*

### ⊛ Brandon Country Park

Tel: (01842) 810185
Off B1106 south of Brandon.
Lake, lawns, tree trail, cycle trail, Victorian walled garden. *Visitor centre open all year, toilets, woodland picnic areas and forest walks. 32 acres. Cycle hire school holidays and weekends. (E/F12)*

### ⊛ Ickworth Park

Horringer, 3 miles
SW Bury St Edmunds, on A143. (NT)
Walks through woodland and by canal. *Leaflet available from machine at car park £1.00. £2.00/50p payable on entrance to park. (F15/16)*

### Nowton Park

Bury St Edmunds  Tel: (01284) 763666
From east exit of A14
for Bury St Edmunds.
Previously a country estate with 170 acres of woodland and pasture. Some formal recreation. All-weather pitch and 2 football pitches. Park Centre open weekends. *Open all year, daily, 0830-dusk. (F/G15)*

### ⊛ West Stow Country Park

West Stow  Tel: (01284) 728718
6 miles NW Bury St Edmunds,
off A1101.
Grassland, heathland, lake and river with many walks. Reconstructed Anglo-Saxon village (see Ancient Monuments section). 125 acres. Children's play area. Visitor centre, car parking, picnicking and toilet facilities. New for 1998, new visitor centre including café and museum housing objects found during excavations. *(F14)*

*The Broads, Norfolk*

## Holidays Afloat on Cruisers, Narrow Boats and Yachts

### Norfolk

#### ⚜ Broom Boats Ltd
Riverside, Brundall
Tel: (01603) 712334
Fax: (01603) 714803
2-9 berth boats. *Weekly hire. (M9)*

#### ⚜ Freshwater Cruisers
Riverside Estate, Brundall
Tel: (01603) 717355
2-6 berth cruisers. *Weekly hire. (M9)*

#### ⚜ VIP Harvey Eastwood
Riverside, Brundall
Tel: (01603) 713345
2-8 berth cruisers. *(M9)*

#### ⚜ King Line Cruisers
Horning  Tel: (01692) 630297
2-6 berth cruisers. *Weekly, day boats by hour, day or week. Riverside cottages with facilities for wheelchairs. (M/N8)*

#### ⚜ Norfolk Broads Yachting Co Ltd
Southgate Yacht Station, Lower Street,
Horning  Tel: (01692) 631330
2-9 berth cruisers, 2-8 berth yachts. *By the day/short break/week. Day boats for hire by the hour or day. (M/N8)*

#### ⚜ Camelot Craft
The Rhond, Hoveton
Tel: (01603) 783096
Yacht hire on the Norfolk Broads, *weekly, weekends and daily hire. Tuition available. (M8)*

#### ⚜ Greenway Marine Ltd
Riverside, Loddon  Tel: (01508) 520397
2-8 berth boats. *Weekly hire. (N10)*

#### ⚜ River Craft
Stalham Yacht Services, The Staithe,
Stalham  Tel: (01692) 580288
2-10 berth Broads cruisers, houseboats, day launches. *Weekly, daily and hourly hire available. (N7)*

#### ⚜ Highcraft
Griffin Lane, Thorpe St Andrew,
Norwich  Tel: (01603) 701701
Motor cabin cruisers. Day, picnic boats and rowing boats from Norwich Yacht Station, Riverside Road. *(L/M9)*

#### ⚜ Blakes Holidays Ltd
Wroxham
Tel: (01603) 782911 (Reservations),
Tel: (01603) 784458 (Brochures)
The largest fleet of holiday yachts on the Norfolk Broads, a wide choice of quality rated cruisers and a few houseboats. Cruises and narrow boats on the Cambridgeshire waterways. Choose from a wide selection from 2-12 berth. *(M8)*

#### ⚜ Broads Tours Ltd
Wroxham, The A1151 to Wroxham
Tel: (01603) 782207
Broads cruises for weekly hire or short breaks. Self-drive day boats. *Open 2 Apr-31 Oct, daily, 0900-1700. (M8)*

#### ⚜ Connoisseur Cruisers
Porter and Haylett Limited, Wroxham
Tel: (01603) 782472
2-8 berth cruisers. *Weekly hire and short breaks. Breaks also available in France. (M8)*

#### ⚜ Moore & Co
Wroxham  Tel: (01603) 783311
2-8 berth cruisers. *Self-drive day launches. (M8)*

### Suffolk

#### ⚜ The Excelsior Trust
Lowestoft  Tel: (01502) 585302
A charitable trust ensuring historic sailing vessels are restored and continue to provide traditional sailing experience for people from all walks of life. *(P11)*

#### ⚜ Snape Maltings, Ethel Ada Thames Sailing Barge
Tel: (0410) 386345/(01728) 688303
Cruise the beautiful unspoilt East Anglia rivers aboard a comfortably converted Thames Sailing Barge. *Sailing weekends, 12-hour day trips, barge matches, sea shanty or bird-watching cruises. Corporate affairs and management training courses. (N16)*

## Day Boat Hire

### Norfolk

#### ⊛ Herbert Woods
Broads Haven, Potter Heigham
Tel: (01692) 670711
All-weather cabin-type day launches, either electric or diesel. Passenger boats make regular trips to Hickling Broad. *Over 100 hire cruisers for weekly hire or short breaks. Fleet of sailing yachts for weekly hire. (N/O7/8)*

#### ⊛ Moore & Co
Hotel Wroxham, Wroxham
Car park   Tel: (01603) 783311
All-weather diesel self-drive day launches and luxury motor cruisers. *(M8)*

### Suffolk

#### ⊛ Outney Meadow Caravan Park
Bungay Tel: (01986) 892338
Rowing boats, skiffs and canoes. *Hourly or daily hire. (M12)*

#### ⊛ The Excelsior Trust
Lowestoft
See entry under Holidays Afloat on Cruisers, Narrow Boats and Yachts.

#### ⊛ Boathouse Hotel
Sudbury Tel: (01787) 379090
Rowing boats for hire by the hour on the Stour, Wed-Sun, Apr-Sep; 1100-1800. *Open Bank Hols. £7-£10 per hour. Afternoon cream teas available. (G18)*

## Regular Excursions

### Norfolk

#### Mississippi River Boat
Horning Tel: (01692) 630262
See the Broads in luxury and style on a double decker paddle steamer. *1.5 hours public trips with bar and commentary. Private hire available. (M/N8)*

#### ⊛ Searle's Hire Boats
South Beach Road, Hunstanton
Tel: (01485) 535455/(0831) 321799
Jul-Sep: D.T.I. motor launch carrying up to 60. Cruises to Seal Island viewing the seals of the Wash. Also 1/2 hour coastal cruises. Fishing trips. Speedboat rides. 20 minute trips in WWII ex-army D.U.K.W., to view Hunstanton from the shoreline. Also 30 minute tour in WWII D.U.K.W., to visit wreck of Sheraton. *(D5)*

*Snape, Suffolk*

#### ⊛ Stalham Water Tours
28 St Nicholas Way, Stalham
Tel: (01692) 670530 answerphone
All-weather luxury cruiser for 1-2.5 hours Broads cruises. Light refreshments. Departs Richardson's Boatyard, Stalham. *Visit to How Hill Gardens, Mon-Fri, Sun afternoons. (N7)*

#### ⊛ Broads Tours Ltd
Wroxham Tel: (01603) 782207
1.25, 1.5, 2 and 3.5 hour Broadland tours in all-weather cabin-type day launches and electric picnic boats. Passenger boats (traditional-style and double decker boats). *Largest boat takes 170. May-Sep. (M8)*

### Suffolk

#### ⊛ Snape Maltings
Snape Tel: (01728) 688303
One-hour trip on the River Alde aboard Edward Alan John, a covered boat carrying up to 70 passengers. Departure times dependent on tides. Reduction for pre-booked groups. *Details and times on request. (N16)*

#### ⊛ Waldringfield Boat Yard
Waldringfield Tel: (01473) 736260
Cruises on the River Deben. *1, 2 and 3 hour morning, afternoon and evenings. Reservations must be made. (M18)*

## Boat Hire for Groups

### Norfolk

#### ⊛ Wherry Yacht Charter
Barton House, Hartwell Road,
The Avenue, Wroxham
Tel: (01603) 782470
Broadland cruising on historic wherry yachts `Olive' and `Norada' and pleasure wherry `Hathor'. *For groups of up to 12 on each. (M8)*

### Suffolk

#### ⊛ The Excelsior Trust
Lowestoft
See entry under Holidays Afloat on Cruisers, Narrow Boats and Yachts.

*Sport for all*

## Golf Courses

### Norfolk

#### ⊛ Barnham Broom Hotel
Barnham Broom, Norwich
Tel: (01603) 759393
Fax: (01603) 758224
Extensive leisure complex offering two mature 18 hole golf courses, indoor swimming pool, gymnasium, squash and tennis courts, sauna and steam room, hair and beauty salon and a solarium. The golf courses are complimented by a five acre practice ground with three academy holes. Professional tuition is available. *(J9)*

### Suffolk

#### Fynn Valley Golf Centre
Witnesham, Ipswich
Tel: (01473) 785267
Situated 3 miles from Ipswich on B1077 Westerfield/Debenham road.
Full 18 hole course plus driving range (some bays undercover and floodlit), chipping green, practice bunker, putting green and par 3, 9 hole course. Open to non-members. Tuition from qualified staff and club hire. Shop, bar and restaurant open to all golfers and public. Leisure centre opens spring 1999. *Open: Weekdays 0800-2100, Sat-Sun 0800-1800. Admission price on request. (K17)*

*Wells-next-the-Sea, Norfolk*

*Norfolk ● Suffolk*

### ✿ Thorpeness Hotel and Golf Club

Thorpeness  Tel: 01728 452176
Mature heathland coastal course. The 18 holes are pleasantly varied with several difficult par 4's guaranteed to test the average player and provide interest for the scratch golfer. Individuals and societies are welcomed for the day, or staying over night at the hotel. Handicap certificate required. The Clubhouse offers morning coffee, breakfast, snacks and evening meals for those playing the course. The restaurant over looks the third tee and above is an attractive roof garden. *The hotel and Golf Club has a variety of all year round packages to suit all standards of golfer. (O16)*

## Leisure Centres
### Norfolk

#### ✿ Norwich Sport Village & Broadland Aquapark

Drayton High Road, Hellesdon
Tel: (01603) 788912
Indoor and outdoor tennis, squash, multi sports hall, health and fitness centre including gymnasium, sauna/steam rooms, plunge and spa pool, bars, restaurants and hotel. The Aquapark is a 6 lane, 25m competition pool and has 2 giant water flumes. *(K/L8/9)*

### ✿ The Splash Leisure Pool
Weybourne Road, Sheringham
Tel: (01263) 825675
Giant waterslide and splash pool, wave pool, children's paddling pool and walrus slide. Health and fitness club. *(K4)*

## Suffolk

### ✿ Felixstowe Leisure Centre
Undercliff Road West, Felixstowe
Tel: (01394) 670411
Features include leisure swimming pool, learner pool, sauna, sunbeds, bowls hall, multi-purpose entertainment and conference hall and amusement area. *(M19)*

## Outdoor Activities
### Suffolk

#### ✿ Alton Water Sports Centre
Alton Water, Stutton
Tel: (01473) 328268
Windsurfing, sailing, canoeing and cycle trail. Tuition and equipment hire. Cafeteria. RYA Approved Centre. *(K19)*

#### ✿ Byways Bicycles
Darsham, Saxmundham
Tel: (01728) 668764
A choice of cycles for hire - follow a planned route or choose your own. *(N/O14)*

## Racing

### ✿ Horseracing at Fakenham
Tel: (01328) 862388 *(G/H6)*

### ✿ Horseracing at Newmarket
Tel: (01638) 663482 *(D15)*

# *Specialist holidays & Activities*
## Norfolk

### ✿ Awayadays
Tel: (01263) 732322
Personalised Norfolk and other tours for groups, individuals and people with special interests. All packages include attractions, accommodation and luxury travel. No car needed. Awayadays, West End Farm, Ingworth, Norwich, Norfolk NR11 6PM. *(K6)*

### ✿ Hilltop Adventure
Tel: (01263) 824514
Outdoor activity centre with conference and training facilities. Activities include: assault course, archery, orienteering, mountain bikes, canoeing, climbing wall and high ropes. Hilltop Adventure, Oldwood, Beeston Regis, Sheringham, Norfolk. *(K4/5)*

*Alton Water Sports Centre, Suffolk*

*Norfolk • Suffolk*

### ❀ Kingswood
Runton Sands  Tel: (0870) 609 6000

A residential summer camp with climbing, archery, swimming, motorsports and caving plus specialist courses for tennis, horseriding and languages. Parents are not accommodated. Kingswood, Runton Sands, Kingswood Centre, West Runton, Cromer, Norfolk NR27 9NF. *(K4/5)*

### ❀ Norfolk Church Tours
Tel: (01603) 811542

Half day tours throughout the year of four country churches accompanied by an informed and enthusiastic guide who will enhance your knowledge and understanding of Norfolk's rich heritage or medieval churches. Cost £4.95 per person. Travel in your own car. Norfolk Church Tours, 20 Central Crescent, Hethersett, Norwich, Norfolk, NR9 3EP. *(Blakeney I4, Heydon J7, Lodden N10, Shettisham D5/6)*

## Suffolk

### ❀ Byways Bicycles
Tel: (01728) 668764

A choices of cycles for hire, to suit all ages. Follow a planned route showing you local places of interest. Pubs, tearooms, picnic places or choose your own. Cycling holidays also arranged. Byways Bicycles, Darsham, Saxmundham, Suffolk, IP17 3QD. *Open Easter and May-Oct, 1000-1800. At other times by appointment. Closed Tue. (N/O14)*

### ❀ Equine Tours
Tel: (01638) 667333

Tailor made tours behind the scenes of the horseracing industry with experienced guides. Can include horses on gallops, their swimming pool, a trainer's yard, the National Stud, Animal Health Trust, Royal Newmarket, the museum and a visit to the races. Equine Tours, 99 High Street, Newmarket, Suffolk CB8 8JL. *Open any time, except 24 Dec-6 Jan. (D15)*

### ❀ Grand Touring Club
Tel: (01449) 737774

Enjoy the nostalgia of touring the by-ways of Suffolk and Norfolk in one of the great British sports car of the 60s and 70s? Carefully-chosen itineraries include three nights at one of the region's best character hotels, including dinner. We can enhance the short break of a lifetime with a gourmet picnic hamper, concert or balloon flight. Grand Touring Club, Model Farm, Rattlesden, Bury St. Edmunds, Suffolk, IP30 0SY. *(H16)*

### ❀ Kids Klub
Tel: (01449) 675907

Easter and summer multi-activity holidays for children and teenagers. Also group programmes available all year round. Choose from four centres and over 50 activities. Call for a brochure. Kids Klub, The Lodge, Great Finborough, Stowmarket, Suffolk, IP14 3EF. *(I16)*

### ❀ Snape Maltings
Tel: (01728) 688305

Painting, crafts and decorative arts courses based at this converted riverside maltings which also include: shops, galleries, restaurants and the world famous concert hall. Snape Maltings, Snape, Saxmundham, Suffolk, IP17 1SR. *(N16)*

### ❀ Suffolk Cycle Breaks
Tel: (01449) 721555

Cycling holidays throughout the county of Suffolk. Holidays to suit your needs. Luggage transportation and accommodation arranged to suit. Walking holidays also available. Suffolk Cycle Breaks, Bradfield Hall Barn, Alder Carr Farm, Creeting St. Mary, Ipswich, Suffolk, IP6 8LX. *(J16)*

### ❀ Thornham Field Centre
Tel: (01379) 788153

Private country estate with residential field centre with shop, cafe, craft workshop and a network of footpaths. Thornham Field Centre, Thornham Magna, Eye, Suffolk, IP23 8HH. *(J14)*

### ❀ Thorpeness Hotel and Golf Club
Tel: 01728 452176

This fascinating seaside village on the Suffolk coast was built in the 1920's. Thorpeness Hotel and Golf Club offers three crown accommodation and a superb 18 hole golf course. The "Dolphin Inn" offers bed and breakfast and the best of pub food and restaurant facilities, ideal for families visiting the village. In the summer there is an outside bar and BBQ area. The Country Club has seven tennis courts available for hire. The original wings have been sympathetically converted into apartments, with function and bar facilities. Guests staying in our village accommodation enjoy a variety of holiday packages all year round. *(O16)*

*Lowestoft, Suffolk*

*Norfolk ● Suffolk*

With such a coastline, it's hardly surprising that fish and sea food has always been a notable part of the region's diet.

Lowestoft is the centre of the fishing industry, but at many beaches along the coast you can buy fresh fish straight from the fisherman - and what better way to enjoy it? Lowestoft also has its smoke houses, curing North Sea herring by traditional methods to produce kippers and bloaters.

Just south of Lowestoft and down as far as Felixstowe, juicy lobsters are caught, while at Butley, Orford and Brancaster the harvest is oysters. Brancaster also harvests mussels - a product of clean, pollution free waters, and nearby Stiffkey is known for its native blue shelled cockle - the famous "Stiffkey blue". And of course, there are the Cromer crabs, known for the mild creaminess of the brown flesh. Why should Cromer crabs taste so much better than any other? It's all to do with the chalk sea bed around North Norfolk. Crabs love calcium and this chalky habitat is their perfect breeding ground.

One other product of the coastal marshes which flourishes particularly in North Norfolk, is samphire. This juicy green delicacy is cooked and eaten like asparagus - although because it is so rich in soda, many years ago it was used for making soap!

Since the 17th century, Suffolk and Norfolk have been famous for rearing turkeys, geese and ducks. Huge flocks used to be walked from here all the way to London. Some of the old fashioned breeds including the flavoursome Bronze and Norfolk Black are still reared here. Suffolk ham is renowned, and how better to eat it than with a spot of mustard, made by Colmans of Norwich!

Apples, pears, damsons and plums all flourish here, and this is cereal producing country too. It's not surprising that we turn some of this basic product into beer - tasty ales are brewed by traditional methods at St Peter's Brewery and by Adnams of Southwold.

# Restaurants

## Norfolk

### Blakeney
#### Morston Hall
Morston, Holt NR25 7AA
Tel: (01263) 741041
Fax: (01263) 740419
E-mail:
reception@morstonhall.demon.co.uk
Internet:
www.morstonhall.demon.co.uk
Dating back to the 17th century, Morston Hall is set in secluded gardens and retains its original charm and character. Six large bedrooms; restaurant with a set four course menu changing daily. Galton Blackiston the Chef-Patron is acknowledged as one of the best Chefs in the country. *(I4)*

### Burgh Castle
### (Nr Great Yarmouth)
#### Church Farm Public House
Church Road NR31 9QG
Tel: (01493) 780251
Church Farm nestles beside Breydon Water where the rivers Waveney and Yare meet opposite the Berney Arms Windmill, giving the most spectacular views of Norfolk. The towns of Gorleston and Great Yarmouth are 10 minutes drive away with their entertainments, beaches and shops. *(O9)*

### Easton
#### Des Amis
Dereham Road,
Easton, Norwich NR9 5EJ
Tel: (01603) 880966
(mobile 07771 53780)
Patio dining and 60 seat non-smoking restaurant (smoking lounge). Full menu includes Creole, Cajun and French cooking. Outside catering available for Caribbean style weddings with steel band. Jazz Pianist Saturday nights. Lunch approx. £8, Dinner approx. £18. *Open: Tues-Sat 1800-1130, Sundays lunch only 1200-1500. Weekdays lunch bookings taken. (J/K9)*

### Grimston (Nr. King's Lynn)
#### The Orangery Restaurant
AT CONGHAM HALL   AA**
Congham Hall Country House Hotel
Tel: (01485) 600250
Chef Andrew Dixon interprets "modern English cooking" intelligently. The restaurant and "Orangery" is delightfully decorated in the Georgian manner. On summer days we recommend Congham's outdoor lunches - ask about the luncheon club. Eating in the dining room or on the lawn, gives the feeling of being part of an English "country home". A member of the "Pride of Britain" consortium and Johansens Hotel of the Year 1993. ETB England for Excellence - Silver Award. *Open: daily. Average prices: lunch table d'hôte from £9.50, Sunday lunch £18.50, dinner from £25.00. (E7)*

### Hethersett
### (5 miles south of Norwich)
#### Park Farm Country Hotel
#### & Restaurant
Hethersett, Norwich NR9 3DL
Tel: (01603) 810264
Fax: (01603) 812104
Set amidst beautiful landscaped gardens, Park Farm Country Hotel has earned a well deserved reputation for good food, a warm welcome and excellent service. Park Farm menus offer a good selection, from daily table d'hôte menu to a seasonal à la carte menu. *Bar Meals are served from Monday to Friday from 1200-2130, Saturdays 1200-1730, Sundays 1830-2100. Morning coffee and afternoon teas are available. Coach Parties welcome by appointment. Average prices: TDH lunch £12.75, dinner £18.50, ALC from £20.00-£25.00, Sunday lunches £13.75. (K10)*

### Norwich
### ❀ Adriano's Trattoria & Pizzeria
68 London Street
Tel: (01603) 622967

"Highly Commended", National Pizza and Pasta Restaurant Award 1996. Authentic Italian cooking, homemade pasta dishes and stone baked pizzas a speciality. Full menu from Saltimbocca Alla Romana to chargrilled sword fish steak. Good value 2 course lunch and theatre suppers. *Open Monday-Saturday noon-2330. Set lunch £6.50. Approximately £15 for 3 courses without wine. (L9)*

### Norwich
### ❀ Barnham Broom Hotel
Barnham Broom, Norwich NR9 4DD
Tel: (01603) 759393
Fax: (01603) 758224

Set in 250 acres of beautiful Norfolk countryside only 10 miles west of Norwich. Flints Restaurant offers fine cuisine from the extensive A La Carte or Table d'Hote menus. Sports Buttery/Bar serves light meals and snacks all day. *Bar snacks £1.20-£10.50. Flints evening menu priced from £17.00. (J9/10)*

### Norwich
### ❀ Boswells
24 Tombland
Tel: (01603) 626099

Open "all day, every day" Boswells is "continentally unique". At night, live jazz and blues, and dancing until 2am. During the day, a brasserie-style menu, varied and delicious, ranges from spectacular sandwiches to three-course meals served indoors or out on its fully licensed terrace facing Tombland. Situated along the forewall of the Cathedral, Boswells is a landmark in the historic heart of the city. *Open Monday to Saturday 12 noon to 2am, Sunday 12 noon to 6pm. Average price under £6. (L9)*

### Norwich
### ❀ Pizza One Pancakes Too!
24 Tombland
Tel: (01603) 621583

Norwich's first and oldest pizza, pasta and French crèperie. The produce is still homemade after twenty years, and is a favourite haunt for families, businessmen, students and tourists. Situated along the Cathedral wall in Tombland, the historic heart of the city, this atmospheric restaurant spot for lunch or dinner at "best value for money" prices. *Average price is £6.50 with student discount on food available. (L9)*

### Norwich
### ❀ The Trafalgar Restaurant
Hotel Nelson, Prince of Wales Road
Tel: (01603) 760260

We highly recommend the newly refurbished Trafalgar Restaurant. It presents a choice of simple but interesting main courses as well as desserts and traditional puddings from the display. The restaurant is fully air-conditioned with pleasant views of the River Wensum. *Light meals, snacks and informal dining is available in the Quarter-deck conservatory and bar (open every day). Trafalgar Restaurant - Open: each evening for dinner & Sunday lunch. Average prices: lunch £11.50, table d'hôte £15.50, à la carte dinner from £16.50. (L9)*

### Norwich
### ❀ Walnut Tree Shades
Old Post Office Court
Tel: (01603) 620166

With the Castle Mall only 5 minutes walk away, it is packed with American style posters and an original Wurlitzer juke box. It attracts families with it's children menu. The adult menu has a variety of American style starters like Spicy Chicken Wings to a more conventional Prawn Cocktail. Main courses are also varied from Chicago style Hot Dogs to Cajun Chicken. A stunning cocktail list ranges from Margarita's to Sangria with special reduced cocktail on offer each night. The wine list offers some interesting wines from California and South Africa. *Open: Mon-Sat, 1145-1415 and 1830-late. Average price: £12.00 (excluding wine) for 3 courses. (L9)*

### West Runton
### The Pepperpot Restaurant
Water Lane, West Runton NR27 9QP
Tel: (01263) 837578

Tucked away down a lane leading to the beach, this beamed restaurant offers a feeling of comfort and intimacy under the

new management of Antoine and Debbie Foucher. The emphasis is on high quality traditional French cuisine. The à la carte menu offers dishes such as fish soup, confit of duck with port sauce, our famous shank of lamb in red wine and our selection of fresh fish and lavish desserts.

*Price per head without wine: 3 course luncheon menu £11.95, à la carte £15.00-£25.00. Garden open to diners, weather permitting. Car park to rear. Open all year round. (K4)*

*Brancaster Staithe, Norfolk*

### Wolterton (North Norfolk)
### ⊛ The Norfolk Mead Hotel
Church Loke
Tel: (01603) 737531
Fax: (01603) 737521

The Fleming family has given this elegant Georgian country house a dazzling facelift. Standing in 12 acres of secluded ground by the River Bure with its own marina. There's also an open-air swimming pool. Chef Terry Westall has good links with local fisherman, forages for wild fungi and seeks out top-quality supplies. Seasonal menus take in such dishes as pan-fried halibut, spinach and orange and basil sauce and hot Grand Marnier soufflé. The well chosen wine list fits the bill perfectly. *Open daily for morning coffee, afternoon tea, lunches and dinners. Table d'hôte menu £18.50, à la carte about £21.00 for three courses without wine. Sun lunch £12.95. (K6)*

### Wolterton (North Norfolk)
### ⊛ The Saracen's Head 'With Rooms'
Tel: (01263) 768909

Only 20 minutes drive from Norwich, the Saracen's Head is a civilised free house without piped music or fruit machines. Built in the early 19th century as a coaching Inn. Impeccably maintained and run by chef/proprietor Robert Dawson-Smith. There are log fires and wicker chairs. It is more a restaurant than a pub. Typical dishes include braised local rabbit, grilled fillets of smoked mackerel, venison, duck and steaks. Desserts are traditional favourites such as bread and butter pudding and treacle tart. The wine list is from Australia, South Africa, Spain and France. *Open 7 days a week 1100-1500, 1800-2300. (K6)*

## Suffolk

### Bungay
### ⊛ St. Peter's Hall
St. Peter South Elmham
St. Peter's Brewery Co Ltd
Tel: (01986) 782322
Fax: (01986) 782505

Among the Saints, in this beautiful part of Suffolk, enjoy a meal or a drink in the Great Hall of St. Peter's. For lunch try freshly made soup or beef casserole; a chocolate gateau for tea. In the evening a seafood chowder, Tournedos Rossini and a Treacle and Ginger Tart feature on the menu. Traditional English Ales brewed on the premises. Marriages may be solemnized in the chapel. *Average prices: lunch £6, dinner (3 courses) £20. Open Fri & Sat 1100-2300, food 1200-2100 (1830 dinner); Sun 1200-1900 both menus and roast. (M12)*

### Bury St Edmunds
### ⊛ The Angel Hotel
Angel Hill
Tel: (01284) 753926

This fine hotel with its Dickensian connections is owned and run by the Gough family. With three dining areas to choose from, the cosy Pickwick bar, the vaults, a medieval undercroft or handsome Regency restaurant, the food ranges from homely venison sausages and mashed potatoes to classic Chateaubriand with bearnaise sauce. Adnams and Green King supply the beers. *Special weekend rates offered from £65.00 per person per night including full English breakfast and dinner allowance of £20.00. Conferences, banquets and weddings ranging from an intimate dinner for 6 to an extravaganza for 120. (F/G15)*

### Bury St Edmunds
### ⊛ Linden Tree
7 Out Northgate
Tel: (01284) 754600

In two bars and conservatory restaurant, overlooking the garden, homemade dishes of fish, grilled meat and vegetarian are served, plus daily specials. Families welcome and play area provided. *Average prices: Bars £1.50-£3.99. Restaurant (non-smoking) 2 courses £9.50. Open 7 days 1100-1500, 1700-2300; food 1200-1400 (1500 Sundays), 1800-2130. (F/G15)*

### Fressingfield, Nr.Eye
### ⊛ The Fox and Goose Inn
Fressingfield, Eye IP21 5PB
Tel: (01379) 586247

Set in the heart of the village on the Norfolk/Suffolk border some 23 miles from Norwich. The building, which dates back to 1509 is still owned by the Church which is clearly visible across the graveyard. A fine example of a truly unspoilt old English restaurant! Boasting a diverse menu from Peking style crispy duck to Morecambe Bay potted brown shrimps. A famous restaurant with a brilliant reception, and an unfailingly warm welcome. Proprietors Tim and Pauline O'Leary. Head Chef Maxwell Dougal. *Open every day for lunch, dinner and bar meals. (L13/14)*

*Norwich, Norfolk*

### Hadleigh
### The Marquis of Cornwallis

Upper Street, Upper Layham, Hadleigh, Ipswich IP7 5JZ  Tel: (01473) 822051

Nestled in Constable countryside, the Marquis of Cornwallis offers a truly traditional welcome. The candle-lit ambience provides the perfect atmosphere for sampling and enjoying its real ales, country wines and traditional English country menu. Perched on the rim of the valley, the Marquis' garden rolls down to the River Brett and provides the perfect location to watch the sun set over the vale. *Open daily, we have no petty restrictions with patrons able to sit in one of the bars, the dining room or the garden. (I18/19)*

### Ipswich
### Mortimer's on the Quay

Wherry Quay
Tel: (01473) 230225
Fax: (01473) 230225

Mortimer's seafood restaurant overlooks the old working and pleasure quay of Ipswich. The lofty glass-roofed dining room and upper room are hung with pictures by the 19th century artist Thomas Mortimer after whom the restaurant is named. There is a fine selection of starters including oysters and smoked fish. The main dishes such as plaice, halibut, sole and daily specials are served in a straight forward manner with new potatoes, allowing the freshness of the fish to shine through. *Open Mon-Fri, lunch, 1200-1400; Mon-Sat, dinner, 1815-2115. Average prices, starters £2.50-£7; main dishes £7-£15.65, luncheon special £4.35. (K18)*

### Lavenham
### ⚜ The Angel Hotel

Market Place, Lavenham CO10 9QZ
Tel: (01787) 247388

In the heart of England's finest medieval town. Choice of formal/informal dining styles. Well-kept local beers and good wine list. *Open: 1200-1415 and 1845-2115. 3 courses £10-£18, bar snacks from £2.75. Accommodation 3 Crowns 'Highly Commended'. AA Rosettes in 1996, 1997 and 1998 and Good Pub Guide  Suffolk Dining Pub 'and national Pub of the Year' 1997. (G/H17)*

### Nayland
### The White Hart

11 High Street, Nayland CO6 4JF
Tel: (01206) 263382 (reservations)
Tel: (01206)263655 (office)

Relax in the comfortable restaurant with open fires or enjoy eating 'Al Fresco' in the summer months on our beautiful terrace. *Set price lunch menu with à la carte in the evenings. Daily specials on blackboards. Open seven days a week, lunch and dinner. (H19/20)*

### Newmarket
### The Chifney Restaurant at Tattersalls

Park Paddocks, The Avenue
Tel: (01638) 666166
Fax: (01638) 666099

In the midst of horseracing country is Newmarket's highest noted restaurant with two AA red rosettes. Enjoy your meal in the high-windowed dining room overlooking the paddock and stables. The lunch menu proposes an interesting choice such as duck boudin to start or a fricassée of mussels and samphire to follow. Many other unusual delights are to be found. *Table d'hôte 2 courses £12.75, 3 courses £15.75, à la carte from £22.50. The adjacent Horseshoe Bar has a daily lunch menu with a choice of portion size £3.95-£8.50. Open Tue-Sat and Sun lunch. (C/D15)*

*Cavendish, Suffolk*

*Norfolk ● Suffolk*

*Oulton Broad, Suffolk*

### Woodbridge
### ❀ The Captain's Table
3 Quay Street, Woodbridge,
IP12 1BX   Tel: (01394) 383145

This beautiful 16th century pale yellow secluded restaurant in the centre of picturesque Woodbridge is now home to acclaimed owners Jo and Pascal. The varied menu, supplemented by blackboard specials and a £5.00 luncheon dish of the day, is available at all times except Sunday lunch (four courses, with choice for £15.00). *Fresh home made starters range from £2.75 to £6.00 and main courses from £6.95 to £10.50. All delicious desserts are £3.50. Open: Tuesday to Saturday lunch-12 until 2pm; Sunday lunch -12 until 3pm. Tuesday to Saturday dinner- 6.30 until 9.30pm (Friday and Saturday until 10pm). Open also on Bank Holidays. (L/M17)*

### Oulton Broad
### ❀ The Crooked Barn
Ivy House Farm (hotel), Ivy Lane,
Oulton Broad, Lowestoft NR33 8HY
Tel: (01502) 501353/588144
Fax: (01502) 501539

Described as Oulton Broad's hidden Oasis, the 18th century thatched barn offers a magnificent place to dine. 'New World' is the style of cuisine. Bistro style lunch offers a choice of large or small portions. In the evening table d'hôte and à la carte menus operate. Throughout the year there are special offers for diners who do not want to drive but to stay the night. *Open: daily. Lunch from 1200-1345 and dinner 1900-2130. Average prices: bistro lunch £10.50; Table d'hôte dinner £21.95/ à la carte £30.00 (3 courses). (P11)*

### Witnesham
### The Valley Restaurant
Fynn Valley Golf Club, Witnesham,
Ipswich IP6 9JA
Tel: (01473) 785202

Attractive restaurant in converted farm buildings with wonderful panoramic views over Fynn Valley. Open to the general public and golfers. Excellent food at extremely reasonable prices. Enclosed courtyard area. Bar food available. *Open: Lunches 1200-1430 Mon-Sun, Evening Meals 1800-2130 Tues-Sat. Bar snacks 1030 onwards. Prices: from £1.95 £11.95 (K17/18)*

*Laxfield, Suffolk*

### Wingfield (Nr Diss)
### ❀ De La Pole Arms
Wingfield Tel: (01379) 384545

In the heart of rural Suffolk, close to the 14th century Wingfield Old College is this restored and delightful village pub. In the bar overlooking the churchyard try the fish specialities such as Fish and Chips in St. Peter's wheat beer batter or one of the Seafood Bowls. The menu, in the charming oak framed dining room has also an emphasis on fish but a hearty steak and chunky chips is also featured. *Average prices: Bar £3.95-£7.50, Restaurant (2 courses) £14.50, Sunday Roast £6.95. Open Mon-Sat 1100-1500, 1800-2300; Sun 1200-1600, 1900-2230; Food served 1200-1400, 1900-2100. (L14)*

*afternoon teas*

## Norfolk

### Bressingham
#### ⊛ Pavilion Tea Room
Bressingham Plant Centre,
Diss  Tel: (01379) 687464/688133
3 miles west of Diss on A1066. Special luncheon delights, tasty snacks and tempting tea-time treats in the airy surroundings of our Tea Room. Peaceful setting in our famous 2 acre Plant Centre, with over 5,000 varieties of colourful garden plants. *Open: Daily including Sundays, 0900-1730 except Christmas Day/Boxing Day. See also entry for Bressingham Plant Centre under Nurseries & Garden Centres on page 83 and Bressingham Steam Museum and Gardens under Machinery & Transport on page 76. (J13)*

### Heacham
#### ⊛ Norfolk Lavender Ltd
Caley Mill, Heacham
Tel: (01485)571965/570384
Locally baked cakes and scones and cream teas a speciality. Booked Sunday lunches and home-cooked hot meals daily and log fire October-April. Tearoom and old Miller's Cottage in the middle of lavender/herb gardens and fragrant meadow. *Seats: 38 all year, 88 in summer. Free admission, open daily 1000-1700 except Dec. 25, 26 & Jan 1. Average price: £2.20. (D5)*

### Hethersett
#### ⊛ Park Farm Country Hotel
Hethersett, Norwich NR9 3DL
Tel: (01603) 810264
Set amidst beautiful landscaped gardens, Park Farm Hotel is an ideal peaceful setting to relax, and enjoy morning coffee, lunches and afternoon teas. Our home-made biscuits and cakes are our speciality. Coach parties welcome by appointment. *(K10)*

### King's Lynn
#### ⊛ Caithness Crystal Visitor Centre
9-12 Paxman Road, Hardwick
Industrial Estate
Tel: (01553) 765111/765123
Our licensed coffee shop/restaurant is open for morning coffee, light refreshments, home-cooked lunches and afternoon teas throughout the year. Coach parties and groups most welcome. Special menu available for parties to pre-book meals. *Seats: 84  Open: 7 days a week. (C/D7/8)*

### Thursford
#### ⊛ The Thursford Collection
Thursford, Fakenham
Tel: (01328) 878477
Proprietor: Mr J Cushing Afternoon cream teas on the lawn served from our Garden Conservatory. Teas, light refreshments and hot meals also served in our 'Barn'. *Seats: 92 inside, 150 outside. Admission: £4.60/£2.10/£4.30. (H6)*

### Walsingham
#### Sue Ryder Coffee Room & Retreat House
The Martyrs House, High Street
Tel: (01328) 820622
Light meals and snacks: cakes and pastries home-made. Coach parties welcome by appointment. Bed & Breakfast accommodation available with evening meal if required. *Seats: 60  Open: All year, 0930-1730. (H5)*

### Wroxham
#### ⊛ The Tearooms, Wroxham Barns
Tunstead Road, Hoveton, Norwich
NR12 8QU
Tearooms: Tel: (01603) 783762
Pleasant tearoom set in a craft centre just 1.5 miles from Wroxham. Morning coffees, 'Hot Dishes of the Day', cream teas and home-made cakes are all available. Pre-booked coach parties are welcome. *Seats: 85 (Group maximum 40) Open: All year, excluding 25/26/31 Dec & 1 Jan, 1000-1700. (M8)*

*Castle Rising, Norfolk*

## Suffolk

### Cavendish
#### ⊛ The Sue Ryder Coffee Room and Museum
High Street   Tel: (01787) 280252
Lunches and light refreshments: cakes and pastries home-made. Gift shop. *Seats: 110 Admission to museum: 80p/40p Open: Daily, 1000-1730; Closed 25 Dec. (F18)*

### Debenham
#### ⊛ Carters Teapot Pottery
Low Road, Debenham,
Stowmarket IP14 6QU
Tel: (01728) 860475
Fax: (01728) 861110
Whilst visiting the Teapot Pottery you may like to be served tea from one of our unusual teapots! Tea, coffee, orange juice and biscuits served in our delightful conservatory. *Open: Mon-Fri, 0900-1730; Sat & Bank Hols 1030-1630; Sun from Easter-Christmas. (K15)*

### Ipswich
#### The Stables Restaurant (Sue Ryder Foundation)
The Chantry, Hadleigh Road, Ipswich
Tel: (01473) 218611
Full luncheon menu changed daily - Sunday roasts, coffee, tea, light refreshments. Also private functions - choice of menus. All food home-made and prepared by expert staff - cakes a speciality. *Seats: 65-70. Open: 7 days per week. May-Oct 1000-1730, Oct-Apr 1000-1630. (K18)*

### Lavenham
#### The Vestry Tea Rooms/ 'A Bit of A Do' outside Caterers
The Centre, High Street, Lavenham
Tel: (01787) 247548 or 278299
Cosy tea room set in a converted Victorian chapel. Morning coffee, snacks, afternoon teas, home made cakes. Hot meals available all day. Sunday roast, including sweet and coffee, £6.50. Parking and wheelchair access. Coach parties welcome by appointment. (Licensed). *Seats: 40 Open: All year, daily, 1030-1730. (G/H17)*

### Monks Eleigh
## ❀ Corn-Craft Tearoom & Coffee Shop
Monks Eleigh, Nr Lavenham
Tel: (01449) 740456

Morning coffee, cream teas, delicious home-made cakes and other light refreshments served in converted granary, beautifully set amongst farm buildings adjoining the craft shop. Ample parking. Coach parties welcome by appointment. *Seats: 40 inside, 30 outside. Open: All year, daily, 1000-1700, Sun 1100-1700. (H17/18)*

### Thorpeness
## Gallery Coffee Shop
Barn Hall
Tel: Aldeburgh (01728) 453105

Proprietors: Elliott Family. A licensed restaurant situated next to beach with pleasant garden overlooking boating lake. Specialising in cream teas, gateaux and ice cream desserts, with extensive craft and gift shop. Coach parties welcome by appointment. *Seats: 60 inside, 100 outside Open: All year, 0800 to dusk. (O16)*

### Walberswick
## ❀ The Parish Lantern
On the Village Green,
Walberswick IP18 6TT
Tel: (01502) 723173

Visit our tea room and courtyard garden. Enjoy morning coffee, light lunches, cream teas and home-baked cakes. Original crafts, gifts, clothes and pictures. Set in the unspoilt beauty of Walberswick Village Green. *Open: Daily from 1000 April-Dec; Fri, Sat, Sun only Jan-March. (O/P14)*

*Woolpit, Suffolk*

## Norfolk

### King's Lynn
## ❀ Congham Hall Herb Gardens
Grimston, King's Lynn PE32 1AH
Tel: Mrs C Forecast on Hillington (01485) 600250.

Unique Potager and Herb Garden - based on XVII Century design - featuring around six hundred herbs. Tours of the Gardens including a lunch based on the use of herbs and talk by can be arranged. *Gardens open to the public Apr-Oct 1400-1600 daily except Sat. No facilities for coaches. (C/D7/8)*

## Suffolk

### Ipswich
## ❀ Tolly Cobbold Brewery & The Brewery Tap
Cliff Road, Ipswich, IP3 0AZ
Tel: (01473) 231723 (day);
(01473) 281508 (evening)
Fax: (01473) 280045

Taste the malt and smell the hops on a fully guided tour of this magnificent Victorian Brewery. See both brewhouses - the old and the new - as we guide you through the traditional brewing process. See the Country's largest collection of commemorative bottled beers and the world's oldest brewing vessel. Complimentary beer. Featured on the BBC TV series 'Troubleshooter' with Sir John Harvey-Jones, Britain's best loved businessman. *Group tours all year by arrangement 1000-2000, casual visitors at 12 noon - June-Sept. Admission: £3.90, Group rates: £3.70/£3.50 inc. (K18)*

### Bruisyard
## ❀ Bruisyard Vineyard & Herb Centre
Church Road, Bruisyard,
Saxmundham IP17 2EF
Tel: Badingham (01728) 638281

10-acre vineyard and winery producing the estate-bottled Bruisyard wine, situated west of Saxmundham. Wines, vines, herbs, souvenirs etc for sale. *Open 16 January - 24 December, 1030-1700. Conducted tours, Parties of 20 or more by appointment. Large herb and water gardens, shop, restaurant, children's play area and picnic area. Free wine tasting for vineyard and winery visitors. (N15/16)*

### Bungay
## ❀ St Peter's Brewery Co Ltd
St Peter's Hall, St Peter's
South Elmham, Bungay NR35 1NQ
Tel: (01986) 782322
Fax: (01986) 782505

The brewery was built in 1996 within converted farm buildings adjacent to St Peter's Hall. The site was ideal because of excellent water quality from a deep bore-hole. Locally malted barley, together with Kentish hops produces a range of classical English cask-conditioned ales. We also have a range of superb bottled beers. Visitor Centre, Restaurant, Bar and Shop. St Peter's Brewery also has a selection of other prestigious establishments; Cornwallis Arms, Brome, De La Pole Arms, Wingfield, The Jerusalem Tavern, Clerkenwell, London *Open: Brewery tours available every Friday, Saturday and Sunday. Telephone for details. (M12)*

A teapot factory, a barn selling corn dollies, glassmaking workshops, and woolly jumpers made from black sheep ... you'll find them all in these pages. You'll find a specialist Children's Book Centre tucked away in Norfolk's countryside, and out in Suffolk a pottery which dates back to 1646.

Local craft producers have grouped together in shared premises at Alby Crafts, Wroxham Barns and Taverham Craft Centre and you can often see them at work and find out how things are made. Outstanding design and workmanship is on view in July in Aldeburgh at the annual exhibition of the Suffolk Craft Society.

*Tuesday Market, King's Lynn, Norfolk*

## Norfolk

## VISIT

### THE BLACK SHEEP SHOP

**Aylsham**
⊛ **Black Sheep Shop**
**Black Sheep Jerseys,**
9 Penfold Street, Aylsham  NR11 6ET
Tel: (01263) 733142/732006
Black Sheep is known for its superb range of quality classic countrywear in natural, undyed and dyed wools - grown and made in Great Britain. See the famous Black Sheep range at our showroom; heavy weight jerseys, light weight sweaters, scarves, hats, gloves and much more. Also, don't forget to have a look at our 'promotion of the month' - quality garments at bargain prices. A warm and courteous welcome always awaits you. If you cannot come and visit us then send for a free colour catalogue. *Open: Mon-Sat 0900-1730, Sun 1030-1600. (K6/7)*

# NORFOLK
# CHILDREN'S
# BOOK CENTRE

**between Aylsham and Cromer**
**Norfolk Children's Book Centre**
Tel: (01263) 761402
Find out more about the Centre on
http://www.argonet.co.uk/ncbc
Surrounded by fields, the Centre displays one of the best collections of children's and teachers' books in East Anglia. Here you will find a warm welcome and expert advice. You can browse through the latest and the classics in both fiction and non-fiction. We also sell story cassettes, videos and cards. *Open daily, Mon-Sat, 1000-1700, closed Bank Hols. Teachers welcome anytime, please phone. Find us between Aylsham and Cromer just off the A140. Look out for the signposted turn 500 metres north of Alby Craft Centre. (K/L5/6)*

**Cley-next-the-Sea**
⊛ **Made in Cley**
High Street, Cley-next-the-Sea,
Holt  NR25 7RF
Tel: (01263) 740134
Hand-thrown domestic and sculptural Pottery in stoneware, porcelain and raku, plus contemporary jewellery in silver and gold, and sculptures in marble and other stones. Everything is made on the premises and exhibited in a Regency shop which is itself of historical interest. *Open daily, closed Wednesdays October to June. (I4)*

**Cromer**
⊛ **Bond Street Antiques** (inc BRIGGS)
6 Bond Street, Cromer NR27 9DA
Tel: (01263) 513134
Goldsmiths, Silversmiths and Jewellers, Incorporating Gem Test Centre. Gems, jewellery, Amber, gifts and objets d'art. Top prices paid for gold, silver and antiques. Valuations for Insurance and Probate. Member of The National Association of Goldsmiths and Fellow of The Gemmological Association of Great Britain. *(L4/5)*

### Great Walsingham
#### ❀ Great Walsingham Gallery and Crafts
Great Walsingham, Fakenham NR22 6DR
Tel: (01328) 820900

An attractive range of converted barns comprising:- The Textile Centre Shop - Gifts, casual clothes with an excellent tearoom providing light lunches and cream teas. Great Walsingham Gallery - Exhibitions of paintings, sculptures and a selection of fine-art cards and prints. The Richeldis Candle Company - Hand made candles containing perfumes or beneficial essential oils. Murray Carpets - A wonderful selection of hand-made oriental rugs. Heather Green Woodcarving & Sculpture Studio - Displaying woodcarving and sculptures. *Open: daily, 0930-1700, weekends and Bank Holidays 1000-1700. Tearoom closed Jan-mid Mar. (H5)*

### Great Yarmouth
#### ❀ Candlemaker and Model Centre
Tel: (01493) 750242

Situated 9 miles from Great Yarmouth on the banks of the River Bure, boasts England's largest variety of handcrafted candles, with many that are unique. The Centre also has a good selection of modelling kits. *The candle shop and workshop is open daily from Easter to the end of Oct from 0900-1730 and during Nov and Dec from Thu to Sun 1000-1600 with free admission. Free parking and river moorings in village. (P9)*

## Norfolk Lavender

### Heacham
#### ❀ Norfolk Lavender Ltd
Caley Mill, Heacham, King's Lynn
Tel: (01485) 570384

Set in the ground floor of Caley Mill, the Countryside Gift Shop contains a very wide range of gifts all on a countryside theme. There are items to suit every pocket, masses of choice and frequent new ideas. The Old Barn houses the Lavender Shop where you can buy Norfolk Lavender's fragrant products: The English Lavender, Rose With English Lavender, Night Scented Jasmine, Lily of the Valley, Men of England and Lavender for Men. *Open daily 1000-1700 (closed Dec 25, 26 and Jan 1). (D5)*

## Wroxham BARNS

### Hoveton
#### ❀ Wroxham Barns
Tunstead Road, Hoveton,
Norwich NR12 8QU
Tel: (01603) 783762

Beautifully restored 18th century barns, the main barn is home to the gift and craft shop and houses the Gallery Clothing Collection. The surrounding thirteen craftsmen's workshops house crafts ranging from decorative glass making and pottery to handmade children's clothes. The Tea rooms serves traditional cream teas and light lunches. Choose from a tempting selection of preserves, wines and confectionery in our food and fudge shops. For the children, Williamson's Family Fair and Junior Farm. *Wroxhan Barns opens daily 1000-1700 (closed 25, 26, 31 Dec, 1 Jan). Williamson's Traditional Fair is seasonal 1100-1700. Parking and admission to Wroxham Barns is free - Junior Farm £2.00. (M8)*

*Norwich Market, Norfolk*

### King's Lynn
#### ❀ Caithness Crystal Visitor Centre
9-12 Paxman Road,
Hardwick Industrial Estate,
King's Lynn PE30 4NE
Tel: (01553) 765111/765123
Fax: (01553) 767628

Glassmaking is a magical craft that can transform sand into exquisite glassware using only the heat of a furnace and the skill of hand and eye. Witness it for yourself at our King's Lynn Visitor Centre and marvel at the demonstration of the skills of glassmaking. Unique factory shopping experience, extensive selection of giftware - stemware paperweights and glass animals, as well as ceramics at bargain prices. Superb choice of Royal Doulton products. *Open: seven days a week (Factory Shop/Restaurant); glass making Mon-Fri throughout the year. Free admission. (C/D7/8)*

*Hoxne, Suffolk*

### Langham
#### ◉ Langham Glass
The Long Barn, North Street,
Langham, Holt  NR25 7DG
Tel: (01328) 830511

In a large beautiful Norfolk barn complex, teams of glassmakers can be seen working with molten glass using blowing irons and hand tools that have been traditional for hundreds of years. There is an enclosed children's adventure playground, factory gift shops, museum, restaurant, video, rose & clematis walled garden, also a newly converted Antiques and Collectable shop. Salt dough, and enamel painting onto ceramics. Woodturning and Pyrography. *Open 7 days a week all year 1000-1700. Glassmaking Easter-31 October (everyday); 1 Nov-Easter (Mon-Fri). Group visits welcome. (J5)*

*Woodbridge, Suffolk*

### Norwich
#### ◉ Black Horse Bookshop
8 & 10 Wensum St, Norwich
Tel: (01603) 626871 and 613828

Latest books on a wide range of subjects, including almost everything in print about East Anglia. Other departments include maps, art books, architecture and reference books. Books posted to all parts of the world. *Open 6 days a week. Official agent for The Stationery Office. (L9)*

### Sutton
#### ◉ Sutton (Windmill) Pottery
Church Road, Sutton,
Norwich  NR12 9SG
Tel: (01692) 580595

1.5 miles southeast of Stalham, 0.75 miles east of A149 to Great Yarmouth (16 miles). Norwich 16 miles. Malcolm Flatman designs and produces a large range of wheel-made microwave and dishwasher safe stoneware pottery and tableware items in a choice of glazes. Many lamps and decorative pieces are 'one-offs'. Commissions accepted. Visitors welcome in the small workshop throughout most of the year to see work in progress and purchase from a selection of finished pieces. *Price list available. Full postal service. Open: Please telephone before a special journey and weekend visits. Free admission. (N7)*

*Norwich, Norfolk*

*Norfolk ● Suffolk*

### Taverham
### ⊛ Taverham Craft and Country Shopping Centre
Fir Covert Road, Taverham,
Norwich NR8 6HT
Tel: (01603) 860522

A purpose-built centre for the finest in traditional crafts, hand made on the premises by local crafts people. You'll find many different crafts, from embroidery and lacemaking to sugar craft, painting and framing. Watch crafts people at work, talk to them about their skills, and come away with a pretty and practical keepsake. Plus garden centre, coffee bar, pet food and corn stores. Facilities for the disabled: coach parties welcome. Free car parking for 1000 cars. *Open Mon-Sat, 1000-1700, Sun 1100-1700. Coaches very welcome (telephone for catering requirements). Please phone before calling for specific crafts and opening hours. (K8)*

*Lavenham, Suffolk*

## Suffolk

### Aldringham
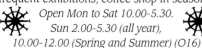
### ⊛ Aldringham Craft Market
Aldringham, Near Leiston,
IP16 4PY  Tel: 01728 830397
Family business, established 1958. Three relaxed and friendly galleries offering wide and extensive ranges of British craft products, original paintings, etchings and prints, studio, domestic and garden pottery, wood, leather, glass, jewellery, toys, kites, games, books, maps and many other good things including ladies' clothes, toiletries and hardy perennial plants. We only stock sensibly-priced, high quality products  Easy and ample car parking; children's play area; frequent exhibitions; coffee shop in season.
*Open Mon to Sat 10.00-5.30.
Sun 2.00-5.30 (all year),
10.00-12.00 (Spring and Summer) (O16)*

## NURSEY & SON LTD
### Bungay
⊛ 12 Upper Olland St, Bungay
Tel: (01986) 892821
Established 1790. Men's and ladies flying jackets, leather and suede jackets, leather trousers, sheepskin coats, slippers, gloves, hats, rugs etc. The factory shop has a good selection especially for Gifts, also a wide variety of sub-standard Products and Oddments. *Mon-Fri 1000-1300, 1400-1700. Closed 24 July. Re-open 9 August. Access, Visa. (M12)*

### Bury St Edmunds
### Art Gallery and Shop
The Market Cross, Bury St Edmunds
Tel: (01284) 762081
Robert Adam's only public building in the East of England. The magnificent cruciform upper floor is used for a programme of changing exhibitions across the visual arts with a special emphasis on contemporary craftwork. The Craft shop offers a wide selection of British-made ceramics, jewellery and glass; also books, cards and children's gifts. Disabled access. *Open: All year Tues-Sat 1030-1700, closed 25 Dec-1 Feb. Adults: 50p, concessions 30p. (F/G15/16)*

### Debenham
### ⊛ Carters Teapot Pottery
Low Road, Debenham,
(Stowmarket) IP14 6QU
Tel: (01728) 860475
Fax: (01728) 861110

It doesn't have to be tea time to visit this Pottery making highly collectable teapots, in the beautiful village of Debenham. Visitors can see from the viewing area how these world renowned teapots are made and painted by hand. Pottery shop selling teapots, mugs and quality seconds. Situated just off the High Street, follow the teapot signs. Parking available. Tea and coffee in the conservatory. *(K15)*

### Snape
### ⊛ Snape Maltings Riverside Centre
Saxmundham IP17 1SR
Tel: (01728) 688303/5

Situated on the banks of the River Alde, Snape Maltings is an historic collection of Victorian granaries and malthouses, now housing shops, galleries and restaurants. These include House & Garden (Fine Foods, Kitchen Shop and Furnishings), Snape Craft Shop, The Gallery, Countrywear, Beachcomber, Maltings Music and Books & Toys. Fresh home-cooked food is served in the Granary Tea Shop, and Plough & Sail pub. During the summer visitors can also take a 1 hour River Trip or join a Painting or Craft Course. No admission charge. *Open every day, all year 1000-1700 (1800 in summer). (N16)*

### Wattisfield
### ⊛ Watson's Potteries
Wattisfield
(A143 between Bury and Diss)
Tel: (01359) 251239

Earliest record of Wattisfield potters is 1646. The Watson family have perpetuated the craft for nearly 200 years. Original Suffolk collection of printed terracotta ware includes kitchen and gift items, unique terracotta wine coolers, herb, spice and storage jars, lasagne dishes, bread bakers, etc. See original kiln, tour factory by appointment, visit shop selling our own quality seconds. See page 106 for further information. (I14)

### Monks Eleigh
### ⊛ Corncraft
Bridge Farm, Monks Eleigh
Tel: (01449) 740456

In the heart of the Suffolk countryside between Hadleigh and Lavenham, Corn Craft specialise in growing and supplying corn dollies and dried flowers. A wide range of their own products, along with an extensive selection of other British crafts is available from the craft shop and new flower shop. Coffee, cream teas, home made cakes and other light refreshments are served in the converted granary adjoining the shop. Ample space and easy parking. Evening demonstrations of corn dolly making are given by arrangement. Contact Mrs Win Gage. *Open every day throughout the year from 1000-1700, Sunday 1100-1700. (H17/18)*

### Walberswick
### ⊛ Tel: (01502) 723173

Set in a grade II listed Georgian building with courtyard garden, the Parish Lantern offers good quality crafts, gifts, clothes and pictures, as well as delicious cream teas and light lunches. The unspoilt sea-side village of Walberswick has long attracted writers and artists, and was once the home of architect and designer Charles Rennie Mackintosh. Close to Minsmere R.S.P.B. Reserve and Dunwich Heath, and just a short ferry ride (in summer) or a pleasant walk from Southwold. *Open daily from 1000. Fri, Sat & Sun only during Jan, Feb and March. (O/P14)*

### Woolpit
### ⊛ Elm Tree Gallery
The Old Bakery, Woolpit,
Nr Bury St. Edmunds IP30 9QG
Tel/Fax: (01359) 240255

An Aladdin's cave of attractive, good quality crafts and gifts, housed in The Old Bakery, a timber-framed building dating from c.1550. The extensive range includes jewellery, textiles, wood, ceramics - including locally crafted Clarecraft figures and Andean cooking vessels, children's gifts include Ty Beanie Babies, and one of the best selections of greetings cards in the region. Light refreshments available all day but limited seating available. *Open: All year, Mon-Sat 1000-1800 (inc. Bank Holidays). Sun 1400-1700. (H15/16)*

# *discovery tours*

### Spinning Yarns
- weave your way through the land of the medieval wool industry
**Starting point:** Lavenham, Suffolk *(G/H17)*
**Mileage:** 10m
**Morning** - explore Britain's best preserved medieval town, and learn about the wool industry at the Guildhall. Then take the unclassified road to *Long Melford* (now a fantastic antiques centre). Visit the magnificent church.
**Afternoon** - visit *Kentwell Hall*, where you might find yourself listening to the yarns of Tudor times, at one of the annual re-creations. Then take the A1092 to *Clare*, to end the day in this beautiful country town.

### Salty tales of the Sea
- discover the maritime heritage of the East Coast
**Starting point:** Gt. Yarmouth, Norf *(P9)*
**Mileage:** 21m
**Morning** - visit the popular resort of *Gt. Yarmouth*, famous for its beaches and seaside fun. Explore the *Maritime Museum* with its tales of the coastline, then don't miss the Quayside area, where you can go aboard the *Lydia Eva Steam Drifter* to learn about the great Herring industry.
**Afternoon** - head down the A12 to the important fishing town of *Lowestoft*. Visit the *East Point Pavilion & Maritime Heritage Museum*. End the day by taking the A12/B1127 to *Southwold*, a place literally 'lost in time'. Enjoy a pint of ale from the town's very own brewery, beside the famous white lighthouse.

### Under Starter's Orders
- explore the horseracing capital of the world
**Starting point:** Newmarket, Suff *(C/D15/16)*
**Mileage:** varied (depending on tour taken)
**Morning** - go 'behind the scenes' of racing establishments/stables on a unique 'equine tour', including *The National Stud*. Then explore racing history and ride a horse simulator at the *National Horseracing Museum*.
**Afternoon** - enjoy an exciting afternoon at the races, where you can cheer your favourite to the winning post!

*Historic Re-Creation, Kentwell Hall, Suffolk*

### Bloomin' Beautiful
- enjoy the spectacular colours and delicate fragrances of some of England's finest gardens.
**Tour 1: Starting point:**
Bury St. Edmunds, Suff *(F/G15)*
**Mileage:**
Bury St. Edmunds & Ickworth House 3m
Bury St. Edmunds & Bressingham Gardens 20m
**Morning** - explore *Bury St. Edmunds* award-winning gardens and floral displays.
**Afternoon** - two choices, either take the A143 southwest to Horringer, and enjoy the Italian garden of *Ickworth House*. Or alternatively, take the A143 northeast to Botesdale, where you turn left onto the B1113 to South Lopham. At the junction with the A143, turn right and head to the world-renowned *Bressingham Gardens*.

**Tour 2:**
**Starting point:** King's Lynn, Norf *(C/D7/8)*
**Mileage:** 23m
**Morning** - leave King's Lynn on the A17 to Terrington St. Clement, and visit the colourful *African Violet Centre*. Retrace your steps to King's Lynn and take the A149 north. After 6m, turn right onto the B1439 to *Sandringham*.
**Afternoon** - enjoy the 60 acres of grounds, containing the Queen's favourite blooms. When you are ready to leave, take the B1440 to Dersingham. At the T-junction, turn right and follow the road to the roundabout with the A149. Head north along the A149 to Heacham and end the day at the sweet-smelling *Norfolk Lavender Limited*.

*Newmarket Races, Suffolk*

**Family Favourites**
- three ideas to keep dad, mum and the children happy in North Norfolk.

**Tour 1:**

**Starting point:** Fakenham, Norf *(G/H6)*

**Mileage:** 14m

**Morning** - take the A1067 to visit *Pensthorpe Waterfowl Park*, then retrace your steps to Fakenham and follow the A148 towards Cromer. After 4m, turn left (following signs) to the musical *Thursford Collection*.

**Afternoon** - return to the A148 and head to the pretty town of *Holt*. Take a ride aboard the *North Norfolk Railway*, along the coast to seaside *Sheringham*. Enjoy a walk along the prom with an ice cream!

**Tour 2:**

**Starting point:** Fakenham, Norf *(G/H6)*

**Mileage:** 12m

**Morning** - leave Fakenham on the B1105 to explore *Wells-next-the-Sea*, a quaint fishing town. Then jump aboard the little steam railway, to pay a visit to the pretty pilgrimage centre of *Little Walsingham*.

**Afternoon** - return to Wells, and take the A149 westwards to visit the magnificent *Holkham Hall*.

**Tour 3:**

**Starting point:** Fakenham, Norf *(G/H6)*

**Mileage:** 25m

**Morning** - leave Fakenham on the A148 towards Cromer. After 8m, turn left onto the B1156 to Langham. Visit the *Langham Glass* workshops, then remain on the B1156 to Blakeney. Follow the coast road (the A149) to Weybourne, and visit the tanks/military displays of *The Muckleburgh Collection*.

**Afternoon** - take the A149 to cliff-top Cromer and enjoy a crab tea overlooking the famous pier.

*Great Yarmouth, Norfolk*

**Things that go Bump in the Night**
- let us send a shiver down your spine on all things spooky and strange!

**Starting point:** Norwich, Norf *(L9)*

**Mileage:** varied (depending on tour taken)

**Morning** - begin in the historic city of Norwich. Wander the ancient streets and lanes (such as *Elm Hill*) and visit the magnificent *Cathedral*. Then take a 'creepy' tour of the *Castle's* dungeons and try out the witches chair.

**Afternoon** - take the A1151 to *Wroxham*, and enjoy a tour of the reed-fringed Norfolk Broads. Scare yourself silly with tales of black devil dogs, ghostly drummer-boys and revengeful skeletons. End the day by leaving Wroxham on the B1354 (via Aylsham) to the beautiful 17th century *Blickling Hall*, haunt of Anne Boleyn.

**A Painters Inspiration**
- visit the places and landscapes which inspired two of Britain's greatest painters

**Starting point:** Ipswich, Suff *(K18)*

**Mileage:** 21m

**Morning** - visit *Christchurch Mansion*, to see the important collection of Constable and Gainsborough paintings. Then head south along the A12 for about 6m, to join the B1070 to *East Bergholt*. See the site of Constable's birthplace, then continue to nearby *Flatford Mill*, scene of "The Haywain".

**Afternoon** - return to the A12, and take the B1068 (via pretty *Stoke-by-Nayland*) to the junction with the A134. Turn right and follow the road to the market town of *Sudbury*. Visit the birthplace of Thomas Gainsborough.

*Haunt of Anne Boleyn, Blickling Hall, Norfolk*

**Strange Tales & Curiosities**
- discover the flipside of the east, its customs, stories and local characters

**Tour 1:**

**Starting point:** King's Lynn , Norf *(C/D7/8)*

**Mileage:** 46m

**Morning** - meet Lynn's witches and highwaymen at *The Old Gaol House*. Then take the A47 to *Swaffham*, where there are tales of the Pedlar and his treasure to discover.

**Afternoon** - take the A1065 to Mundford, then the A134 towards Thetford. After 2m, turn right to descend into the bat-infested flint mines of *Grimes Graves*. Continue along the A134 (via Thetford) to *Bury St. Edmunds*, to see the book bound in human skin at *Moyse's Hall Museum*. End the day with a pint in Britain's smallest pub.

**Tour 2:**

**Starting point:** Woodbridge, Suff *(L/M17)*

**Mileage:** 28m

**Morning** - visit the unique *Tide Mill* and *Sutton Hoo's* treasure-filled burial site. Then take the B1084, via UFO country (Rendlesham Forest) to *Orford*. Climb the magnificent *Castle* and discover the Merman story.

**Afternoon** - return along the B1084 for 2.5m, then join the B1078 to Tunstall. Turn right here onto the B1069 to visit the shops/galleries of *Snape Maltings*. Remain on the B1069 to the T-junction, where you turn right onto the A1094 to the unspoilt town of *Aldeburgh*. Hunt out the 'Snooks' dog statue and visit the lifeboat station. End the day by taking the coast road north (2m) to 'eccentric' *Thorpeness*, and its 'House in the Clouds'.

*Norfolk* ● *Suffolk*

# IMPORTANT NEWS - NEW FOR 1999

**Two brand new publications will be available to buy in 1999 about the region and its gardens and connections with aviation heritage.**

## Gardens in the East of England 1999

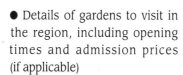

This is an exciting and informative guide to the many gardens to visit in this region. This handy A5 sized full colour publication features:

● Details of gardens to visit in the region, including opening times and admission prices (if applicable)

● Contributions from some of the region's most famous gardeners: Lady Salisbury (Hatfield House), Alan Mason (Harlaxton Manor and Gardens), Adrian Bloom (Bressingham Gardens) and Hugh Johnson (Saling Hall and Gardens), including a helpful handy hint for your garden!

● A Calendar of the Seasons, indicating when is the best time to see certain flowers/shrubs in bloom, and where you can view them in the East of England.

● A Calendar of Gardening Events, Shows and Festivals throughout the region in 1999.

● A themed listing of the places where certain types of gardens can be seen eg. Kitchen, Knot, Scent, Water, including those gardens with links to famous gardeners.

● Key gardening highlights from around the region including the 'Tulipland' of Lincolnshire, the 'Garden Cities' of Hertfordshire.

● Suggested tours around the region, linking together gardening attractions.

● Plus lots more to help you explore the many gardens of the East of England.

Copies of this guide will be available in late January 1999 from the East of England Tourist Board at the address shown opposite.

*Cover illustrations shown above may change.*

## Quest for the Sky
Aviation Heritage in the East of England

This full colour A5 publication will bring together the story of the East of England's rich aviation heritage. Produced in consultation with one of the region's leading aviation historians, this guide will include:

● Special features on key aviation connections in the East of England, such as The Dambusters, Glenn Miller, Scott and Black and the De Havilland Company, to name just a few.

● A calendar highlighting aviation shows and events in the region throughout 1999.

● Suggested day tours, linking together aviation attractions and connections.

● Special sections containing listings of aviation memorials/monuments, plus airfields (past and present) listing a selection of connections, squadrons, memorials etc.

Copies of this guide will be available in March 1999 from the East of England Tourist Board at the below address.

**To order your copy of either of the above publications please contact:**

The East of England Tourist Board
Toppesfield Hall, Hadleigh, Suffolk IP7 5DN
Tel: 01473 822922  Fax: 01473 823063
Email:
eastofenglandtouristboard@compuserve.com
Internet:
http://www.visitbritain.com/east-of-england/

# Bedfordshire, Essex & Hertfordshire

There's plenty to do in *Bedfordshire, Essex* and *Hertfordshire*. Anyone who lives here will tell you we're spoilt for choice when it comes to deciding where to go for days out. We have grand houses, wild animals, Roman treasures, many years of transport history, great shopping, and attractive countryside too. What more could you want?

Let's look at the scenery first, starting over in the west of the area where the *Chilterns* escarpment runs through Bedfordshire and Hertfordshire. Part of this is the *Ashridge Estate*, with over 4,000 acres of unspoiled, rolling countryside with commons and ancient woodland. For breathtaking views over three counties, climb the steep, winding staircase to the top of the monument to the Third Earl of Bridgewater. The view is worth the effort!

*Woodland, water and hilltop walks*

*Below: Aldbury, Hertfordshire*
*Left: Maldon, Essex*

The 'picture postcard' village of *Aldbury* is delightful. Fine cottages are grouped around a village pond and the village stocks are a reminder of the punishment for miscreants.

Nearby are the Tring Reservoirs, a home for wildlife and popular with walkers. The bustling little town of *Tring* has been important since the 17th century but had its heyday when the Rothschild family lived in the mansion and brought employment to the town. Today the zebra head pavement recalls Walter Rothschild's interest in zoology, when emus and kangaroos would roam the estate, and zebras were trained to pull carriages.

Further north are the *Dunstable Downs* - rolling chalk hills which are just great for flying kites, as well as for walking and gasping at the views! Watch out for the lions, and we don't just mean those at Whipsnade Wild Animal Park, there's also one made of chalk!

The *Grand Union Canal* wends its way through this western part of the area. A walk along the towpath is always interesting, or if you prefer to sit back and watch the world go by, take a trip on a historic canal boat. *Leighton Buzzard* is on the canal and is worth exploring. It has a wide Georgian high street, charming mews shops and an ancient street market.

Travel east a bit and you'll reach the *Lee Valley Park*. It is 23 miles long and follows the course of the River Lea from *Ware* to London's East End. The park is an unusual combination of purpose-built sports and leisure facilities set in vast areas of countryside and nature reserves, for every sport from boating to biking to birdwatching.

For walking or birdwatching, the ancient wooded landscapes of *Hatfield Forest* and *Epping Forest* are favourites. There are waymarked trails and attractive stretches of water amongst the trees.

North east of here, bordering Suffolk, is the lovely *Stour Valley*, its landscape and wide skies well known from the paintings of John Constable. Come here and see the settings for his famous paintings. At the heart of Constable Country is *Dedham*. Perhaps its pastel washed cottages and houses, and interesting church might inspire any of us to paint!

Travel east a bit more until you can't go any further. You have reached the *Essex Coast* -

## Secret waters of the smugglers' coast

so keep an eye open for smugglers still hiding in the creeks and inlets of this mysterious edge of England. The "Secret Waters" of Arthur Ransome's stories were here in the backwaters behind *Walton-on-the-Naze*, and the flat saltmarshes and mudflats are a precious habitat for wildlife both here and elsewhere along the coast.

Three river estuary towns are centres of maritime heritage and yachting. *Maldon* is full of interesting historical buildings, including the 15th century Moot Hall in the High Street. The quay is home to several Thames sailing barges - a magnificent sight. *Brightlingsea* has one of the best stretches of sailing on the East Coast, and superb walks along the banks of the creek. *Burnham-on-Crouch* has a picturesque charm created by the historical character of the buildings on the waterfront and along the High Street.

*Southend-on-Sea, Essex*

Stay by the River Crouch if your interest is in antiques, as *Battlesbridge* is a lively antiques centre.

Most of the Essex coast has been designated an Environmentally Sensitive Area, but it is still more famous for its seaside resorts.
Sunshine resorts

*Southend-on-Sea* is one of the best loved and most friendly of resorts. It has the longest pleasure pier in the world, and seven miles of beaches with seaside awards. There's an amusement park, sea life centre, and Never Never Land, as well as

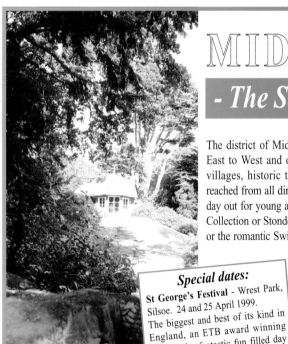

# MID-BEDFORDSHIRE
## - The Scenic Route

The district of Mid Bedfordshire stretches in an arc from East to West and offers a "Scenic Route" of enchanting villages, historic towns and amazing attractions. Easily reached from all directions with both the M1 and A1 passing through, the 70 mile "Scenic Route" is an ideal day out for young and old alike. If you like vintage aircraft and transportation why not visit the Shuttleworth Collection or Stondon Transport Museum. Perhaps you like gardens - we're sure you would enjoy Wrest Park or the romantic Swiss Garden. Alternatively, if you prefer charming historic houses, the magnificent Woburn Abbey is hard to equal especially when combined with the exciting Safari Park. For beautiful countryside and picturesque villages come to Mid Beds.

### Perfectly placed for enjoyment.

### Special dates:
St George's Festival - Wrest Park, Silsoe. 24 and 25 April 1999. The biggest and best of its kind in England, an ETB award winning event and a fantastic fun filled day out for all the family.

The Bedfordshire Millennium Festival - Shuttleworth, Old Warden Park. 28,29,30 August 1999. Celebrating the last 1000 years and looking forward to the future, this massive Festival has something for everyone to enjoy, no matter what their age!

### New for 1999:
We are pleased to introduce coach trips for your social groups, the itineraries include our popular Scenic Route, combined with visits and lunch at the best attractions in the area. Your party will require a minimum of 30 people

For more information and free "Scenic Route" brochure, please contact the award winning: Sandy Tourist Information Centre. A1 Sandy Roundabout, Girtford Bridge, Sandy, Beds SG19 1NA. Tel: 01767 682728, Fax: 01767 681713.

museums and an art gallery. *Southend* has won awards for its magnificent floral displays in parks and gardens and you'll realise why when you see for yourself. Last year it opened its vast new indoor entertainment complex, the Kursaal, with bowling, ice and roller skating, retail units and restaurants. Next to *Southend*, *Leigh-on-Sea* is an old fishing village where the cockle boats can be seen unloading their catch every day.

*Clacton-on-Sea's* south-facing long sandy beach is part of the sunshine holiday coast of Essex. There are plenty of amusements for all ages at this resort. On the largest fun pier in Europe you can ride on the dodgems or go on a Reptile Safari. Close by is *Frinton-on-Sea*, quiet, secluded and unspoilt with high quality shopping in its main street. Walton is a jolly, quaint resort with plenty of seaside entertainment.

The seaside resorts are a well known feature of this part of the world, and so are *Historic centres* the historic centres of *Colchester* and *St Albans*. *Colchester* is Britain's oldest recorded town with over 2,000 years of history involving the Romans, the Saxons and the Normans. The town's history is brought to life in Colchester Castle Museum where you can get thoroughly involved in finding out about the past. Here you can touch Roman pottery, feel what it is like to wear medieval clothes, and experience the murkier past by visiting the castle prisons. Surrounding the castle is Castle Park, a good place for a stroll before returning to the present to visit the big stores and specialist shops of modern *Colchester*.

The city of *St Albans* has been important since ancient times. An important treasure from the past is Verulamium, the site of the country's third largest Roman city. You can still see the remains of Roman walls, and the Hypocaust in a lovely parkland setting, surrounded by fine trees and a lake and river which provide a haven for ducks, herons and kingfishers.

The magnificent Abbey Church dominates the skyline. It was built in 1077, close to the resting place of Alban, Britain's first Christian martyr, after whom the city is named.

The Clock Tower in the market place is the only medieval town belfry in England. It was built as a political statement by the town, asserting its freedom and wealth in the face of the powerful Abbey, allowing it to sound its own hours and curfew. From the Clock Tower are fine views over the city and surrounding countryside.

The ancient town of *Saffron Walden* has many timber framed buildings, many of *Antiques, rogues and villains* which are decorated with pargetting. At the heart of the town is its market - still the focal point as it has been for generations. The church, reputed to be the biggest in Essex, dominates the town, and nearby are the ruins of the Norman Castle. On the common is a rare earth maze, and there is a restored hedge maze also at Bridge End Gardens. The Saffron Crocus can be seen in autumn, flowering outside the museum.

Close by is *Thaxted* with three easily recognised landmarks. The tall spire of its church soars above the town; the half timbered medieval guildhall is compact and unusually wedge shaped; and John Webb's windmill on its vantage point, gives outstanding views of town and surrounding countryside.

Both towns are good centres for antiques, as are *Coggeshall* with its many fine medieval timber framed buildings, *Baldock*, where little has been built since the mid 19th century, and *Hertford* whose many old buildings, including the castle, give this

*Market day, St Albans, Hertfordshire*

quiet town a special character. *Ampthill* too, with its fine Georgian architecture, has several quaint antique shops.

*Woburn* is also a good place to seek out antiques. Houses and shop-fronts from the 18th and 19th centuries line the high street of this small and beautifully preserved Georgian town, and it deserves its reputation as one of the most important historic towns in England.

With so many good haunts for antique collectors around here, it's no surprise that this is "Lovejoy Country" where many episodes of the Lovejoy series were filmed. Indeed on one occasion the Tourist Information Centre at Saffron Walden was the centre of the action when an episode was filmed in which Lovejoy's assistant Eric fell in love with the lady working in the information centre.

We have our share of rogues in this part of the world. Dick Turpin's daring exploits to relieve the rich of their money and jewels are well known. The highwayman's birthplace was at *Hempstead* and he worked as a butcher in *Thaxted*. Because of debt he turned to cattle stealing, and then to robbery, working the busy coach route from

London to *Cambridge* and *Norwich*, using a cave deep in the forest of *Epping* as his hideout. After his arrest he found refuge in the attractive group of villages known as 'The Rodings'.

Hardly a rogue, but nevertheless a notorious and fascinating character also from these parts, was Matthew Hopkins, Witchfinder General. He came from the tiny and attractive market town of *Manningtree*, and used his talent for unmasking witches to sentence many women to death.

Rogues and villains are not the only famous characters from hereabouts. A whole host *Creative* of creative talent is *Talent* associated with this part of the world. As well as Constable, we can claim Henry Moore, whose home and studio were at Perry Green. He developed a parkland garden here where his sculptures could be shown to their best advantage.

Graham Greene was born at *Berkhamsted* and went to school here. Sir James Barrie often visited friends in *Berkhamsted* and the five sons of this household were the inspiration for "Peter Pan".

George Orwell wrote "The Road to Wigan Pier" whilst living in the village of *Wallington*. "Animal Farm" is set in the fictitious Manor Farm, Willingdon, said to be based on Manor Farm at *Wallington*, just a few steps from his front door.

George Bernard Shaw used to write in the summerhouse at his home, set in a woodland clearing in *Ayot St Lawrence*. His house is now owned by the National Trust and is kept unchanged - his pens are still on his desk, his hats in the hall.

John Bunyan, preacher and writer of works including "The Pilgrim's Progress", has his roots in Bedfordshire. He grew up in the village of *Elstow*, a village with many charming timber framed houses and a medieval Moot Hall which now houses a museum. Nearby in *Harlington*, the church has a commemorative stained glass window.

John Bunyan lived and was imprisoned for his beliefs in the riverside town of *Bedford* during the 1660s and '70s. Here the new Bunyan Museum illustrates his life and times with a collection of books and artefacts. There is a series of stained glass windows, one of which shows Bunyan deep

*Elstow Moot Hall, Bedfordshire*

in thought. It was a postcard of this window which gave hope and courage to Terry Waite during his four years in solitary confinement in Beirut. As well as this museum, there are other interesting places to visit in *Bedford*, plus a modern shopping centre and pleasant walks along the embankment gardens beside the river.

*Bishop's Stortford* is a fascinating ancient market town on the River Stort with fine buildings including the 16th and 17th century inns and the remains of a Norman Castle. *Hitchin* is a medieval market town with many Tudor and Georgian buildings based around a market

*More towns to visit*

square. *Berkhamsted's* elegant High Street is close to the romantic ruined castle with its unique double moat.

*Ware* is a delightful town on the navigable section of the River Lee. It has many historic buildings and its Grotto, decorated with flints, minerals and shells, is one of the finest in England.

*Dunstable* and *Luton* were once famous centres for the straw plait and hat making industry, replaced in *Luton* now by modern industries including car manufacture. In contrast, traditional rural trades are the nostalgic subject of the Stockwood Craft Museum, and in a series of workshops, contemporary crafts are being made by today's craft workers. *Dunstable* was built

by the Romans at the junction of the Icknield Way and Watling Street and was once a coaching town.

*Braintree* and *Halstead* have a long history in the textile trade, first with wool, and since the 18th century with silk weaving, an industry which continues to prosper today. To see the story of silk weaving brought to life, visit the Working Silk Museum at *Braintree*. *Halstead* has a 600 year old church, country style shops, clapboard watermill.

*Watford* is the largest town in Herts with a prosperous centre - much developed since the middle ages when it was a market town. The Harlequin Shopping Centre draws shoppers from afar.

*Bedfordshire ● Essex ● Hertfordshire*

These recently-built towns are interesting examples of our modern heritage and good *Garden Cities, New Towns* centres for shopping. *Letchworth Garden City* was the world's first garden city and will be a hundred years old in 2003. In *Welwyn Garden City* the residential and industrial areas are laid out along tree-lined boulevards, with a neo-Georgian town centre. *Stevenage* was Britain's first New Town and was developed in the 1940's to provide good quality housing set in pleasant surroundings amongst open spaces and trees. Great care has been taken to preserve the attractive historic buildings in the High Street which is now a conservation area. *Hemel Hempstead* also, unlike most new towns, developed around a charming old town.

There are lots of attractive villages in this part of England, and perhaps the most special "showpiece" villages are *Traditional villages* *Finchingfield*, with picturesque cottages and church grouped around the village pond, and *Much Hadham* which was for 800 years the country seat of the Bishops of London. *Old Warden* was created in a style fashionable in the 19th century, with Swiss chalets and charming thatched cottages. *Turvey* is a delightful 19th century estate village, with cottages built of limestone beside the River Ouse.

*Harrold* is a large village with thatched cottages built of limestone. Its Old Manor in the High Street dates back to 1600. On the triangular green is the octagonal market house and behind it a circular stone lock up built in 1824 to detain wrong-doers. *Great Bardfield* too, still has its village 'cage' where drunks and delinquents could be held

overnight. It also has attractive houses, some decorated with pargeting, and its own tiny museum.

You'll find interesting architecture at *Castle Hedingham*, as well as a castle which has one of the finest Norman keeps in England, approached by a beautiful Tudor bridge which spans the dry moat.

At *Ashwell* you will see the springs which are the very start of the River Cam. At *Chipperfield*, the 100 acres of common land includes 400 year old chestnut trees, and the apostles pond is surrounded by twelve trees, each representing one apostle. At *Ickwell* old traditions are kept alive. Every year the village children dance around the maypole which, unusually, is a permanent fixture in the village. They say that in former days the May Day celebrations would last a whole two months!

*Colchester Castle, Essex*

*Bedfordshire* ● *Essex* ● *Hertfordshire*

# Tourist Information Centres

With so much to see and do in this area, it's impossible for us to mention all of the places you can visit. You will find Tourist Information Centres (TICs) throughout Bedfordshire, Essex and Hertfordshire, with plenty of information on all the things that you can do and the places you can visit. TICs can book accommodation for you, in their own area, or further afield using the 'Book A Bed Ahead Scheme'. They can be the ideal place to purchase locally made crafts or gifts, as well as books covering a wide range of local interests. A list of the TICs in this area can be found below.

\* Not open all year

## Bedfordshire

**Bedford**, 10 St Pauls Square,
Tel: (01234) 215226 (D15)
**Dunstable**, The Library, Vernon Place,
Tel: (01582) 471012 (C19)
**Luton**, The Bus Station, Bute Street,
Tel: (01582) 401579 (D19)
**Sandy**, A1 Sandy roundabout,
Girtford Bridge, London Road,
Tel: (01767) 682728 (E15)

## Essex

**Braintree**, Town Hall Centre, Market Square, Tel: (01376) 550066 (N19)
**Brentwood**, Pepperell House,
44 High Street, Tel: (01277) 200300 (L23)

**Chelmsford**, County Hall, Market Road,
Tel: (01245) 283400 (M/N21)
**Clacton-on-Sea**, 23 Pier Avenue,
Tel: (01255) 423400 (T20)
**Colchester**, 1 Queen Street,
Tel: (01206) 282920 (R19)
**Harwich**, Iconfield Park, Parkeston
Tel: (01255) 506139 (U/V18)
**Maldon**, Coach Lane, Tel: (01621) 856503 (P21)
**Saffron Walden**, 1 Market Place,
Market Square, Tel: (01799) 510444 (K16/17)
**Southend-on-Sea**, 19 High Street,
Tel: (01702) 215120 (P24)
**Thurrock**, Granada Motorway Service Area, M25, Grays, Tel: (01708) 863733 (L24/25)
**Waltham Abbey**, 4 Highbridge Street,
Tel: (01992) 652295 (I22)

## Hertfordshire

**Birchanger**, Welcome Break Service Area, J8 M11 Motorway, Tel: (01279) 508656 (J19)
**Bishop's Stortford**, The Old Monastery, Windhill, Tel: (01279) 655831 (J19)
**Hemel Hempstead**, Marlowes,
Tel: (01442) 234222 (D21)
**Hertford**, 10 Market Place
Tel: (01992) 584322 (G/H20)
**St Albans**, Town Hall, Market Place,
Tel: (01727) 864511 (E21)

## Blue Badge Guides:

There are also experts available to help you explore some of our towns and cities. These Registered Blue Badge Guides have all attended a training course sponsored by the East of England Tourist Board. Below are some of the tours offered by these Guides - you can obtain further information by contacting the appropriate Tourist Information Centre, unless otherwise indicated. Some Blue Badge Guides have a further qualification to take individuals or groups around the region for half day, full day or longer tours if required.

## Essex

### Colchester
**Regular Town Tours:** 1.75 hours from Visitor Information Centre. 1 Jun-30 Sep, daily 1100. £2.00/£1.00/£1.50.

**Group Tours:** May be booked at any time of year.

## Hertfordshire

### St Albans
**Regular City Walks:** from Clock Tower, Wed, Sat; 1500, Sun 1115 and 1500, Easter-Oct. Ghost walk last Wed in month Easter-Oct; 2000. Verulamium walk departs Verulamium Museum, Easter-Oct, Sun, 1430.
Guides also on duty Roman Theatre, Easter-Oct, Sun, 1430-1700. Tel: Tours Secretary (01727) 833001 or TIC (01727) 864511.

*Leighton Buzzard, Bedfordshire*

*Bedfordshire* ● *Essex* ● *Hertfordshire*

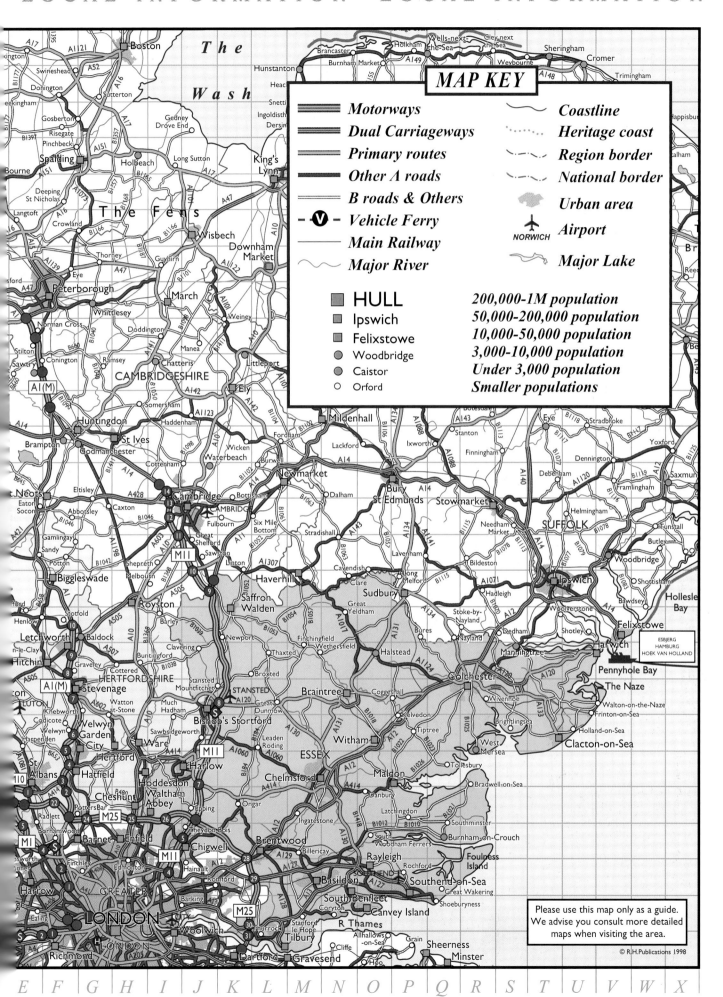

## MAP KEY

**Motorways**
**Dual Carriageways**
**Primary routes**
**Other A roads**
**B roads & Others**
**- V - Vehicle Ferry**
**Main Railway**
**Major River**

**Coastline**
**Heritage coast**
**Region border**
**National border**
**Urban area**
**Airport**
NORWICH
**Major Lake**

■ **HULL**          *200,000-1M population*
■ Ipswich          *50,000-200,000 population*
■ Felixstowe       *10,000-50,000 population*
● Woodbridge       *3,000-10,000 population*
● Caistor          *Under 3,000 population*
○ Orford           *Smaller populations*

ESBJERG
HAMBURG
HOEK VAN HOLLAND

Please use this map only as a guide.
We advise you consult more detailed
maps when visiting the area.

© R.H.Publications 1998

## Historic houses

This area has many links with aviation and you will find air museums and memorials to airmen who lost their lives on flights from this part of England. Airships were build at Cardington where the hangars can still be seen looming over the village, and at Hatfield, aircraft such as the Mosquito, the Comet and Trident were built. England's first balloon flight set off from London and landed at the village of Standon End Green where a sandstone boulder marks the event.

The history of flying comes to life at the Shuttleworth Collection. The oldest aeroplane here is almost 100 years old. All are kept in working condition and can be seen flying in regular displays.

You can also visit the secret moated hideout, Salisbury Hall, where the wooden Mosquito bomber was developed.

History is always fun when it comes to life, and for a fascinating experience of everyday life in Roman Britain, come and get involved at the Verulamium Museum. Or, to get the feel of life in Norman times, come to the recreated Mountfitchet Castle. From a number of dwellings and workplaces within the castle, the lifelike inhabitants tell you about their life and work.

*Woburn Abbey, Bedfordshire*

## Bedfordshire

### Elstow

#### ⬡ Elstow Moot Hall
Elstow Green, Church End
Tel: (01234) 266889
A medieval market hall containing exhibits of 17thC life including beautiful period furniture. Publications and antique maps for sale. *Open 1 Apr-28 Oct, Tue-Thu, Sat, Bank Hol Mon, 1400-1700; Sun, 1400-1730. £1.00/50p/50p. (D15/16)*

### Woburn

#### ⬡ Woburn Abbey
Tel: (01525) 290666
An 18thC Palladian mansion, altered by Henry Holland, the Prince Regent's architect, containing a collection of English silver, French and English furniture and art. *Please contact for details. £7.50 / £3.00 / £6.50. (B17/18)*

## Essex

### Coggeshall

#### ⬡ Grange Barn
The National Trust, Grange Hill
Tel: (01376) 562226
A restored 12thC barn, the earliest surviving timber-framed barn in Europe with a small collection of early 20thC farm carts and wagons. *Open 28 Mar-10 Oct, Tue, Thu, Sun, Bank Hol Mon, 1400-1700. £1.50/75p/£1.50. (O/P19)*

### Coggeshall

#### ⬡ Paycockes
West Street Tel: (01376) 561305
A half-timbered merchant's house, built in the 16thC with a richly-carved interior and a small display of Coggeshall lace. Very attractive garden. *Open 28 Mar-10 Oct, Tue, Thu, Sun, Bank Hol Mon, 1400-1730; last admission 1700. £2.00/£1.00/£2.00 (O/P19)*

### Finchingfield

#### Finchingfield Guildhall
Church Hill Tel: (01371) 810456
A 15thC guildhall housing a museum of local items including Roman remains (open Sundays only). There is an exhibition hall (the old school room) holding art exhibition events. *Open 28 Mar-26 Sep, Sun, Bank Hol Mon, 1430-1730. (M18)*

### Gosfield

#### Gosfield Hall
Tel: (01787) 472914
A Tudor house built around a courtyard with later alterations, an old well and pump house with a 100ft Elizabethan gallery with oak panelling. *Open Grounds 5 May-23 Sep, Wed, Thu, 1400-1700; Tours, 1430, 1515. £2.50/£1.50/£2.50. (O18)*

### Ingatestone

#### ⬡ Ingatestone Hall
Hall Lane Tel: (01277) 353010
Tudor house and gardens, the home of the Petre family since 1540 with a family portrait collection, furniture and other heirlooms on display. *Open 3 Apr-11 Jul, Sat, Sun, Bank Hol Mon, 1300-1800; 14 Jul-3 Sep, Wed-Sun, Bank Hol Mon, 1300-1800; 4-26 Sep, Sat, Sun, 1300-1800. £3.50/£2.00/ £3.00. (M22)*

### Layer Marney

#### ⬡ Layer Marney Tower
Tel: (01206) 330784
A 1520 Tudor-brick gatehouse, 8 storeys high with Italianate terracotta cresting and windows. Gardens, deer and rare breeds farm. There is a nearby church. *Open 1 Apr-4 Oct, daily except Sat, 1200-1700; Bank Hol Sun and Mon, 1100-1700. £3.25/£1.75/ £3.25. (Q19/20)*

### Saffron Walden

#### ⬡ Audley End House and Park
Audley End Tel: (01799) 522399
A palatial Jacobean house remodelled in the 18th-19thC with a magnificent Great Hall with 17thC plaster ceilings. Rooms and furniture by Robert Adam and park by 'Capability' Brown. *Open 1 Apr-30 Sep, Wed-Sun, Bank Hols, 1100-1800; House and Grounds, 1-31 Oct, Wed-Sun, 1000-1500. Guided tour only in October. £5.75 / £2.90 / £4.30. (K17)*

### Widdington

#### ⬡ Priors Hall Barn
Tel: (01604) 730320
One of the finest surviving medieval barns in south east England, representative of the type of aisled barn in north west Essex, 124 x 30 x 33 ft high and little altered. *Open 27 Mar-26 Sep, Sat, Sun, 1000-1800. (K18)*

### Writtle

#### ⬡ Hylands House
Park and Gardens, Hylands Park
Tel: (01245) 606812
An historic house, originally built in 1730. The first phase of restoration open to view includes 4 restored areas, an exhibition on history and a view into the unrestored areas. *Please contact for details of opening times. (M21/22)*

## Hertfordshire

### Ayot St Lawrence
#### Shaw's Corner
Tel: (01438) 820307

The home of George Bernard Shaw from 1906 until his death in 1950 with literary and personal relics in 5 rooms maintained as in his lifetime. *Open 1 Apr-31 Oct, Wed-Sun, Bank Hol Mon, 1300-1700; groups by written application only; last admission 1630 except 18-20 Jun, 3, 4, 23-25 Jul, 1530; closed 2 Apr. £3.30/£1.65/£3.30. (F20)*

*Ingatestone Hall, Essex*

### Gorhambury
#### Gorhambury
Tel: (01727) 854051

A classical-style mansion built from 1777-1784 by Sir Robert Taylor with 16thC-enamelled glass, 17thC carpet and historic portraits of the Bacon and Grimston families. *Open 6 May-23 Sep, Thu, 1400-1700. £4.00/£2.50/£2.00. (D21)*

### Hatfield
#### ❀ Hatfield House and Gardens
Tel: (01707) 262823

Magnificent Jacobean house, home to the Marquess of Salisbury. Exquisite gardens, collection of model soldiers and park trails. Home of Queen Elizabeth I. *Please contact for details of opening times. £6.00/£3.00. (F21)*

### Hoddesdon
#### ❀ Rye House Gatehouse
Rye House Quay, Rye Road

A 15thC moated building, the scene of the 'Rye House Plot' to assassinate King Charles II in 1683. Features include an exhibition and a shop. *Open 2 Apr-26 Sep, Sun, Bank Hols, 1100-1700; Whitsun and summer school hols, 1100-1700. (H/I21)*

### Knebworth
#### ❀ Knebworth House, Gardens and Park
Tel: (01438) 812661

A Tudor manor-house, re-fashioned in the 19thC by Bulwer-Lytton, housing a fine collection of manuscripts, portraits, a Jacobean banquet hall, adventure playground and gift shop. *Please contact for details of opening times. £6.00/£5.50/£5.50. (G19)*

### Ware
#### ❀ The Priory
High Street  Tel: (01920) 460316

Founded in 1338 as a Franciscan friary and dissolved 200 years later by Henry VIII when it became a private house. It is now home to Ware Town Council. *Open all year, Mon-Fri, 0900-1700; closed Bank Hols, 25, 26 Dec, 1 Jan. (H20)*

# Ancient Monuments

## Bedfordshire

### Ampthill

**Houghton House**
Tel: (01536) 402840

The ruins of a 17thC country house, built in the 'heights' near Ampthill and believed to be the 'House Beautiful' in Bunyan's 'The Pilgrim's Progress'. *Open at any reasonable time. (D17)*

### Colmworth

**⊛ Bushmead Priory**
Tel: (01234) 376614

A small Augustinian priory founded in about 1195 with a magnificent 13thC timber roof of crown-post construction. There are also medieval wall paintings and stained glass. *Open 4 Jul-29 Aug, Sat, Sun, 1000-1300, 1400-1800. £1.60/80p/£1.20. (D/E14)*

### Flitton

**De Grey Mausoleum**
Tel: (01536) 402840

A large mortuary chapel of the Greys of Wrest Park containing fine sculptured tombs of monuments from 16th-19thC and some brass and alabaster. *Open Sat, Sun, please contact key keeper on Tel: (01525) 860094. (D17)*

## Essex

### Billericay

**St Mary Magdalene Church**
Church Street, Great Burstead

Saxon church with 14thC medieval wall paintings. Christopher Martin, the church warden, led the Pilgrim Fathers' journey to Billericay near Boston in the USA. *Open 4 Apr-26 Sep, Sun, 1400-1700. (M24)*

### Bradwell-on-Sea

**Saint Peters-on-the-Wall**
East End Road
Tel: (01621) 776203

A 7thC Saxon chapel which is always open and offers a small exhibition about its history and a bookstall. *Evening services every Sunday at 1830 during July and August. Open daily, 24 hours a day. (R21)*

### Castle Hedingham

**⊛ Hedingham Castle**
Tel: (01787) 460261

The finest Norman keep in England, built in 1140 by the deVeres, Earls of Oxford. Visited by Kings Henry VII and VIII and Queen Elizabeth I and besieged by King John. *Open 27 Mar-31 Oct, daily, 1000-1700; please contact for opening times to view the snowdrops. £3.50/£2.50/£3.00. See page 125 for further details. (O18)*

### Chelmsford

**⊛ Chelmsford Cathedral**
Cathedral Office, New Street
Tel: (01245) 294480

A late-medieval church, reordered in 1983 and blending old with new. Became a cathedral in 1914 when the Diocese of Chelmsford was created. Modern sculpture and tapestry. *Open all year, Mon-Sat, 0815-1730; Sun, 0730-1900. (M/N21)*

*Saint Botolphs Priory, Colchester, Essex*

### Colchester

**⊛ Saint Botolphs Priory**
Tel: (01728) 621330

The remains of a 12thC priory near the town centre with a nave which has an impressive arcaded west end. One of the first Augustinian priories in England. *Open at any reasonable time. (R19)*

### Colchester

**Saint Michael and All Angels Church**
Church Road, Copford Green
Tel: (01621) 815434

A 12thC church with 12thC wall paintings. *Open all year, daily, 0915-dusk; Sun service, 1100-1200. (R19)*

### Cressing

**⊛ Cressing Temple**
Witham Road
Tel: (01376) 584903

The site of a Knights Templar settlement dating from 1137. Two magnificent timber-framed barns survive. The Barley Barn c1200 and the Wheat Barn c1250. *Open 4 Apr-29 Oct, Mon-Fri, 0900-1630; Sun, Bank Hol Mon, 1030-1730. £3.00/£2.00/£2.00. See page 125 for further details. (O19)*

### East Tilbury

**Coalhouse Fort**
Princess Margaret Road
Tel: (01375) 844203

A Victorian Thames defence fortress housing the Thameside Aviation Museum with military vehicles, artillery displays, rifle range and park. Also a River Thames foreshore walk. *Please contact for details of opening times. £2.00/£1.00/£2.00. (L/M26)*

### Great Stambridge

**Parish Church of St Mary The Virgin and All Saints**
Stambridge Road
Tel: (01702) 258272

A pre-Conquest church of Saxon origin with a fine Victorian interior with a stained-glass window commemorating John Winthrop, founder of Boston and Governor of Massachusetts. *(P24)*

*Mountfitchet Castle,
Stansted Mountfitchet, Essex*

### Greensted
**Greensted Church**
Greensted Road
Tel: (01277) 364694
The oldest wooden church in the world. The oldest wooden building standing in Europe. *Open all year, daily, dawn-dusk. (K22)*

### Hadleigh
**◉ Hadleigh Castle**
Tel: (01760) 755161
Familiar from Constable's painting, the castle stands on a bluff overlooking the Leigh Marshes with a single, large 50-ft tower and 13thC and 14thC remains. *Open at any reasonable time. (O24)*

### Harwich
**Harwich Redoubt Fort**
Behind 29 Main Road
Tel: (01255) 503429
An anti-Napoleonic circular fort commanding the harbour. Eleven guns on battlements. *Open 3 Jan-25 Apr, Sun, 1000-1200, 1400-1600; 1 May-31 Aug, daily, 1000-1700; 5 Sep-19 Dec, Sun, 1000-1200, 1400-1600. £1.00/free/£1.00. (U/V18)*

### Little Tey
**St James the Less Church**
Church Lane
A 12thC church with 13thC and 14thC wall paintings which have been uncovered and conserved without any restoration. They are virtually untouched since their original painting. *Open all year, Thu-Sun, Bank Hol Mon, 0930-dusk. (P19)*

### Mistley
**◉ Mistley Towers**
Tel: (01604) 730325
Two towers designed by Robert Adam in 1776 as part of the parish church. A rare example of Robert Adam's ecclesiastical work. *Open at any reasonable time, key keeper (01206) 393884. (S/T18)*

### Stansted Mountfitchet
**◉ Mountfitchet Castle**
Tel: (01279) 813237
A re-constructed Norman motte-and-bailey castle and village of the Domesday period with a Grand Hall, church, prison, siege tower and weapons. Domestic animals roam the site. *Open 14 Mar-14 Nov, daily, 1000-1730. Please contact for details. (J/K19*

*Bedfordshire ● Essex ● Hertfordshire*

### Tilbury
#### ◎ Tilbury Fort
No 2 Office Block, The Fort
Tel: (01375) 858489

One of Henry VIII's coastal forts, re-modelled and extended in the 17thC in continental style. *Open 1 Jan-19 Mar, Wed-Sun, 1000-1600; 22 Mar-31 Oct, daily, 1000-1800/1800 or dusk in Oct; 1 Nov-31 Dec, Wed-Sun,1000-1600; closed 24-25 Dec. £2.20/£1.10/£1.70. (L/M26)*

### Waltham Abbey
#### Waltham Abbey Church
Highbridge Street
Tel: (01992) 767897

A Norman church, the reputed site of King Harold's tomb. There is a lady chapel with a crypt which houses an exhibition of the history of Waltham Abbey and a shop. *Open daily, Mon, Tue, Thur-Sat, 1000-1600; Wed, 1100-1600; Sun, 1200-1600, 1800 during British Summer Time; closed 25 Dec. (I22)*

### Willingale
#### Willingale Churches
The Street

Two ancient churches in one churchyard, side by side. On site since Norman times. A village setting on the Essex Way. *Open all year, daily, dawn-dusk. (L21)*

## Hertfordshire

### Berkhamsted
#### Berkhamsted Castle
Tel: (01536) 402840

The extensive remains of an 11thC motte-and-bailey castle which was the work of Robert of Mortain, half brother of William of Normandy, who learnt he was king here. *Open all year, daily, 1000-1600, contact the key keeper, Mr Stevens on Tel: (01442) 871737. (C21)*

### Bishop's Stortford
#### ◎ Castle Mound
The Castle Gardens
Tel: (01279) 655261

The remaining mound of a castle built by William I, set in a pleasant spot in the gardens just minutes from the town centre. Key to gate available from Bishop's Stortford Tourist Information Centre. *Open all year except Bank Hols, Mon-Fri, 0930-1530. (J19)*

### Gorhambury
#### Roman Theatre of Verulamium
Tel: (01727) 854051

The only completely exposed Roman theatre in Britain with the remains of a townhouse and underground shrine. *Open 1 Jan-28 Feb , daily, 1000-1600; 1 Mar-31 Oct, daily, 1000-1700; 1 Nov-31 Dec, daily, 1000-1600; closed 25, 26 Dec. £1.50/50p/£1.00. (D21)*

### Hertford
#### ◎ Hertford Castle
10 Market Place
Tel: (01992) 584322

A 15thC Edward IV gatehouse, Mayor's parlour and robing room with 15thC stone, brick and timber screens. The town's insignia is also on display on special open days. *Please contact for details of opening times. (H20)*

### Royston
#### Royston Cave
Melbourn Street

A man-made cave with medieval carvings made by the Knights Templar dated from around the end of the 13thC. Possible secret meeting place for initiations. *Open 3 Apr-26 Sep, Sat, Sun, Bank Hol Mon, 1430-1700. £1.00/free/£1.00. (H16)*

*Cathedral and Abbey Church of St Alban, Hertfordshire*

### St Albans
#### ◎ Cathedral and Abbey Church of St Alban
The Chapter House
Tel: (01727) 860780

A Norman abbey church on the site of the martyrdom of St Alban, Britain's first Christian martyr. The 14thC shrine has been restored and is a centre of ecumenical worship. *Open all year, daily, 0900-1745; closed 25 Dec from 1300. £1.50/£1.00/£1.50. (E21)*

### St Albans
#### Clock Tower
Market Cross
Tel: (01727) 853301

A curfew tower, built in approximately 1405 with small exhibitions on aspects of local history. The belfry and 1866 clock mechanism can be viewed. Fine views from the roof. *Open 3 April-12 Sep, Sat, Sun, Bank Hol Mon, 1030-1700. 25p/10p/25p. (E21)*

### Ware
#### Scott's Grotto
Scott's Road
Tel: (01920) 464131

Grotto (English Heritage) extending 67ft into the hillside, including passages and 6 chambers decorated with fossils, shells, pebbles and flints. Unlit so torches are necessary. *Open 3 Apr-25 Sep, Sat, Bank Hol Mons, 1400-1630. (H20)*

# Museums & heritage Centres

## Bedfordshire

### Bedford
#### ⊕ Bedford Museum
Castle Lane  Tel: (01234) 353323
The Museum has interesting displays of local archaeology, social and natural history and geology and a full programme of exhibitions, children's activities and events. *Open all year, Tue-Sat, 1100-1700; Sun, Bank Hol Mon, 1400-1700; closed 2 Apr, 25, 26 Dec. (D15)*

### Bedford
#### ⊕ Cecil Higgins Art Gallery and Museum
Castle Close, Castle Lane
Tel: (01234) 211222
A Victorian mansion built in 1846 and furnished late 19thC style. A large collection of English watercolours, glass, ceramics and porcelain in modern galleries. *Open all year, Tue-Sat, 1100-1700; Sun, Bank Hol Mon, 1400-1700; closed 2 Apr, 25, 26 Dec, 1 Jan. (D15)*

### Bedford
#### John Bunyan Museum and Bunyan Meeting Free Church
Mill Street  Tel: (01234) 213722
Museum housing the personal effects of John Bunyan (1628-1688) and copies of 'The Pilgrim's Progress' in 169 languages, together with other works by Bunyan. *Open 2 Mar-11 Dec, Tue-Sat, 1100-1600. Donations accepted. (D15)*

*Selection from costume collection, Chelmsford and Essex Museum (photographer Paul Starr)*

### Elstow
#### Elstow Moot Hall
See entry in Historic Houses Section

### Luton
#### ⊕ John Dony Field Centre
Hancock Drive, Bushmead
Tel: (01582) 486983
A natural history site whose facilities include displays featuring local history, natural history, conservation and archaeology. *Open all year, Mon-Fri, 0930-1630; Sun, 0930-1300; closed 25, 26 Dec, 1 Jan, 2-5 Apr. (D19)*

### Luton
#### ⊕ Luton Museum and Art Gallery
Wardown Park  Tel: (01582) 546739
A Victorian mansion set in 50 acres of parkland with costume lace and hat-making displays, Victorian 'street' displays, natural history and the archaeology of South Bedfordshire. *Open all year, Tue-Sat, 1000-1700; Sun, 1300-1700; closed 25, 26 Dec, 1 Jan. Guided tours available by appointment. (D19)*

### Luton
#### Mossman Collection
Stockwood Country Park, Farley Hill
Tel: (01582) 738714
The Mossman Collection is Britain's largest collection of horse-drawn carriages which are displayed in a new purpose-built building. *Open 3 Jan-29 Mar, Sat, Sun, 1000-1600; 31 Mar-31 Oct, Tue-Sat, 1000-1700, Sun, Bank Hol Mon, 1000-1800; 7 Nov-19 Dec, Sat, Sun, 1000-1600. Guided tours available, please contact for details. (D19)*

### Luton
#### ⊕ Stockwood Craft Museum and Gardens
Stockwood Park, Farley Hill
Tel: (01582) 738714
Housed in an 18thC stable block and featuring Bedfordshire craft displays and workshops including a blacksmith, wheelwright, saddler, shoemaker and thatcher. *Open 2 Jan-28 Mar, Sat, Sun, 1000-1600; 1 Apr-31 Oct, Tue-Sat, 1000-1700; Sun, Bank Hol Mon, 1000-1800; 1 Nov-19 Dec, Sat, Sun, 1000-1600; closed 25, 26 Dec. Guided tours available, please contact for details. (D19)*

## Essex

### Basildon
#### Langdon Conservation Centre and Plotland Museum
Third Avenue, Lower Dunton Road
Tel: (01268) 419095
Langdon contains a bungalow which was built in 1934. It illustrates the lifestyle of a family during the war years. The trail route passes the ruins of former homes. *Open 1 Jan-28 Mar, Tue-Sun, 0900-1700; 30 Mar-26 Oct, Tue-Sun, Bank Hol Mon, 0900-1730; 28 Oct-31 Dec, Tue-Sun, 0900-1700, closed 25, 26 Dec. Reserve, all year, daily, dawn-dusk. (M/N24)*

### Billericay
#### ⊕ Barleylands Farm Museum and Visitor Centre
Barleylands Road  Tel: (01268) 282090
A unique visitor's centre comprising a rural museum, animal centre, working craft studios, a glass-blowing studio with a viewing gallery, miniature steam railway and a restaurant. *Open 1 Mar-31 Oct, daily, 1000-1700. £3.00/£1.50/£1.50. (M23)*

### Billericay
#### Cater Museum
74 High Street  Tel: (01277) 622023
A folk museum of bygones with a Victorian sitting room and bedroom. *Open all year, Mon-Sat, 1400-1700; closed Bank Hol Mon, 22-31 Dec. (M23)*

### Bradwell-on-Sea
#### ⊕ Bradwell Power Station and Visitor Centre
Tel: (01621) 873395
Exhibits in the centre on energy production, the environment and nuclear power. Visits are arranged to the reactors and the generating station. *Open 1 Mar-31 Oct, daily, 1000-1600. (R21)*

### Braintree
#### ⊕ Braintree District Museum
Manor Street  Tel: (01376) 325266
`Threads of Time' is a permanent exhibition housed in a converted Victorian school, telling the story of Braintree district and its important place in our history. *Open 2 Jan-9 Apr, Tue-Sat, 1000-1700; 10 Apr-31 Dec, Tue-Sat, Bank Hol Mon, 1000-1700; Sun, 1400-1700; closed 25-26 Dec, 1 Jan. £2.00/£1.00/£1.00. (N19)*

### Brentwood
#### Brandler Galleries
1 Coptfold Road  Tel: (01277) 222269
A gallery selling exhibitions of work by major British artists and prints by European masters at affordable prices. *Open all year, Tue-Sat, 1000-1730; please phone to confirm not closed for an outside show. (L23)*

Get in touch with your past at

Colchester Castle Museum

where you'll find 2000

years of history

all under

one roof!

STRETCH YOUR
**IMAGINATION**

COLCHESTER

See yourself as a Norman soldier
See how Boudica took her revenge on the Romans

**See it**

Eavesdrop on a 'witch's' confession
Listen to the Romans as they await their fate
at the hands of Boudica

**Hear it**

Feel the weight of Roman armour
Smell the aromas of a
17th century apothecary shop

**Do it**

Discover why Colchester was chosen
as the first capital of Roman Britain
Find out what the Castle looked like when it was first built

**Know it!**

Enquiries &
admission details
☎ 01206 282931/2
Group visits
☎ 01206 282937
Fax
01206 282925

*Open* 10am to 5pm
Monday to Saturday
all year round
*and* 2-5pm
on Sundays from
March to November
Last admission 4.30pm

Colchester **CASTLEMUSEUM**

*Holytrees Museum, Colchester, Essex*

### Brentwood
**Brentwood Museum**
Cemetery Lodge, Lorne Road
Tel: (01277) 224012
A small cottage museum covering social and domestic history with special reference to Brentwood. It includes a 1930s kitchen, toys, games and memorabilia from 2 world wars. *Open 4 Apr-3 Oct, first Sun of each month, 1430-1630. (L23)*

### Brentwood
**⊛ Kelvedon Hatch
Nuclear Bunker**
Kelvedon Hall Lane, Kelvedon Hatch
Tel: (01277) 364883
A large, 3-storey, ex-government regional headquarters buried some 100ft below ground, complete with canteen, BBC studio, dormitories, plant room and plotting floor. *Please contact for details of opening times. £5.00/£3.00/£5.00. (K22/23)*

### Brightlingsea
**Brightlingsea Museum**
1 Duke Street
The maritime and social history museum of Brightlingsea (a limb of the Cinque Port of Sandwich) showing collections relating to the town's Cinque Port connections. *Open 1 Apr-30 Sep, Mon, Thu, 1400-1700; Sat, 1000-1600. 50p/25p/25p. (S20)*

### Burnham-on-Crouch
**Burnham-on-Crouch
and District Museum**
Tucker Brown Boathouse,
Coronation Road,
A small museum devoted to local history with maritime and agricultural features of the Dengie Hundred. *Open 2 Apr-28 Nov, Wed, Sat, 1100-1630; Sun, Bank Hols, 1400-1630. 50p/20p/50p. (Q23)*

### Canvey Island
**Dutch Cottage Museum**
Canvey Road  Tel: (01268) 794005
An early 17thC cottage of one of Vermuyden's Dutch workmen who was responsible for drainage schemes in East Anglia. *Open 31 May-29 Sep, Sun-Wed, 1430-1700; Bank Hol Mon, 1030-1300, 1430-1700. (N/O25)*

### Canvey Island
**Heritage Centre**
Canvey Village, Canvey Road
Tel: (01268) 512220
The Heritage Centre is housed in the now redundant parish church of St Katherine, built in 1876. It contains an art and craft centre and a folk museum. *Open 2 Jan-28 Mar, Sat, Sun, 1200-1500; 3 Apr-31 Oct, Sat, Sun, 1100-1600; 1 Nov-26 Dec, Sat, Sun, 1200-1500. (N/O25)*

### Chelmsford
**⊛ Chelmsford and Essex Museum
& Essex Regiment Museum**
Oaklands Park, Moulsham Street
Tel: (01245) 353066
Permanent collections of fossils and rocks, archaeology, costume, decorative arts, glass, natural history and the Essex Regiment Museum. Temporary exhibition programmes. *Open all year, Mon-Sat, 1000-1700; Sun, 1400-1700; closed 2 Apr, 25, 26 Dec. (M21)*

### Colchester
**⊛ Colchester Castle**
Tel: (01206) 282931
A Norman keep on the foundations of a Roman temple. The archaeological material includes much on Roman Colchester (Camulodunum). *Open 2 Jan-27 Feb, Mon-Sat, 1000-1700; 1 Mar-30 Nov, Mon-Sat, 1000-1700; Sun, 1400-1700; 1-31 Dec, Mon-Sat, 1000-1700; closed 24, 25 Dec. £3.60/£2.30/£2.30. (R19)*

### Colchester
**⊛ Firstsite at the Minories**
74 High Street  Tel: (01206) 577067
A Grade A gallery showing a programme of temporary exhibitions of contemporary art and housed in a converted Georgian house. *Open 2 Jan-31 Mar, Mon-Sat, 1000-1600; 1 Apr-30 Oct, Mon-Sat, 1000-1700; 1 Nov-31 Dec, Mon-Sat, 1000-1600. (R19)*

### Colchester
**⊛ Hollytrees Museum**
High Street  Tel: (01206) 282931
A collection of toys, costume and decorative arts from the 18th-20thC, displayed in an elegant Georgian town house, built in 1718. *Open all year, Tue-Sat, 1000-1200, 1300-1700; 24 Dec, 1000-1200; closed 25 Dec, 1 Jan. (R19)*

*Cecil Higgins
Art Gallery
and Museum,
Bedford*

*Barleylands Farm Museum and Visitors Centre, Billericay, Essex*

### Colchester
#### ⊛ Natural History Museum
All Saints Church, High Street
Tel: (01206) 282932

A 13thC church housing the natural history of Colchester and Essex with dioramas. Recently re-displayed to a high standard with 'hands-on' activities for children. *Open all year, Tue-Sat, 1000-1300, 1400-1700; 24 Dec, 1000-1200; closed 25 Dec, 1 Jan. (R19)*

### Colchester
#### ⊛ Tymperleys Clock Museum
Trinity Street  Tel: (01206) 282931

A fine collection of Colchester-made clocks from the Mason collection, displayed in a 15thC timber-framed house which Bernard Mason restored and presented to the town. *Open 1 Apr-30 Oct, Tue-Sat, 1000-1200, 1300-1700. (R19)*

### Dedham
#### Dedham Art and Craft Centre
High Street  Tel: (01206) 322666

A Constable Country converted redbrick church in this famous Dedham village with 3 floors of craft units, resident artists, workshops, galleries and a small toy museum. *Open 1 Jan, 1200-1700; 2 Jan-31 Mar, Tue-Sun, 1000-1700; 1 Apr-31 Dec, daily, 1000-1700; closed 25-27 Dec; Toy Museum, please phone for details. 50p/30p/30p. (S17/18)*

### Dedham
#### The Sir Alfred Munnings Art Museum
Castle House, Castle Hill
Tel: (01206) 322127

The house, studio and grounds where Sir Alfred Munnings, KCVO, lived and painted for 40 years. The collection also includes pictures on loan from private collections. *Open 2 May-28 Jul, Wed, Sun, Bank Hol Mon, 1400-1700; 1-29 Aug, Wed, Thu, Sat, Sun, 1400-1700; 1 Sep-3 Oct, Wed, Sun, Bank Hol Mon, 1400-1700. £3.00/50p/£2.00. (S17/18)*

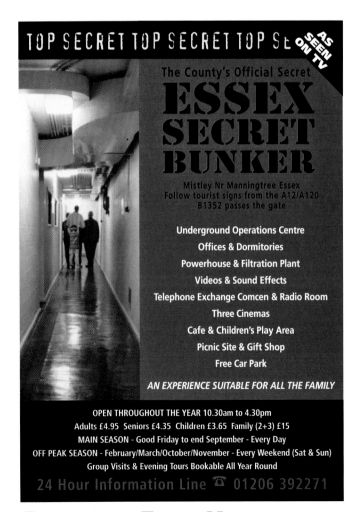

*Ha'penny Pier Visitors Centre, Harwich, Essex*

### Dedham
### ⊛ Toy Museum
Dedham Centre, High Street
Tel: (01206) 322666
A collection of dolls, teddies, toys, games, play houses and pictures displayed in a section of the beautifully converted church with a 'touch and try' corner. *Open 2 Jan-31 Mar, Wed, Sat, Sun, 1000-1700; 1 Apr-31 Dec, Wed-Sun, 1000-1700; open daily during school hols; closed 25, 26, Dec, 1 Jan. 50p/30p/30p. (S17/18)*

### Finchingfield
### Finchingfield Guildhall
See entry in Historic Houses section.

### Grays
### Thurrock Museum
Thameside Complex, Orsett Road
Tel: (01375) 382555
An interesting display of artefacts, maps and models showing Thurrock's history from prehistoric to modern times. *Please contact for details of opening times. (L26)*

### Great Bardfield
### Bardfield Cage
Bridge Street
Great Bardfield cage is a 19thC village lock-up. *Open 27 Mar-26 Sep, Sat, Sun, Bank Hol Mon, 1400-1730. (M18)*

### Great Bardfield
### Cottage Museum
Dunmow Road
A 16thC charity cottage with a collection of mainly 19th and 20thC domestic and agricultural artefacts and some rural crafts. Mainly straw plaiting and corn dollies. *Open 27 Mar-26 Sep, Sat, Sun, Bank Hol Mon, 1400-1730. (M18)*

### Harlow
### Harlow Museum
Passmores House, Third Avenue
Tel: (01279) 454959
Museum housing 5 galleries covering the history and geology of the area. Also a temporary exhibition gallery. *Open all year, Thu, Fri, 1000-1645; Sat, 1000-1230, 1330-1645; closed 23 Dec-6 Jan. (I/J21)*

### Harlow
### Harlow Study and Visitors Centre
Netteswellbury Farm
Tel: (01279) 446745
A visitor's centre in a medieval tithe barn containing an exhibition telling Harlow's 'New Town' story. The Study Centre is housed in a 13thC church. *Open all year, Mon, Wed, Thu, 0930-1600; closed Bank Hol Mon. (I/J21)*

### Harwich
### Ha'penny Pier Visitor Centre
The Quay
Visitor Information Centre for everything in Harwich with a small local history exhibition. *Open 1 May-31 Aug, daily, 1000-1700. (U/V18)*

### Harwich
### Harwich Lifeboat Museum
Timberfields, off Wellington Road
The Lifeboat Museum contains the last Clacton off-shore 37ft lifeboat, the Oakley class and a fully-illustrated history of the lifeboat service in Harwich. *Open 1 May-31 Aug, daily, 1000-1700; 5-26 Sep, Sun, 1000-1200, 1400-1700. 50p/50p. (U/V18)*

### Harwich
### Harwich Maritime Museum
Low Lighthouse, The Green
Tel: (01255) 503429
A museum with special displays related to the Royal Navy and commercial shipping with fine views over the unending shipping movements in the harbour. *Open 4-25 Apr, Sun, 1000-1200, 1400-1700; 1 May-31 Aug, daily, 1000-1700; 5-26 Sep, Sun, 1000-1200, 1400-1700. 50p/free/50p. (U/V18)*

### Kelvedon
### Feering and Kelvedon Local History Museum
Maldon Road
Tel: (01376) 570307
A museum containing artefacts from the Roman settlement of Camonium, manorial history, agricultural tools and bygones. *Open 3 Jan-21 Feb, Sat, 1000-1230; 1 Mar-25 Oct, Mon, 1400-1700, Sat, 1000-1230; 6 Nov-26 Dec, Sat, 1000-1230; closed Bank Hol Mon. (P19/20)*

*Dedham Toy Museum, Essex*

*House on the Hill Toy Museum,*
*Stansted Mountfitchet, Essex*

### Leigh-on-Sea
**Leigh Heritage Centre**
13A High Street  Tel: (01702) 470834
A photographic exhibition with historical, interpretative displays, Granny's kitchen and a number of local artefacts. *Open all year, daily, 1100-1500; (subject to volunteers); closed 25 Dec. (P24/25)*

### Linford
**Walton Hall Farm Museum**
Walton Hall Road  Tel: (01375) 671874
The main collection is housed in a 17thC English barn and other farm buildings. *Open 28 Mar-23 Dec, Thu-Sun, school holidays, 1000-1700. £3.00/£1.50/£1.50. (M25/26)*

### Lindsell
**Lindsell Art Gallery**
Old Crown House  Tel: (01371) 870777
An art gallery specialising in paintings, prints and greetings cards by local artists. The pictures are largely of local interest. *Open all year, daily, 0900-1800; closed 25-31 Dec. (L18/19)*

### Maldon
**Maeldune Centre**
Plume Building, Junc of Market Hill and High Street  Tel: (01621) 851628
The Maeldune Centre has changing exhibitions of paintings and local history. It also contains Maldon Embroidery and a tour of Moot Hall can be undertaken by prior arrangement. *Open 2 Jan-31 Mar, Mon-Sat, 1030-1630; 1 Apr-30 Sep, daily, 1030-1630; 1 Oct-31 Dec, Mon-Sat, 1030-1630; closed 24, 27-31 Dec, 1 Jan. £1.50/75p/75p. (P21/22)*

### Maldon
**Maldon District Museum**
47 Mill Road  Tel: (01621) 842688
A small museum devoted to Maldon town with many articles of a general and domestic nature in a charming, small Listed building. *Open 1 Mar-29 Nov, Wed, 1400-1600; Thu, 1400-1600; Sat, 1300-1700; Sun, 1300-1700. £1.00/50p/50p. (P21/22)*

### Maldon
**Maldon Embroidery**
The Maeldune Centre, High Street
Tel: (01621) 851628
Embroidery in 7 panels depicting 1000 years of Maldon's history. The embroidery was produced to commemorate the 1000th anniversary of the Battle of Maldon. *Open all year, daily, 1030-1615. £1.50/75p/75p. (P21/22)*

### Manningtree
**Manningtree and District Local History Museum**
Manningtree Library, High Street
Tel: (01206) 392747
A local history museum with displays of old photographs, artefacts, books, local maps and plans. Some permanent displays with 2 major exhibitions of local interest yearly. *Open all year, Fri, 1000-1200, 1400-1600; Sat, 1000-1200; closed 2 Apr. (S18)*

### Mistley
**⊛ Essex Secret Bunker**
Crown Building, Shrublands Road
Tel: (01206) 392271
Former Essex county nuclear war headquarters bunker with operation rooms, communications rooms, a command centre, cinema with authentic film and an AV theatre presentation. *Open 6 Feb-28 Mar, Sat, Sun, 1030-1630; 2 Apr-30 Sep, daily, 1030-1630; 2 Oct-28 Nov, Sat, Sun, 1030-1630. £4.95/£3.65/£4.35. (S/T18)*

*Dedham Art and Craft Centre, Essex*

### Purfleet
**Purfleet Heritage and Military Centre**
Royal Gunpowder Magazine,
Centurion Way  Tel: (01708) 866764
The Royal Gunpowder Magazine dates from 1760. The Heritage Centre displays local history, photographs, artefacts and 1939-1945 memorabilia. *Open 3, 4, 17, 18 Apr, 1, 2, 15, 16 May, 5, 6, 19, 20 Jun, 3, 4, 17, 18 Jul, 7, 8, 21, 22 Aug, 4, 5, 18, 19 Sep, 2, 3, 16, 19 Oct, 1000-1630. £1.00/25p/£1.00. (K25/26)*

### Saffron Walden
**Fry Public Art Gallery**
Bridge End Gardens, Castle Street
Tel: (01799) 513779
A permanent exhibition of 20thC British artists who have lived and worked in north west Essex. Two or three changing exhibitions additionally are on show in parallel. *Open 4 Apr-31 Oct, Sat, Sun, Bank Hol Mon, 1445-1730. (K17)*

### Saffron Walden
**⊛ Saffron Walden Museum**
Museum Street  Tel: (01799) 510333
A friendly, family-sized museum of local history, decorative arts, ethnography with the Great Hall gallery of archaeology and early history and an ancient Egyptian room and tomb. *Please contact for details of opening times. £1.00/free/50p. (K17)*

*Prittelwell Priory, Southend-on-Sea, Essex*

### Southend-on-Sea
### ⊛ Central Museum and Planetarium
Victoria Avenue  Tel: (01702) 215131
An Edwardian building housing displays of archaeology, natural history, social and local history. Also housing the only planetarium in south east England outside London. *Open all year, Mon-Sat, except Bank Hol Mon, 1000-1700; closed 2, 5 Apr, 27, 28, 31 Dec. £2.15/£1.60/£1.60. (P24)*

### Southend-on-Sea
### ⊛ Prittlewell Priory
Priory Park, Victoria Avenue
Tel: (01702) 342878
The remains of a 12thC priory with later additions housing displays of natural history, medieval religious life, radios, gramophones and televisions. *Open all year, Tue-Sat, 1000-1300, 1400-1700; closed 10 Apr, 25-27 Dec, 1 Jan. (P24)*

### Southend-on-Sea
### Southend Pier Museum
Southend Pier, Marine Parade
Tel: (01702) 611214
Situated in redundant pier workshops underneath the pier station (shore end). Depicts the history of the longest pier in the world from 1830. Pictures and antique slot machines. *Open 4 May-30 Oct, Fri-Mon, 1100-1700; school hol, 1100-1800; 26 Dec, 1200-1600. 50p/free/50p. ( P24)*

### Southend-on-Sea
### Southend Planetarium
Central Museum, Victoria Avenue
Tel: (01702) 215131
The only public planetarium in the south east outside London. The projector provides a clear illusion of the night sky with stars and the Milky Way which lasts 40 minutes. *Open all year, Wed-Sat, 1000-1600; pre-booked groups have priority; closed 2 Apr, 25, 26 Dec. £2.15/£1.60/£1.60. (P24)*

### Southend-on-Sea
### ⊛ Southchurch Hall Museum
Southchurch Hall Gardens,
Southchurch Hall Close
Tel: (01702) 467671
A moated, timber-framed 14thC manor-house set in attractive gardens with rooms laid out in medieval, Tudor and Victorian period settings. *Open all year, Tue-Sat, 1000-1300, 1400-1700; preference given to schools in the morning; closed 2, 5 Apr, 25, 26 Dec, 1 Jan. (P24)*

### Stansted Mountfitchet
### ⊛ House on the Hill Toy Museum
Tel: (01279) 813237
An exciting, animated toy museum covering 7,000 sq ft and featuring a huge collection of toys from Victorian times to the 1970s. Offers a nostalgic trip back to childhood. *Open 14 Jan-14 Dec, daily, 1000-1730. Please contact for details of admission prices. (J/K19)*

### Thaxted
### Thaxted Guidhall
Town Street  Tel: (01371) 831339
A 15thC building housing a permanent display of old photographs and relics, mainly relating to the history of Thaxted. Exhibitions on some weekends and a small museum. *Open 28 Mar-26 Sep, Sat, Sun, Bank Hol Mon, 1400-1800. 25p/10p/25p. (L18)*

### Tiptree
### Tiptree Tearoom, Museum and Shop
Wilkin and Sons Ltd
Tel: (01621) 815407
Tearoom and shop with a museum displaying how life was and how the art of jam-making has advanced over the years at Tiptree. *Open 5 Jan-30 Jun, Mon-Sat, 1000-1700; 4 Apr, 1000-1700; 1 Jul-31 Aug, daily, 1000-1700; 1 Sep-24 Dec, Mon-Sat, 1000-1700. (P20)*

### Waltham Abbey
### Epping Forest District Museum
39-41 Sun Street  Tel: (01992) 716882
Tudor and Georgian timber-framed buildings with a herb garden, a Tudor-panelled room, temporary exhibitions, the social history of Epping Forest and many special events. *Open all year, Mon, Fri-Sun, 1400-1700; Tue, 1200-1700. (I22)*

### Walton-on-the-Naze
### Walton Maritime Museum
East Terrace
A 100-year-old former lifeboat house, carefully restored with exhibitions of local interest particularly maritime, urban, geological seaside and development. *Open 2-5 Apr, Fri-Mon, 1300-1500; 1 Jul-30 Sep, daily, 1400-1600; 3-31 Oct, Sat, Sun, 1400-1600. 50p/free/50p. (V19)*

### Westcliff-on-Sea
### ⊛ Beecroft Art Gallery
Station Road  Tel: (01702) 347418
An Edwardian building with panoramic estuary views which houses a permanent collection of works of art plus a varied programme of temporary exhibitions. *Open all year, Tue-Sat, 0930-1300; 1400-1700; closed 2, 5 Apr, 27, 28, 31 Dec. (P24)*

### West Mersea
### Mersea Island Museum
High Street  Tel: (01206) 385191
Museum of local, social and natural history with displays of methods and equipment used in fishing and wildfowling. Fossils and a mineral display. Also special exhibitions. *Open 2 May-30 Sep, Wed-Sun, Bank Hol Mon, 1400-1700. 50p/25p/25p. (R20)*

# Hertfordshire

### Ashwell
### Ashwell Village Museum
Swan Street
A collection of village bygones and agricultural implements set in a small but interesting timber building. *Open all year, Sun, Bank Hol Mon, 1430-1700; closed 27 Dec. £1.00/25p/£1.00. (G16)*

### Bishop's Stortford
### Rhodes Memorial Museum and Commonwealth Centre
South Road  Tel: (01279) 651746
The birthplace of Cecil John Rhodes with 2 Victorian villas made to look as one. Fifteen rooms with photographs and memorabilia of Rhodes' life and times, refurbished in 1992. *Open all year, Tue-Sat, 1000-1600; closed Bank Hols, 25 Dec, 1 Jan. £1.00/free/50p. (J19)*

*House on the Hill Toy Museum, Stansted Mountfitchet, Essex*

*Southchurch Hall, Southend-on-Sea, Essex*

### Hatfield
**Mill Green Museum and Mill**

Mill Green  Tel: (01707) 271362

An 18thC watermill, restored to working order, with a museum in the adjoining miller's house displaying local and social history, archaeology, craft tools and a Victorian kitchen. *Open all year, Tue-Fri, 1000-1700; Sat, Sun, Bank Hol Mon, 1400-1700. Donations welcome. (F21)*

### Hertford
**⊛ Hertford Museum**

18 Bull Plain  Tel: (01992) 582686

A 17thC building with main exhibits on the archaeology, natural and local history of Hertfordshire with a collection of Hertfordshire Regiment regalia and changing exhibitions. *Open all year, Tue-Sat, 1000-1700; closed 2 Apr, 24-28 Dec. (G/H20)*

### Hitchin
**Hitchin Museum and Art Gallery**

Paynes Park  Tel: (01462) 434476

A converted 19thC house on 2 floors with displays of costume, local history, a Victorian chemist's shop, a physic garden and temporary art exhibitions. *Open all year, Mon-Sat, 1000-1700; Sun, 1400-1630; closed Bank Hol Mon, 24-27 Dec, 1 Jan. (E/F18)*

### Hoddesdon
**Lowewood Museum**

High Street  Tel: (01992) 445596

A Georgian house with a museum on the first floor with local artefacts concerning Broxbourne Borough along with temporary exhibitions. *Open all year, Wed, Fri, Sat, 1000-1600; closed 25,26 Dec, 2 Apr. (H/I21)*

### Letchworth
**First Garden City Heritage Museum**

296 Norton Way South
Tel: (01462) 482710

A museum housing displays relating to the Garden City movement and the social history of Letchworth including a collection of Parker and Unwin architectural drawings. *Open all year, Mon-Sat, 1000-1700; closed 25 Dec. (F18)*

### Letchworth
**Letchworth Museum**

Broadway  Tel: (01462) 685647

A museum which features local natural history, archaeological displays and a programme of temporary exhibitions. *Open all year, Mon-Sat, 1000-1700; closed Bank Hols. (F18)*

### Rickmansworth
**Batchworth Lock Canal Centre**

99 Church Street  Tel: (01923) 778382

A canal information centre about restoration of narrow boat 'Roger' being undertaken over 3-year period. Canal history, shop and 'Roger' exhibition. Explore the working boat cabin. *Open 1 Mar-30 Apr, Mon, Tue, Thu, Fri, 1000-1700; 1 May-30 Sep, Mon, Tue, Thu, Fri, 1000-1500; Sat, Sun, 1200-1700; 1-29 Oct, Mon, Tue, Thu, Fri, 1000-1700. (D23)*

### Royston
**Royston and District Museum**

Lower King Street  Tel: (01763) 242587

An old Sunday school converted to a museum housing local history and archaeology. The Royston tapestry and the Hertfordshire collection of ceramics and glass. *Open all year, Wed, Thu, Sat, 1000-1700; 7 Mar-24 Oct, Sun, Bank Hol Mon, 1400-1700. (H16)*

### St Albans
**⊛ Museum of St Albans**

Hatfield Road  Tel: (01727) 819340

Purpose-built as a museum in 1898, displays include craft tools and local and natural history telling the St Albans story from Roman times to the present day. Wildlife garden. *Open all year, Mon-Sat, 1000-1700; Sun, 1400-1700; closed 25, 26 Dec. (E21)*

### St Albans
**Saint Albans Organ Museum**

320 Camp Road  Tel: (01727) 851557

A collection of organs by Mortier, DeCap, Bursens, Weber and Steinway, duo-art reproducing pianos, Mills violano-virtuoso music boxes and Wurlitzer and Rutt theatre pipe organs. *Open all year, Sun, 1400-1630. £2.00/60p/£1.50. (E21)*

### St Albans
**⊛ Verulamium Museum**

St Michaels  Tel: (01727) 819339

The museum of everyday life in Roman Britain. Award-winning displays of re-created Roman rooms, 'hands-on' areas and videos of coins to coffins and mosaics to mercury. *Please contact for details of opening times. £2.80/£1.60/£1.60. (E21)*

### Stevenage
**Stevenage Museum**

St George's Way  Tel: (01438) 218881

A lively award-winning museum which tells the story of Stevenage from the Stone Age to the present. Displays include a 1950s living room and a programme of exhibitions. *Open all year, Mon-Sat, 1000-1700; closed Bank Hol Mon. (F/G19)*

### Ware
**Ware Museum**

The Priory Lodge, 89 High Street
Tel: (01920) 487848

An independent museum featuring the 'Story of Ware' from the Roman town through the malting industry of the 18th-20thC and modern times. *Open 10 Jan-28 Mar, Sat, 1100-1600; Sun, 1400-1600; 4 Apr-24 Oct, Sat, 1100-1700; Sun, 1400-1600; Bank Hol Mon, 1400-1700; 6 Nov-26 Dec, Sat, 1100-1600; Sun, 1400-1600; 1 Jan, 1400-1600. (H20)*

### Watford
**Watford Museum**

194 High Street  Tel: (01923) 232297

A museum building, built in 1775 with displays of local history, brewing, printing and archaeology, local art school exhibits in the art gallery and changing exhibitions. *Open all year, Mon-Fri, 1000-1700; Sat, 1000-1300, 1400-1700; 24 Dec, 1000-1200; 31 Dec, 1000-1300; closed 10, 13 Apr, 25, 26 Dec, 1 Jan. (D23)*

### Welwyn
**Welwyn Roman Baths**

Welwyn Bypass  Tel: (01707) 271362

The baths are a small part of a villa which was built at the beginning of the 3rdC AD and occupied for over 150 years. The villa had at least 4 buildings. *Open all year, Sat, Sun, Bank Hol Mon, 1400-1700/dusk; school holidays, daily, 1400-1700/dusk, except December. £1.00/free/£1.00. (F20)*

# machinery & transport

*Baby Peugeot, Shuttleworth Collection, Bedfordshire*

## Bedfordshire

### Biggleswade

ⓦ **Shuttleworth Collection**
Old Warden Aerodrome
Tel: (01767) 627288

A unique historical collection of aircraft from a 1909 Bleriot to a 1942 Spitfire in flying condition and cars dating from an 1898 Panhard in running order. *Open 1 Jan-31 Mar, daily 1000-1600; 1 Apr-31 Oct, daily 1000-1700; 1 Nov-31 Dec, daily, 1000-1600; please phone for Christmas and New Year opening. £6.00/£4.00/£4.00. (F16)*

*Working Silk Museum, Braintree, Essex*

### Leighton Buzzard

ⓦ **Leighton Buzzard Railway**
Page's Park Station, Billington Road
Tel: (01525) 373888

A preserved industrial railway with steam locomotives from around the world and a diesel collection. This 2ft-gauge railway, built in 1919, offers a return trip of 5.5 miles. *Please contact for details of opening times. £4.50/£1.50/£3.50. (B19)*

### Lower Stondon

ⓦ **Stondon Museum**
Station Road  Tel: (01462) 850339

A museum with transport exhibits from the early 1900s to the 1980s. The largest private collection in England of bygone vehicles from the beginning of the century. *Open all year, daily, 1000-1700; closed 24 Dec-2 Jan. £3.00/£1.00/£3.00. (E17)*

## Essex

### Audley End
**Audley End Miniature Railway**
Tel: (01799) 541354

Steam and diesel locomotives in 10.5 gauge, running through attractive woodland for 1.5 miles. The railway crosses the River Cam twice. *Open 10-19 Apr, 25-31 May, daily, 1400-1700; 6 Jun-18 Jul, Sat, Sun, 1400-1700; 20 Jul-31 Aug, daily, 1400-1700; 5 Sep-17 Oct, Sat, Sun, 1400-1700; 12, 13, 19, 20 Dec, Santa Specials from 1100. £2.00/£1.00/£2.00. (K17)*

### Billericay
ⓦ **Barleylands Farm Museum and Visitor Centre**
See entry in Museums section.

### Braintree
ⓦ **The Working Silk Museum**
New Mills, South Street
Tel: (01376) 553393

The country's last remaining hand-loom silk weavers, using 150-year-old hand looms. See how silk fabric is produced from the raw material to the finished cloth. *Open all year, Mon-Fri except Bank Hols, 1000-1230, 1330-1700. £3.20/£1.70/£2.00. (N19)*

*Shuttleworth Collection, Bedfordshire*

### Burnham-on-Crouch
**Mangapps Railway Museum**
Tel: (01621) 784898
A large collection of railway relics, 2 restored stations, locomotives, coaches and wagons with a working railway line of 0.75 miles. *Please contact for details of opening times. £3.50/£2.00/£3.50. (Q23)*

### Canvey Island
**Canvey Railway and Model Engineering Club**
Waterside Farm Leisure Centre
Two miniature railways. One live steam and one live steam and diesel. *Open 4 Apr, 1000-1700; 2 May-26 Sep, Sun, 1000-1700. (N/O25)*

### Canvey Island
**Castle Point Transport Museum Society**
105 Point Road
Tel: (01268) 684272
A 1935 museum housing a collection of buses, coaches and commercial vehicles in restored condition. Some examples of these vehicles are unique and some are now being restored. *Open 4 Apr-24 Oct, Sun, 1000-1700. (N/O25)*

### Castle Hedingham
**⊛ Colne Valley Railway**
Yeldham Road
Tel: (01787) 461174
An award-winning station. Ride in the most pleasant part of the Colne Valley. A large, interesting collection of operational heritage rolling stock. *Open 1 Mar-23 Dec, daily, 1000-1700/dusk. £2.00/£1.00/£2.00. (O17)*

### Colchester
**⊛ East Anglian Railway Museum**
Chappel Station
Tel: (01206) 242524
A large and varied collection of working and static railway exhibits from the age of steam, set in original surroundings of a once-important Victorian country junction station. *Open all year, daily, 1000-1700; closed 25 Dec. £4.50/£2.50/£3.50. (P18)*

### Epping
**North Weald Airfield**
Tel: (01992) 523010
The ground floor of a fine old house at the former main gate of North Weald Airfield. *Open all year, Sat, Sun, 1200-1600. £1.00/50p/75p. (J22)*

### Goldhanger
**Maldon and District Agricultural and Domestic Museum**
47 Church Street
Tel: (01621) 788647
An extensive collection of farm machinery, domestic items of every kind, products of Maldon Ironworks, printing machines from 1910, a display of photographs and stuffed birds. *Open 4 Apr-31 Oct, Wed, 1400-1800; Sun, Bank Hol Mon, 1000-1800. £1.00/75p/75p. (P21)*

### Harlow
**Mark Hall Cycle Museum**
Off First Avenue, Muskham Road
Tel: (01279) 439680
A unique collection of over 60 cycles and accessories illustrating the history of the bicycle from 1818-1980s, housed in a converted stable block. *Open all year, Tue, Wed, 1000-1630; 3, 17, Jan, 7, 21 Feb, 7, 21 Mar, 4, 18 Apr, 2, 16 May, 6, 20 Jun, 4, 18 Jul, 1, 15 Aug, 5, 19 Sep, 3, 17, Oct, 7, 14 Nov, 5, 19 Dec, Sun, 1100-1600. £2.00/£1.25/£1.25. (I/J21)*

### Pitsea
**National Motorboat Museum**
Wat Tyler Country Park
Tel: (01268) 581093
A museum devoted to the history and evolution of the motorboat racing hydroplanes, powerboats and leisure boats with racing trophies. *Open all year, Thu-Sun, 1000-1630; closed 24 Dec-1 Jan. (N/O24)*

### St Osyth
**East Essex Aviation Society and Museum**
Martello Tower, Point Clear
An exhibition of aircraft parts from local recoveries. There are also displays from World War I up to the late 1940s housed in a 19thC Martello tower. *Open all year, Sun, 1000-1400; Mon, 1900-2200; 2 Jun-29 Sep, Wed, 1000-1400; Sun Bank Hols, 1000-1600. (T20)*

## Hertfordshire

### London Colney
**Mosquito Aircraft Museum**
PO Box 107, Salisbury Hall
Tel: (01727) 822051
Museum showing the restoration and preservation of a range of De Havilland aircraft including the first Mosquito. There are also engines, propellers, missiles and memorabilia. *Open 2 Mar-31 Oct, Tue, Thu, Sat, 1400-1730; Sun, Bank Hol Mon, 1030-1730. £4.00/£2.00/£2.00. (E/F22)*

*East Anglian Railway Museum, Chappel Station, Essex*

## Bedfordshire

### Bromham

#### ⚙ Bromham Mill
Stagsden Road (Bridge End)
Tel: (01234) 824135
Restored watermill in working condition. Static displays of machinery and interpretation of waterways and milling. Art gallery, craft sales, natural history room and picnic site. *Open 3 Mar-31 Oct, Wed-Sat, 1200-1600; Sun, Bank Hol Mon, 1030-1700; last admission 30 mins before closing. £1.50/50p/75p. (C15)*

### Stevington

#### ⚙ Stevington Windmill
Tel: (01234) 228135
A fully-restored 18thC postmill. Entry is via keys which are available from the pubs in the village for a small returnable deposit. *Open all year, daily, collect keys from the pubs in the village. (C14/15)*

## Essex

### Aythorpe Roding

#### ⚙ Aythorpe Roding Postmill
Tel: (01621) 828162
An 18thC postmill restored to working order. *Open 25 Apr, 9, 30 May, 27 Jun, 25 Jul, 29 Aug, 26 Sep, 1400-1700. (K/L20)*

### Colchester

#### ⚙ Bourne Mill
Bourne Road Tel: (01206) 572422
A 16thC fishing lodge converted into a mill with the machinery now in working order. There is also a cottage garden. *Open 4, 5 Apr, 2, 3, 30, 31 May, 29, 30 Aug, 1400-1730; 1 Jun-29 Aug, Tue, Sun, 1400-1730. £1.50/75p/£1.50. (R19)*

### Finchingfield

#### ⚙ Finchingfield (Duck End) Postmill
Tel: (01621) 828162
A small, simple, mid-18thC feudal or 'estate'-type postmill with a wooden wind shaft and 1 pair of stones. *Open 18 Apr-19 Sep, 3rd Sun of each month, 1400-1700; 9 May, Sun, 1400-1700 (National Mills Day). (M18)*

### Mountnessing

#### ⚙ Mountnessing Windmill
Roman Road Tel: (01621) 828162
An early 19thC postmill restored to working order. Visitors may climb the windmill and see the fascinating wooden machinery. *Open 9,16 May, 20 Jun, 18 Jul, 15 Aug, 19 Sep, 17 Oct, 1400-1700. (L/M22)*

### Rayleigh

#### Rayleigh Windmill and Museum
Rear of Mill Hall, Bellingham Lane
Tel: (01268) 774897
A windmill with sails but no mechanism on the ground floor. The museum has local artefacts. The upper floors of the mill are not open. *Open 3 Apr-25 Sep, Sat, 1030-1300. 20p/10p/20p. (O24)*

### Stock

#### ⚙ Stock Towermill
Mill Lane Tel: (01621) 828162
A 19thC towermill, recently restored to working order. *Open 11 Apr, 9 May, 13 Jun, 11 Jul, 8 Aug, 12 Sep, 10 Oct, 1400-1700. (M22)*

*Finchingfield (Duck End) Post Mill, Essex*

### Thaxted

#### John Webb's Windmill
Mill Row Tel: (01371) 830285
The windmill has 4 floors of mill which can be explored. The main machinery is intact and on view. There is a rural museum on the two lower floors. *Open 1 May-26 Sep, Sat, Sun and Bank Hol Mon, 1400-1800. 50p/25p/50p. (L18)*

### Thorrington

#### ⚙ Thorrington Tidemill
Brightlingsea Road Tel: (01621) 828162
An early 19thC tidal watermill, restored by Essex County Council. *Open 28 Mar, 2-5, 25 Apr, 3, 30, 31 May, 27 Jun, 25 Jul, 29, 30 Aug, 26 Sep, Sun, Bank Hol, 1400-1700. (S19/20)*

## Hertfordshire

### St Albans

#### ⚙ Kingsbury Watermill
St Michael's Street Tel: (01727) 853502
A 16thC watermill with working machinery, a collection of farm implements, an art gallery and gift shop. There is also the Waffle House tearoom and restaurant. *Please contact for details of opening times. £1.20/60p/80p. (E21)*

This countryside provides just the conditions for growing watercress and roses. Watercress might have limited appeal, but who can fail to be inspired by the wonderful Gardens of the Rose, where some 30,000 roses form a beautiful garden.

The gardens of Hatfield House are fabulous. They are developed following traditions of design, and using organic methods. The RHS Garden has a woodland garden, spring bulbs, ornamental ponds, shrubs and herbaceous borders, all designed and grown to the high standards you would expect from the Royal Horticultural Society.

In a completely different style, the Swiss Garden is a charming and romantic early 19th century landscape garden. Wander among trees and shrubs from all over the world and enjoy ponds, a fernery and grotto, statues and a tiny thatched Swiss cottage.

At Stockwood Gardens you can see several periods of gardening, in beautifully re-created examples of Knot, Medieval, Victorian and Italian gardens.

20 acres of garden designed by Harold Peto in 1903 have been restored at the Gardens of Easton Lodge, with features which include a balustraded pool in a sunken garden, a tree house and a Japanese garden.

# Gardens & Vineyards

## Bedfordshire

### Old Warden
#### ☸ The Swiss Garden
Biggleswade Road
Tel: (01767) 627666
An attractive garden dating from the 19thC and taking its name from the tiny Swiss thatched cottage in the centre, restored by Bedfordshire County Council. *Open 3 Jan-28 Feb, Sun, 1100-1500; 1 Mar-28 Sep, Mon-Sat, 1300-1800; Sun, Bank Hols, 1000-1800; 3-31Oct, Sun,1100-1500. £2.50/ £1.25/ £1.25. (E16)*

### Silsoe
#### ☸ Wrest Park Gardens
Wrest Park  Tel: (01525) 860152
One hundred and fifty years of English gardens laid out in the early 18thC including painted pavilion, Chinese bridge, lake, classical temple and Louis XV-style French mansion. *Open 3 Apr-31 Oct, Sat, Sun, Bank Hol Mon, 1000-1800/dusk in Oct. £3.20/£1.60/£2.30. (D17)*

### Woburn
#### ☸ Woburn Abbey
See entry in Historic Houses section.

## Essex
### Abridge
#### BBC Essex Garden
Ongar Road  Tel: (01708) 688581
A garden with decorative shrub beds, seed sowing, flower borders, a vegetable plot, 2 greenhouses, a summerhouse and dahlia area. Also an organic garden and a junior trial plot. *Open all year, daily, 0900-1730; closed 25-29 Dec. (J23)*

### Boxted
#### Carter's Vineyards
Green Lane  Tel: (01206) 271136
Vineyards and a winery with an alternative energy project and a conservation area. Fishing facilities (day licence) are available. *Open 13 Apr-30 Sep, daily, 1100-1700. £2.50/£2.50. (R18)*

### Coggeshall
#### ☸ Grange Barn
See entry in Historic Houses section.

### Coggeshall
#### ☸ Marks Hall Estate and Arboretum
The Thomas Phillips Price Trust,
Estate Office, Marks Hall
Tel: (01376) 563796
A country estate and visitor centre with a tea shop, gift sales, ornamental grounds, lakes, cascades, mature avenues, extensive woodlands and waymarked walks. *Open at any reasonable time; Visitor Centre and Arboretum, 28 Mar-31 Oct, Tue-Fri, 1030-1630, Sat, Sun, Bank Hol Mon, 1030-1800. £3.00 per car. (O/P19)*

### Coggeshall
#### ☸ Paycockes
See entry in Historic Houses section.

### Cressing
#### ☸ Cressing Temple
See entry in
Ancient Monuments section.

### Dunmow
#### Little Easton Manor and Barn Theatre
Park Road  Tel: (01371) 872857
Little Easton Manor has gardens, lakes, fountains, a barn theatre, angling, a caravan and rally site and refreshments. *Open 6 May-23 Sep, Thu, 1300-1700; please contact for further details. £2.00/free/£1.50. (L19)*

## Visit COLCHESTER Castle park

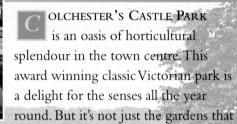

COLCHESTER'S CASTLE PARK is an oasis of horticultural splendour in the town centre. This award winning classic Victorian park is a delight for the senses all the year round. But it's not just the gardens that makes the park such a delight to visit. Castle Park's 33 gently sloping acres (13.5ha) provide the perfect venue for fairs, festivals, open-air concerts and displays.

Variety is the essence of Castle Park. There are formal flower beds and gardens, a Sensory Garden, a children's playground, the Hollytrees toy and costume museum and summertime Pitch & Putt. A magnificent weeping willow provides an impressive backdrop to the children's boating lake and you can take picturesque walks along the river nearby. Stroll up the hill, through the oldest Roman wall in Britain, for a treat in the café near the Victorian bandstand or bring your own picnic.

No trip to Castle Park is complete without a visit to the award-winning Castle Museum, popular for its hands-on displays and holiday events. Visit the Castle Museum and its Roman foundations and discover the major historical events which took place in and around the Castle almost 2000 years ago.

COLCHESTER

FOR FURTHER INFORMATION ABOUT COLCHESTER AND EVENTS IN CASTLE PARK
☞ PLEASE CALL THE COLCHESTER VISITOR INFORMATION CENTRE
1 QUEEN STREET · COLCHESTER · ESSEX · CO1 2PG ☎ 01206 282920

*Saling Hall Garden, Great Saling, Essex*

### Great Leighs
### Rochester Farm
Tel: (01245) 361411

The Great Leighs Maze, set in the countryside. Possibly the worlds largest maze. A great day out for families and individuals alike. *Open 27 Jul-19 Sep, daily, 1000-1900; last admission 1700. £3.50/£2.00/ £2.50. (N20)*

### Great Saling
### Saling Hall Garden
Tel: (01371) 850243

The 17thC house is not open. A 12-acre garden with old walls, fish ponds, water gardens and a well-known landscaped arboretum including many rare trees. *Open 12 May-28 Jul, Wed,1400-1700; 30 May, Sun, 1400-1800. £2.00/free/£2.00. (M18/19)*

### Harlow
### Mark Hall Gardens
Muskham Road, off First Avenue
Tel: (01279) 439680

Three walled gardens developed as an ornamental fruit garden, a 17thC-style garden with a parterre, and a large walled garden demonstrating a number of styles. *Open all year, Mon-Fri, 1000-1530; 1st and 3rd Sun of each month, 1100-1600. (I/J21)*

### Feering
### Feeringbury Manor
Tel: (01376) 561946

A large 6-acre garden with a stream, ponds and the River Blackwater at the bottom of the garden. There are many rare and interesting plants. *Open 6 Apr-1 Aug, Mon-Fri, 0800-1300; closed Bank Hol Mons. Admission to Garden: £2.00/free/£2.00. (P19)*

### Felsted
### Felsted Vineyard
The Vineyards, Crix Green
Tel: (01245) 361504

Showing wine and cider making and vineyard work. Wine and vines may be bought along with other local produce. *Open 1 Apr-30 Sep, Tue-Sun, Bank Hol Mon, 1000-1800; 2 Apr,1200-1430; 9 Oct-19 Dec, Sat, Sun, 1000-1800. (M19)*

### Gosfield
### Gosfield Hall
See entry in Historic Houses section.

### Great Dunmow
### The Gardens of Easton Lodge
Warwick House, Easton Lodge
Tel: (01371) 876979

Gardens created since 1971 on the foundations of Easton Lodge with a courtyard, dovecote, pergolas and forgotten gardens designed by Peto (1903) and now being restored. *Open 2 Apr-24 Oct, Sat, Sun, Bank Hols, 1100-1800; please contact for opening during Feb, Mar for the snowdrop display. £3.30/£1.00/£3.00. (L19)*

### Ingatestone
### ⍟ Ingatestone Hall
See entry in Historic Houses section.

### Layer Marney
### ⍟ Layer Marney Tower
See entry in Historic Houses section.

### Purleigh
### New Hall Vineyards
Chelmsford Road
Tel: (01621) 828343

Guided tours of the vineyards with a trail through the vines and the cellars where wine can be tasted. Also visit the press house with slide shows. See fermentation and bottling. *Open all year, Mon-Fri, 1000-1700; Sat, Sun, 1000-1330. (O/P22)*

*Colchester Castle Park Gardens, Essex*

*RHS Garden, Rettendon, Essex*

### Rettendon
**⊛ R H S Garden**
Hyde Hall  Tel: (01245) 400256
An eight acre garden with all year round interest including greenhouses, roses, flowering shrubs, perennial borders and alpines. *Open 24 Mar-31 Aug, daily, 1100-1800; 1 Sep-31 Oct, daily, 1100-1700. £3.00/70p/£3.00. (N23)*

### Saffron Walden
**⊛ Audley End House and Park**
See entry in Historic Houses section.

### Widdington
**⊛ Priors Hall Barn**
See entry in Historic Houses section.

### Writtle
**⊛ Hylands House**
**Park and Gardens**
See entry in Historic Houses section.

## Hertfordshire

### Ayot St Lawrence
**Shaw's Corner**
See entry in Historic Houses section.

### Frithsden
**Frithsden Vineyard**
Roman Road
Tel: (01442) 864732
A vineyard planted with various grape varieties on a south-facing slope overlooking the village with wine-making equipment. The winery is open, tours and tastings available. *Open all year, Wed-Sat, 1000-1700; Sun, 1200-1500; closed 25, 26 Dec. (C21)*

### Gorhambury
**Gorhambury**
See entry in Historic Houses section.

### Hatfield
**⊛ Hatfield House and Gardens**
See entry in Historic Houses section.

### Hitchin
**Saint Pauls Walden Bury Garden**
Saint Pauls Walden
Tel: (01438) 871218
A formal woodland garden laid out in about 1730 and covering 40 acres with temples, statues, lake, ponds and flower gardens. It was the childhood home of the Queen Mother. *Open 18 Apr, 16 May, 13 Jun, Jul date to be arranged, Sun, 1400-1900. £2.50/50p. (E/F18)*

*Gardens of the Rose, St Albans, Hertfordshire*

### Knebworth
**⊛ Knebworth House,**
**Gardens and Park**
See entry in Historic Houses section.

### St Albans
**⊛ The Gardens of the Rose**
The Royal National Rose Society, Chiswell Green  Tel: (01727) 850461
The Royal National Rose Society's Garden with 27 acres of garden and trial grounds for new varieties of rose. Roses of all types displayed with 1,700 different varieties. *Please contact for details of opening times. £4.00/£1.50/£3.50. (E22)*

### Ware
**⊛ The Priory**
See entry in Historic Houses section.

*Knebworth House, Gardens and Park, Hertfordshire*

*Nurseries*
# &Garden Centres

## Bedfordshire

### nr Henlow Camp
**✿ Stondon Museum and Garden Centre**
Station Road, Lower Stondon,
Nr Henlow Camp SG16 6JN
Tel: (01462) 850339
Transport exhibits from the early 1900's to 1980's and the only garden centre nationally to display Norfolk Greenhouses. Also see entry in Machinery and Transport section on page 135. *(E17)*

## Essex

### Ardleigh
**✿ Notcutts Garden Centres**
Station Road, Ardleigh, Essex
Tel: (01206) 230271

Hatfield Road, Smallford, St. Albans
Tel: (01727) 853224
Notcutts Garden Centres are wonderlands for gardeners. Over 2000 varieties of guaranteed hardy plants. No need to be a specialist. There's plenty of help on hand. Why not spend some time wandering at leisure. There's so much to see - display borders, pools, furniture, stoneware, books, gift ideas and pot plants, plus lots of tips on how to improve your garden. Whatever your interests, there's plenty for you at Notcutts.
Also at
Woodbridge Tel: (01394) 445400
Norwich Tel: (01603) 453155
Peterborough Tel: (01733) 234600

*Ardleigh (R18); St. Albans (F22)*

### Coggeshall
**✿ The Dutch Nursery Garden Centres**
West Street, Coggeshall, Essex
Tel: (01376) 561287
also at
A1000, Brookmans Park Potters Bar,
Hertfordshire Tel: (01707) 653372
Situated in the picturesque town of Coggeshall, The Dutch Nursery with its new shop and plant area has much to interest the keen or even reluctant gardener! Many different varieties of shrubs and trees including more unusual types. Houseplants, cut flowers and seasonal bedding always available. For patio planting our terracotta and container selection takes some beating. Also on site there are extensive water gardens and other retail outlets. Finally, why not stop off at our Flower Pot Coffee Shop for a tea, coffee or light snack. *For further details please phone. (Coggeshall O/P19; Potters Bar F/G22)*

## Hertfordshire

### Great Amwell
**✿ The Van Hage Garden Company**
Great Amwell, Ware SG12 9RP
Tel: (01920) 870811
Fax: (01920) 871861
On A1170 (Junction 25 off M25).
One of Europe's top gardening emporiums offering visitors an outstanding selection of products to meet all gardening requirements. Van Hage's is leisure destination for the whole family with Animal Gardens and Miniature Steam Railway. The term 'garden centre' hardly begins to describe something that's become a complete home, garden, and lifestyle experience in an environment that the whole family enjoys exploring! Disabled, Information, Parking (Ample - FREE) Coaches, WC, Shops, Catering - Hot Meals, Snacks, Beverages, Self-service, Groups (inc. children) welcome. Conference facilities available. Suggested length of visit: 2 hours minimum, 4 hours better. *(H20/21)*

### Potters Bar
**✿ The Dutch Nursery,**
see entry under Coggeshall, Essex

### Smallford
**✿ Notcutts Nurseries**
see entry under Ardleigh, Essex

*family fun*

Drive through the Woburn Safari Park and you can forget about the East of England and believe you are the other side of the world where lions, tigers and monkeys live according to the rules of the wild. Alternatively visit the award-winning Colchester Zoo, with its new elephant kingdom; Spirit of Africa.

For a more gentle experience, two farms side by side at Lee Valley Park show two contrasting styles of farming. One is a modern dairy and arable form, the other an old style farm yard with farm animals. At Woodside Wildfowl Park, you can stroke, handle and feed the farm animals. You can buy eggs and other farm produce and you can even buy animals here.

Have you ever wanted to feel the thrill of drag racing? You can try it here, at the famous Santa Pod raceway. Alternatively there are seaside thrills at the resorts, and at the children's adventure park, Never Never Land, all your favourite fairy tales come alive.

## Bedfordshire

### Dunstable
**Toddler World**
Dunstable Leisure Centre, Court Drive
Tel: (01582) 604307
An indoor adventure play area. *Open all year, daily, 0930-1800; closed 25 Dec. Child £2.50. (C19)*

### Dunstable
**Whipsnade Wild Animal Park**
Zoological Society of London
Tel: (0990) 200123
Whipsnade Wild Animal Park has over 2,500 animals set in 600 acres of beautiful parkland, the Great Whipsnade Railway and free animal demonstrations. *Open 1 Feb-1 Apr, daily, 1000-dusk; 2 Apr-30 Sep, Mon-Sat, 1000-1800; Sun, Bank Hol Mon, 1000-1900; 1-31 Oct, daily, 1000-dusk. Please contact for details of admission prices. (C19)*

### Leighton Buzzard
**Mead Open Farm and Rare Breeds**
Stanbridge Road, Billington
Tel: (01525) 852954
A working farm with a wide range of traditional farm animals and rare breeds, a pet's corner, children's play area and a tearoom. Animals are housed in farm buildings and paddocks. *Open 16 Mar-31 Oct, Tue-Sun, Bank Hol Mon, 1000-1700. £3.00/£2.25/£2.50. (B19)*

### Slip End
**Woodside Farm and Wildfowl Park**
Mancroft Road  Tel: (01582) 841044
A 6-acre park with farm shop, rare breeds, wildlife, farm animals, arts and crafts centre, a children's play area and coffee shop. Also new 'hands-on' operation. *Open all year, Mon-Sat, 0800-1730; closed 25, 26 Dec, 1 Jan. £2.20/£1.70/£1.70. (D20)*

*'Fishing' at the River Stour, Dedham, Eseex*

### Wilden
⚜ **Bedford Butterfly Park**
65 Rennold Road  Tel: (01234) 772773
Set in landscaped haymeadows, park features tropical glasshouse where visitors walk through lush foliage with butterflies flying. Tearoom, gift shop, trails and playground. *Open 1 Mar-30 Nov, Mon-Sat, 1000-1730; Sun, 1000-1700. £4.00/£2.50/£3.00. (D14)*

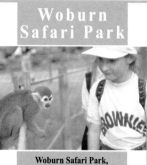

### Woburn
### ✿ Woburn Safari Park

Woburn Park  Tel: (01525) 290407
Drive through the safari park with 30 species of animals in natural groups just a windscreen's width away plus the action-packed Wild World Leisure Area with shows for all. *Open 9 Jan-28 Feb, Sat, Sun, 1100-1500; 3 Mar-1 Nov, daily, 1000-1700; 13 Nov-26 Dec, Sat, Sun, 1100-1500; please contact for Christmas opening times, and for details of admission prices. (B17/18)*

## Essex

### Braintree
### Dorewards Hall Farm

Bocking  Tel: (01376) 324646
Open working farm with farm animals and wildlife. Feature days, dog and horse shows, Christmas festivals. Farm shop and garden centre. Caravan and Camping Club rallies. *Open all year, daily, 0900-1730; closed 25, 26 Dec. (N19)*

### Clacton-on-Sea
### ✿ Clacton Pier
### E and M Harrison (Clacton) Ltd

1 North Sea  Tel: (01255) 421115
The largest fun pier in Europe with 13 fairground rides, arcades, shops, cafes, restaurants, side shows, a pub with children's play area, disco and a sea aquarium. *Open all year, daily, from 1000; closed 25 Dec. ((T/U20)*

*Woburn Safari Park, Bedfordshire*

*Colchester Zoo, Essex*

### Clacton-on-Sea
### SeaQuarium

Clacton Pier, 1 North Sea
Tel: (01255) 422626
SeaQuarium enables visitors to come face-to-face with the world beneath the waves with 15 themed displays showing marine life from around the coast of the UK. *Open 31 Mar-30 Jun, daily, 1000-1700; 1 Jul-31 Aug, daily, 1000-2200; 1 Sep-31 Oct, daily, 1000-1800. £2.50/£1.50/£2.00. (T/U20)*

### Colchester
### ✿ Colchester Zoo

Maldon Road, Stanway
Tel: (01206) 330253
A zoo with 170 species of animals, 40 acres of gardens and lakes, award-winning animal enclosures, picnic areas, a road train, 2 play areas, pony rides and a large soft play area. *Open all year, daily, winter, 0930-1 hour before dusk; summer, 0930-1830; closed 25 Dec. £7.50/£5.25/£5.25. (Q19)*

### Colchester
**Go Bananas**
9-10 Mason Road, Cowdray Centre
Tel: (01206) 761762
A children's indoor adventure playground with a 3-storey play frame for 5-12 year olds, a toddler village and full service cafeteria. *Open all year, daily, 0930-1830; closed 4 Apr, 25, 26, 31 Dec, 1 Jan. Child (under 5) £2.95. (R19)*

### Colchester
**⊛ Quasar at Rollerworld**
Eastgates  Tel: (01206) 868868
East Anglia's largest quasar arena. *Please contact for details of opening times and prices. (R19)*

### Dedham
**Dedham Vale Family Farm**
Mill Lane Tel: (01206) 323111
Many different breeds of farm animals set in the heart of Constable Country. Playground, pets paddock and gift shop. *Open 8 Mar-30 Sep, daily, 1030-1730. £3.35/£2.10/£2.85. (R17/18)*

### Hullbridge
**Jakapeni Rare Breeds Farm**
Jakapeni Farm, Burlington Gardens
Tel: (01702) 232394
Working organic smallholding specialising in rare breeds of farm animals and poultry with a pet's corner, picnic area, fishing and refreshments in 30 acres of rolling countryside. *Open 4 Apr-31 Oct, Sun, Bank Hol Mon, 1030-1730. £1.75/£1.00/£1.25. (O23)*

*Peter Pan's Adventure Island,
Southend-on-Sea, Essex*

### Mistley
**Mistley Place Park**
New Road  Tel: (01206) 396483
Twenty five acres of woodlands and lakeside walks with goats, horses, sheep, rabbits, ducks, hens, a tearoom, gift shop and a nature trail. *Open all year, daily, 1000-1800/dusk. £2.50/£1.50/£2.00. (S/T18)*

### Nazeing
**⊛ Ada Cole Rescue Stables**
Broadlands, Broadley Common
Tel: (01992) 892133
A horse rescue charity with 47 acres of paddocks and stables with a gift shop and information room. *Open all year, daily, 1400-1700; closed 25 Dec. £1.50/free/£1.50. (I21)*

### Southend-on-Sea
**Kids Kingdom**
Garon Park, Eastern Avenue
Tel: (01702) 462747
Kids Kingdom provides an exciting range of indoor adventure play activities such as slides, inflatables, ball ponds, swing bridges, a special under-5 section, diner and gardens. *Open all year, daily, 1000-1800; closed 25, 26 Dec, 1 Jan. For admission prices, please contact for details. (G26)*

### Southend-on-Sea
**Mr B's Space Chase Quasar**
5/8 Marine Parade Tel: (01702) 603947
A quasar arena situated within a family entertainment centre with prize bingo and video games. *Open all year, Mon-Fri, 1200-2300; Sat, Sun, Bank Hol Mon, summer school half terms, 1000-2300; closed 25 Dec. £2.00/£2.00/£2.00. (G26)*

*Clacton Pier, Essex*

### Southend-on-Sea
**Never Never Land**
Western Esplanade Tel: (01702) 460618
A children's fantasy park of 2.5 acres with animated fairytale themes and familiar children's characters. *Open 22 Mar-6 Apr, daily, from 1100; 12 Apr-17 May, Sat, Sun from 1100; 24 May-1 Jun, daily, from 1100; 7 Jun-12 Jul, Sat Sun, from 1100; 19 Jul-31 Aug, daily, from 1100; 6 Sep-25 Oct, Sat, Sun, from 1100. £1.80/£1.20/£1.20. (G26)*

### Southend-on-Sea
**Peter Pan's Adventure Island**
Sunken Gardens West,
Western Esplanade Tel: (01702) 468023
Rides and attractions include a rollercoaster, big wheel, fantasy dome, sky lab, giant pirate ship and a looping barracuda with fast food kiosks. New rides for 1998. *Open 3 Jan-21 Mar, Sat, Sun, 1100-2000; 28 Mar-14 Sep, daily, 1100-2000/dusk; 4 Oct-27 Dec, Sat, Sun, 1100-1800. Please contact for details of ride prices. (G26)*

### Southend-on-Sea
**⊛ Southend-on-Sea Pier**
Western Esplanade Tel: (01702) 215622
Train ride along the pier approx 1.3 miles. Pier Museum at North Station, amusements novelty shop, restaurant, licensed public house. Guided tours at Lifeboat House. *Open all year, daily, 0800-2045. Please contact for details. (G26)*

### Southend-on-Sea
**Southend Sea Life Centre**
Eastern Esplanade Tel: (01702) 601834
The very latest in marine technology brings the secrets of the mysterious underwater world closer than ever before. An amazing underwater tunnel allows an all-round view. *Open all year, daily, from 1000; last admission, 1700; closed 25 Dec. £4.75/£3.50/£3.50. (G26)*

### South Weald
## Old MacDonalds Educational Farm Park
Weald Road   Tel: (01277) 375177
We tell the whole story of British livestock farming, keeping cattle, pigs, sheep, shire horses and poultry. Our wildlife hospital cares for sick and injured local wildlife. *Open all year, daily, 1000-dusk in winter; 1000-1800 in summer; closed 25, 26 Dec. £2.75/£1.75/£2.25. (K23)*

### South Woodham Ferrers
## ◉ Marsh Farm Country Park
Marsh Farm Road  Tel: (01245) 321552
A farm centre with sheep, a pig unit, free-range chickens, milking demonstrations, an indoor and outdoor adventure play areas, nature reserve, walks, picnic area and pet's corner. *Open 14 Feb-1 Nov, Mon-Fri, 1000-1630; Sat, Sun, Bank Hol Mon, summer school hols, 1000-1730; 6 Nov-19 Dec, Sat, Sun, 1000-1730. £2.50/£1.65/£1.65. (O23)*

### Vange
## Basildon Zoo
London Road  Tel: (01268) 553985
The zoo has birds of prey, patting pens, baby animals, a cafe and gift shop. There are big cats, otters, bats, a sand pit, swings and pet shop. Birthday parties arranged. *Open all year, daily, from 1000; winter closes 1 hour before dusk; closed 25, 26 Dec. £3.00/£1.75/£1.25. (M/N24)*

### Waltham Abbey
## ◉ Lee Valley Park Farms
Hayes Hill and Holyfield Hall, Stubbings Hall Lane, Crooked Mile
Tel: (01992) 892781
Two farms in one. Hayes Hill, a traditional-style farm with visitor facilities including tearooms and play area. Holyfield Hall, a modern daily/arable farm. *Open all year, Mon-Fri, 1000-1630; Sat, Sun, Bank Hol Mon, 1000-1800; tearooms closed 25 Dec-1 Jan. £2.75/£1.80/£1.80. (I22)*

### Walton-on-the-Naze
## ◉ Walton Pier
Pier Approach  Tel: (01255) 672288
A pier with arcade, prize bingo, a diner, tenpin bowling centre, fishing, adult and junior rides and Pirate Pete's indoor soft play area. Gala days, including firework display. *Open Pier all year, rides, 27 Mar-16 May, Sat, Sun, Bank Hol Mon, 1030-dusk; 24 May-13 Sep, daily, 1030-dusk; 19 Sep-24 Oct, Sat, Sun, 1030-dusk. (U/V19)*

### Wethersfield
## Boydells Dairy Farm
Boydells Farm  Tel: (01371) 850481
A small dairy farm where you can watch the milking of cows, sheep and goats. *Open 4 Apr-30 Sep, daily, 1400-1700. £2.50/£1.50/£2.50. (M/N18)*

### Widdington
## ◉ Mole Hall Wildlife Park
Tel: (01799) 540400
Park with otters, chimps, guanaco, lemurs, wallabies, deer, owls and waterfowl, a butterfly pavilion, attractive gardens picnic and play areas and a pet's corner. *Open all year, daily, 1030-1800; closed 25 Dec. £4.50/£3.20/£3.80. (K18)*

# Hertfordshire

### Broxbourne
## ◉ Paradise Wildlife Park
White Stubbs Lane
Tel: (01992) 470490
Britain's most interactive wildlife park with many animal activities daily. Also including an adventure playground, children's rides, woodland railway and catering facilities. *Open 1 Jan-28 Feb, daily, 1000-dusk; 1 Mar-31 Oct, daily, 1000-1800; 1 Nov-28 Feb, daily, 1000-dusk. £6.00/£4.00/£4.00. (I21/22)*

### Hatfield
## Activity World
Longmead, Birchwood
Tel: (01707) 270789
A large children's indoor adventure play centre with 6,000 sq ft of giant slides, ball pools and mazes. Birthday parties are catered for and special schemes for playgroups. *Open all year, daily, 0930-1930; closed 25, 26 Dec. Child from £2.50. (F21)*

### Hatfield
## Toddler World
The Galleria, Comet Way
Tel: (01707) 257480
An indoor adventure play area. *Open all year, Mon-Sat, 1000-1800; Sun, 1100-1700; closed 25 Dec. Child £2.50. (F21)*

### Hemel Hempstead
## Bingham Park Farm Shop and Children's Farm
Potten End Hill, Water End
Tel: (01442) 232373
Award-winning farm which provides many activities for children. Farm shop, tea room, outdoor picnic area and seasonal pick-your-own. *Open all year, daily, 0900-1730; closed 25 Dec. £2.50/£2.00/£2.00. (D21)*

*Bingham Park Farm Shop and Children's Farm, Hemel Hemstead, Hertfordshire*

### Hemel Hempstead
## Quasar
179 Marlowes  Tel: (01442) 213200
The largest quasar centre in the world, styled on the crystal maze with 4 game zones. Wild west, future world, medieval and World War II. *Open all year, Mon-Fri, 1500-2300; school holidays, 1200-2300; Sat, Sun, 1000-2300; closed 25, 26 Dec, 1 Jan. £4.00/£4.00/£4.00. (D21)*

### Letchworth
## Standalone Farm
Wilbury Road  Tel: (01462) 686775
An open farm with cattle, sheep, pigs, poultry, shire horses a wildfowl area, natural history museum, farm walk and daily milking demonstration. *Open 1 Mar-30 Sep, daily, autumn half term week, 1100-1700. (F18)*

### Sawbridgeworth
## Adventure Island Playbarn
Parsonage Lane
Tel: (01279) 600907
A £200,000 high-quality barn conversion into an indoor children's play centre incorporating a toddler area for the under 5's, soft play, slides and much more. *Open all year, daily, 1000-1800; closed 24-26 Dec, 1 Jan. Child from £1.00. (J20)*

### Whitwell
## Waterhall Farm and Craft Centre
Tel: (01438) 871256
An open farm featuring rare breeds and offering a 'hands-on' experience for visitors also craft centre and tea-room. *Open all year, Wed-Sun and Bank Hol Mon, 1000-1700; daily during school holidays. Closed 25, 26 Dec, 1 Jan. £2.75/£1.50/£1.50. (E/F19/20)*

*Countryside*

Sports and leisure facilities are great in this part of the world. Lee Valley Park sets the standard, with facilities for every possible activity, indoors and out, all centred around the riverside park.

This area is the home of English golf. In St Albans you can trace historical connections with the Ryder Cup. In the surrounding area we have everything from championship golf courses to those at Wyboston Lakes and Chesfield Downs which are designed for all the family to enjoy.

At The Lodge, the RSPB has set up its headquarters in mature woodland surroundings where a series of nature trails explores birch and bracken slopes, heathland and an artificial lake. Many birds and muntjac deer can be seen.

For fun on the water there is everything from a steamer trip at Southend, to river or canal cruises, to a special voyage on a Thames Sailing Barge. There's great fascination in water and the creeks and inlets of the Blackwater estuary are great places to explore from dry land as well as by boat. The Maldon Maritime Trail will set you off in the right direction.

## Nature Reserves

### Bedfordshire

#### Lodge Nature Reserve
Sandy  Tel: (01767) 680551
On the B1042
Sandy to Cambridge road
A reserve with mixed woodland and heathland supporting a wide variety of birds and wildlife. There are also formal gardens which are run by organic methods open to the public. *Open all year, Mon-Fri, 0900-1700; Sat, Sun, 1000-1700; closed 25-27 Dec. Admission to nature reserve, £2.00/50p/£1.00. (F15)*

### Essex

#### Abberton Reservoir
Layer-de-la-Haye  Tel: (01206) 738172
3 miles S of Colchester on the B1026
(EWT)
Bird-watching over the 1200-acre reservoir, a wildlife centre with a observation room, shop, toilets and hides. *Open all year, daily except Mon, 0900-1700; closed 25, 26 Dec. (Q/R20)*

#### Belfairs Nature Reserve
Leigh-on-Sea  Tel: (01702) 520202
From Southend take the A13 (London bound) for approximately 3 miles. Turn right into Eastwood Road. Go left at roundabout. 92-acre nature reserve, with woodland gardens and walks. *Open all year, daily, 0730-dusk. (O24)*

#### Fingringhoe Wick Nature Reserve
Fingringhoe  Tel: (01206) 729678
7 miles SE Colchester (EWT)
125 acres of woodland and lakes by the Colne estuary. Nature trails, observation room, tower and 8 hides. Conservation centre. *Open all year, daily, 0900-1900; centre and shop open all year, daily, 0900-1700 closed 25, 26 Dec. (R19)*

#### ⊛ Hatfield Forest National Nature Reserve
Tel: (01279) 870678
Bishops Stortford at Takeley
signposted off A120 ( NT)
The last surviving Royal Hunting Forest. Nature trail, lake and 18thC shell house. *Open all year. Car park charge. (K19/20)*

#### Langdon Nature Reserve
Basildon  Tel: (01268) 419095
B148 to Laindon (EWT)
Conservation centre, gift shop, toilets, refreshments and displays. 460 acres of meadow and woodland. 18 miles of footpaths and bridle ways. Coaches must pre-book. *Conservation centre, all year, Tue-Sun, Bank Hol Mon, 0900-1700; closed 25, 26 Dec. (L/M24)*

*Dunstable Downs, Bedfordshire*

### ❀ Stour Estuary Nature Reserve

Great Oakley  Tel: (01255) 886043
Off A1352 beyond Wrabness (RSPB)
Mixed woodland and mudflats. Beautiful
surroundings which helped inspire
Constable. Provides a refuse for large
numbers of wintering wildfowl and waders.
*Coaches must pre-book. (T/U18)*

### ❀ Thorndon Countryside Centre

Tel: (01277) 232944
1 mile S of Brentwood off A128
(EWT and Essex County Council)
In the Thorndon Country Park North which
includes some fine areas of woodland and
nature trails. Centre has activity displays,
gift and bookshop, separate education
room, toilets and refreshments. It was built
mainly of wood blown down in the 1987
storm. Park mobility buggy available. *Open
daily except Mon, 1000-1700. (L24)*

## Hertfordshire

### ❀ Fowlmere
### Nature Reserve RSPB

Fowlmere  Tel: (01763) 208978
From the A10 Royston to Cambridge
road, take the Fowlmere turning
An 86-acre nature reserve incorporating a
nature trail and 4 bird-watching hides.
Attractions include unspoilt wetland
scenery and birdlife including the kingfisher.
*Admission £1.00/50p/£1.00. (I16)*

### ❀ Rye House
### Marsh Nature Reserve

Hoddesdon  Tel: (01992) 460031
Off the A1170, A10 and A414
A nature reserve offering good views of wild
birds and different marshland habitats with
good paths and observation hides
throughout; a common tern colony and
kingfisher bank. *Open all year, daily, 1000-
1700/dusk if earlier; closed 25, 26 Dec.
Admission £2.00/50p/£1.00. (H/I21)*

---

### Naturalists' Organisations & Other Abbreviations used in this section

| | |
|---|---|
| EBWS | Essex Bird-watching Society, The Saltings, 53 Victoria Drive, Great Wakering, Southend-on-Sea, Essex. |
| EWT | Essex Wildlife Trust, Fingringhoe Wick Nature Reserve, South Green Road, Fingringhoe, Colchester CO5 7DN. Tel: (01206) 729678. |
| ❀ NT | The National Trust, Blickling, Norwich, Norfolk NR11 6NF. Tel: (01263) 733471. |
| ❀ RSPB | Royal Society for the Protection of Birds, HQ: The Lodge, Sandy, Beds SG19 2DL. Tel: (01767) 680541. East Anglia Regional Office, Stalham House, 65 ThorpeRoad, Norwich NR1 1UD. Tel: (01603) 661662. |
| SSSI: | Site of Special Scientific Interest |

## Country Walks

## Bedfordshire

### Circular Walks

Leaflets are available for 14 Circular Walks
around the county, and are based around
Harrold-Odell Country Park, Dunstable
Downs, Totternhoe and Eaton Bray villages
and Whipsnade and Studham villages, to
name but a few.

### The Icknield Way

Path passes through south Bedfordshire, as
it follows part of the oldest road in Britain
for over 120 miles.

*Harrold-Odell Country Park, Bedfordshire*

---

### Lea Valley Walk

50 mile walk, starts at the source of the
River Lea in Leagrave, and follows
waymarked routes through Luton to East
Hyde, and on through Hertfordshire to the
River Thames Bow Locks.

### Three Shires Way

A long distance bridleway which runs for 37
miles through Buckinghamshire, north
Bedfordshire and Cambridgeshire.

New leaflets are regularly produced to
accompany the above walks. For more
information of routes in the Bedfordshire
area, contact:

❀ Bedfordshire County Council
County Hall, Cauldwell Street, Bedford
MK42 9AP. Telephone: (01234) 228310.

## Essex

### Essex Way

A long distance path stretching across the
county of Essex, from Epping in SW to the
port of Harwich in NE. A distance of 81
miles, following footpaths and ancient
green lanes. *Guidebook £3.00 from Essex
County Council.*

### Forest Way

25 miles of gentle walking along footpaths
and ancient green lanes between the forests
of Epping and Hatfield. *Booklet £2.50 from
Essex County Council.*

### Harcamlow Way

140 miles in the form of a 'figure-of-eight'
footpath walk from Harlow to Cambridge
and back. *Booklet £2.50 from Essex County
Council.*

### St Peters Way

45-mile walk from Chipping Ongar to
ancient chapel of St Peter-on-the-Wall at
Bradwell-on-Sea. *Booklet £1.20 from Essex
County Council.*

### The Roach Valley Way

A 23 mile circular walk around south-east Essex leading you through a rich variety of landscapes from the ancient woodlands of Hockley to the expansive coastal margins of the Roach and Crouch estuaries. *Guidebook £2.50 from Essex County Council.*

### Three Forests Way

60 mile circular walk linking the forests of Epping, Hatfield and Hainault. *Booklet £1.00 from Essex County Council.*

For more information of routes in the Essex area, contact:
⊛ Essex County Council
Planning Department, County Hall,
Chelmsford CM1 1LF.
Telephone: (01245) 437530.

## Hertfordshire

### The Hertfordshire Way

166 mile circular walking route taking in some of Hertfordshire's best countryside, and some of the major towns and villages. Waymarked throughout but use of the detailed guide is advised. "The Hertfordshire Way A Walker's Guide". 1998. Ed. Bert Richardson. Castlemead Publications, Ware. Also from a range of book shops.

### The Icknield Way

105 mile route following the line of one of Britain's oldest known tracks with origins in the Neolithic era (4-2000BC) waymarked with a prehistoric stone axe. "The Icknield Way Path A Walker's Guide" from a range of bookshops or The Icknield Way Association, 19 Boundary Road, Bishops Stortford, Hertfordshire CM23 5LE. 'The Icknield Way Path A Guide for Horseriders, Cyclists and Others' from East Anglian Trails, Pip's Peace, Kenton, Stowmarket IP14 6JS. Tel: (01728) 860429.

### Lea Valley Walk

50 mile Regional Route from the Thames to the source of the River Lea at Luton. Its waymark is a swan. It uses towpaths, field paths, former railway tracks and park paths to link with rights of way. *Details from: the Lea Valley Park Authority, Tel: (01992) 717711. Hertfordshire County Council, Tel: (01279) 843067. Bedfordshire County Council, Tel: (01234) 228342.*

For more information of routes in the Hertfordshire area, contact:
⊛ Hertfordshire County Council
Environmental Land Management Service,
County Hall, Pegs Lane, Hertford, SG13 8DN.
Telephone: (01992) 555237.

*Ayot Green, Hertfordshire*

## Country Parks

## Bedfordshire

### Dunstable Downs
Tel: (01582) 608489
Off the B4541 from Dunstable

Scenic views over the vale of Aylesbury. Countryside Centre where kites, souvenirs and publications can be purchased. Site of Specific Scientific Interest. *Open at any reasonable time; countryside centre, 3 Jan-29 Mar, Sat, Sun, 1200-1600; 1 Apr-30 Sep, Tue-Sat, 1300-1630; Sun and Bank Hols, 1200-1800; 3 Oct-27 Dec, Sat, Sun, 1200-1600. (C19/20)*

### Stockgrove Country Park
Leighton Buzzard Tel: (01525) 237760
Off the A5 and the A418

Approximately 80 acres of parkland, oak and conifer woodlands with a small ornamental lake. One hundred and five acres of woodland access adjoining the park. *(B18)*

### Sundon Hills Country Park
Sundon
Signposted from the A6 at Streatley

Chalk downland within the Chilterns Area of Outstanding Natural Beauty, a Site of Specific Scientific Interest, adjoining the Icknield Way long distance footpath. *(D18)*

## Essex

### Cudmore Grove Country Park
On Mersea Island Tel: (01206) 383868
10 miles south of Colchester

Situated next to the entrance of the Colne estuary, the Park consists of grassland and a sandy beach, ideally suited to walking, picnics, informal games and wildlife watching. *Open all year, daily, 0800-dusk. Car park £1.10. (S20)*

### Flitch Way and Rayne Station Centre
Rayne Tel: (01376) 340262
Rayne Station Centre is
3 miles west of Braintree

Fifteen miles of linear country park along the old Bishop's Stortford to Braintree railway. Rayne Station Centre has been renovated and now has an exhibition of local heritage. *Flitch Way open all year, daily, dawn-dusk; Rayne Station Centre open all year, daily, 0900-1700; Exhibition Room open all year, Sun, 1300-1600. (M/N19)*

### ⊛ Hatfield Forest
3 miles E Bishop's Stortford
1,000 acres of wooded medieval landscape and nature reserve with lake. Miles of peaceful woodland walks including waymarked trail. *Car parking charge. (K19/20)*

### High Woods Country Park
Colchester  Tel: (01206) 853588
Accessible from Mile End Road
(A134) and Ipswich Road
A 330-acre (134-hectare) country park situated to the north of central Colchester with a variety of landscape and wildlife, visitor's centre, toilets, bookshop and car parks. *Open all year, daily, at any reasonable time; Visitors Centre, 3 Jan-29 Mar, Sat, Sun, 1000-1600; 1 Apr-30 Sep, Mon-Sat, 1000-1630; Sun, Bank Hol Mon, 1100-1730; 3 Oct-27 Dec, Sat, Sun, 1000-1600. (R19)*

### Holland Haven Country Park
Holland-on-Sea
Located on the B1032
Frinton Road
Situated on the coast between Clacton-on-Sea and Frinton-on-Sea, the country park offers over 100 acres of unspoilt scenic coastline which is ideal for bird-watching. *Open all year, daily, dawn-dusk. (U20)*

*Lee Valley Park, Essex*

### Langdon Hills Country Park
Corringham  Tel: (01268) 542066
Signed from the A13 and B1007
Country park consisting of Westley Heights and One Tree Hill. Picnic areas, wildflower, meadows and ancient woodlands overlooking the Thames estuary. *Open all year, daily, 0800-dusk. (N24/25)*

### ⬢ Marsh Farm Park
Tel: (01245) 321552
South Woodham Ferrers,
(Essex County Council)
320 acres of country park operating as a modern livestock farm. Country walks around the sea wall, farm tracks and nature reserve. Visitors centre, tearoom and picnic area. See also Family Fun section. *(O23)*

*Lee Valley Park Information Centre, Waltham Abbey*

### ⬢ Lee Valley Park Information Centre
Waltham Abbey Tel: (01992) 702200
Signposted from
junction 26 on the M25
Open countryside with lakes and wildflower meadows within Lee Valley Park, which stretches along the river Lee from Waltham Abbey, Essex to Broxbourne in Hertfordshire. *(H/I21/22)*

### ⬢ Thorndon Countryside Centre
Brentwood  Tel: (01277) 211250
1 mile S. Brentwood
(Essex County Council)
540 acres. Thorndon North is almost totally woodland with pleasant walks and a bridle way. Thorndon South has woodland walks, fishing and some extensive views of the Thames Estuary. Ranger service. Park mobility buggy available. Countryside Centre. *(L24)*

### Wat Tyler Country Park
Pitsea  Tel: (01268) 550088
Off the A13 at Pitsea, Basildon
A nature reserve with additional attractions including a marina, museums, arts and crafts studios and a heritage area.
*Open all year, daily, 0800-dusk. (M/N25)*

### ⬢ Weald Country Park
South Weald  Tel:(01277) 216297
1 mile NW Brentwood
(Essex County Council)
428 acres of wood land, lakes and open parkland, open to the public for informal recreation. Fishing and horse riding. Visitors Centre, ranger service. *(K23)*

## Hertfordshire

### Aldenham Country Park
Elstree  Tel: (0181) 9539602
Take A411 and A41 - A1 Sterling Corner. Junction 5, M1,
take the A41 Harrow
The 175 acres of meadow and woodland with rare breeds farm, playgrounds, angling, nature trail, horse-riding and refreshments. Site of 'Winnie the Poohs wood'. *Open 1 Jan-31 Mar, daily, 0900-1600; 1 Apr-31 May, daily, 0900-1700; 1 Jun-30 Sep, daily, 0900-1800; 1 Oct-31 Dec, daily, 0900-1700; closed 25 Dec. (E23)*

### Ashridge Estate
Ringshall  Tel: (01442) 851227
Between Northchurch and Ringshall
just off the B4506
About 4500 acres of wood, heath and downs including the 700ft Ivinghoe Deacon and the Bridgewater Monument. *Open Estate at any reasonable time; Visitor's Centre, Monument and Shop, 3 Apr-31 Oct, Mon-Thu, 1400-1700; Sat, Sun, Bank Hol Mon, 1400-1730. Admission: £1.00/50p. (B/C20/21)*

### Fairlands Valley Park
Tel: (01438) 353241
1 mile east of Stevenage
near the town centre.
A 120-acre park with an 11-acre lake for windsurfing and sailing. The Park has a boating lake, play area, paddling pools and a wildfowl sanctuary. *Open at any reasonable time, except Christmas Day and New Years Day. Open Boxing Day, morning only. (G19)*

*On the Water*

**Holidays Afloat on Cruisers, Narrow Boats and Yachts**

## Essex

### ⊛ Blackwater Boats
on the Chelmer and Blackwater Navigation Tel: (01206) 853282
4-berth luxury narrow boats. Day hire, short breaks and long holidays. *(N-S21/22)*

## Hertfordshire

### ⊛ Lee Valley Boat Centre
Broxbourne  Tel: (01992) 462085
Traditional narrow boats for hire by the week or short break. *(H21)*

### ⊛ Adventuress Cruises
Sawbridgeworth  Tel: (01279) 600848
Adventuress cruises on the historic River Stort Navigation, through the rural countryside on the borders of Essex and Hertfordshire. Departure from and return to Sawbridgeworth. *(J20)*

## Day Boat Hire

## Essex

### ⊛ Mill Race Nursery
Tel: (01206) 242521
New Road, Aldham, Colchester
(just off the A604 at Ford Street)
Rowing boats, riverside garden, restaurant and plant centre. *(P/Q19)*

## Hertfordshire

### ⊛ Arcturus Day Cruises
Watford 1959-1999
Tel: (01438) 714528
Our 40th Anniversary of passenger-carrying with seating for 50 on scheduled public trips, Sundays and Bank Hols, Easter-Oct; Tue and Thu in Aug. Group charter. *(D23)*

## Boat Hire for Groups

## Bedfordshire

### ⊛ Leighton Lady Cruises
Brantoms Wharf, Leighton Buzzard
Tel: (01525) 384563
70 foot narrow boat. Heated passenger saloon with cushioned seats, seating up to 54. Cream teas and buffet available on request. *Phone for public trips list. (B19)*

*River Stour, Dedham, Essex*

*Sport for all*

## Golf Courses

### Essex

#### ⊛ Colchester and Lexden Family Golf Centre

Bakers Lane  Tel: (01206) 843333

Learn to play golf in a friendly and relaxed format under the direction of experienced professionals on a structured beginners course. 18-hole pay and play course, covered floodlit driving range with 12 additional bays. 9-hole pitch 'n' putt course and putting green. Visitors welcome. *(Q19)*

### Hertfordshire

**Malton Golf**

See entry on page 45

#### ⊛ Whitehall Golf Centre

Dane End, Ware  Tel: (01920) 438495

18 hole golf course plus range, shop and lounge/bar. Course open every day except 25 Dec, 0700-dusk. Open to members and non-members. *Please contact for full details of opening times for the range. (H20)*

## Leisure Centres

### Bedfordshire

#### ⊛ Bedford Oasis Beach Pool

Cardington Road, Bedford
Tel: (01234) 272100

Fun pool with 2 giant waterslides, spa baths, toddlers paddling area, lazy river ride, outside water lagoon, water cannon, wave machine, water mushroom and depth charge. *(D15)*

### Essex

#### ⊛ Colchester Leisure World

Cowdray Avenue, Colchester
Tel: (01206) 766500

Extensive leisure complex offering a wide range of facilities including leisure pool, bubble lounge, children's fountain, 25m competition pool and teaching pool. Also badminton courts, sauna, jacuzzi, bar and restaurant and concert hall. *(R19)*

#### ⊛ Blackwater Leisure Centre

Maldon  Tel: (01621) 851898

Leisure pool with flumes, baby/toddlers pool, health and fitness area, solarium and cafeteria. *(P21)*

### Hertfordshire

#### ⊛ Gosling Sports Park

Stanborough Road,
Welwyn Garden City
Tel: (01707) 331056

Gosling Sports Park offers a wealth of sporting facilities, housed in a 52 acre complex in the heart of Welwyn Garden City in Hertfordshire. *Please contact for details of opening times. (G20)*

#### ⊛ Lee Valley Leisure Pool

Old Nazeing Road, Broxbourne,
contact Lee Valley Park
Information Centre
Tel: (01992) 702200

This includes a free form leisure pool with wave machine, a learner pool, toddlers play area and tree house, fitness suite, a health suite, aerobics studio and a cafe. Located in the Lee Valley Regional Park, it is due to open late Spring 1999 and is an ideal place for all the family. *(H21)*

## Indoor Activities

### Essex

#### ⊛ Rollerworld

Eastgates, Colchester
Tel: (01206) 868868

Great Britain's largest roller-skating rink, 25m x 50m maple floor. RollerHire, RollerCafe and RollerBar - stunning sound and light show. Quasar at Rollerworld, the earths favourite laser game. *(R19)*

#### ⊛ Grand Central

*(formerly RollerBowl)*
Collier Row Road,
Collier Row, Romford
Tel: (0181) 924 4000 (General)
Tel: (0181) 924 2222 (Bookings)

Major new entertainment concept offering a diverse range of unique attractions under one roof. 34 lanes of GLOW Ten Pin Bowling, Mid City Bar & Diner, Old Orleans Restaurant, Sports Bar with American Pool, Function Suites, State Fair Amusements area, Health & Fitness Club. Free secure parking. *Free admission to centre. Individual game rates. (J24)*

### Ice Skating

### Essex

#### ⊛ Riverside Ice and Leisure Centre

Victoria Road, Chelmsford
Tel: (01245) 269417

Ice rink, 3 pools, 6 court sports hall, gymnasium, squash courts, snooker hall and health suite. *(M/N21)*

## Specialist Holidays and Activities

### Bedfordshire

#### ⊛ Shirescapes

Walk and Discover the Shires
Tel: (01234) 326010

Escorted and self-guided walking and cycling holidays, many based on a local theme in unspoilt corners of Bedfordshire, Cambridgeshire and Hertfordshire. Leisurely short breaks offering a package of quality accommodation, meals, transport and luggage transfer. Escorted walking and cycling days available throughout the year. Brochure available. Shirescapes Holidays Ltd, 15 Winifred Road, Bedford, MK40 4ET.

### Hertfordshire

#### ⊛ Hertfordshire Rail Tours

Tel: (01438) 715050

Day excursions by chartered train and luxury weekend tours to Scotland. 28 Chestnut Walk, Welwyn, Hertfordshire AL6 0SD.

## Restaurants

*Dedham Vale, Essex*

### Essex

The Essex coast specialises in Dover sole, plaice and sea bass during the summer months, followed by herring, cod and whiting in the colder weather. But in the protected waters of the Thames estuary, the speciality is whitebait. At Leigh-on-Sea the quay is a hive of activity when the daily catch of cockles and brown shrimps comes in. Hurry down there and sample the fare! The harvest at Colcheseter is oysters, and every year the Oyster Festival at East Mersea celebrates this delicacy.

Inland, the climate and conditions are perfect for soft fruit, and the juicy strawberries of Essex have to be tasted to be believed! No wonder that jam producers Wilkin & Sons and Elsenham both made this their home. See how the art of jam making has advanced over the years, and taste the results at Wilkin & Son's museum and tearoom at Tiptree.

Be sure to stop for afternoon tea at Woburn Abbey. The tradition of afternoon tea was invented here - and it's certainly a tradition worth preserving!

In such excellent cereal growing countryside, it's not surprising to find Jordans' mill at Biggleswade. This long established family business believes in using best quality ingredients to produce delicious recipes for a healthy lifestyle, so why not visit their excellent shop to test the goodies!

**Great Yeldham**
### The White Hart
Tel: (01787) 237250

The White Hart was built in 1505. The timbered exterior is matched by the heavily beamed interior, complete with four fireplaces. The huge gardens run along both sides of a stream. It is now part of 'Hunstsbridge', a partnership of Chefs who each serve the highest quality food within the relaxed, informal atmosphere of an inn of character. Chef Patron is Roger Jones, previously of The Pheasant at Keyston in Cambridgeshire, where he received acclaim from all the guide books. Real ales and Huntsbridge's renowned selection of wines complete the picture. *Open: daily. Average prices: lunch or dinner à la carte £16; bar food from £2.95. (N17)*

## Afternoon teas

### Essex

**Aldham**
### ✿ Mill Race Nursery Coffee Shop
New Road, Aldham, Colchester
(just off the A1124, formerly
A604 at Ford Street)
Tel: (01206) 242521

Enjoy home-made and speciality cakes, cream teas or light lunches in our conservatory style coffee lounge or courtyard garden. Riverside garden and boat hire, large plant centre, silk and dried flower shop and giftware. *Open daily including Sundays 0930-1700. (P18/19)*

*Woburn, Bedfordshire*

### Essex

We are spoilt for choice when it comes to shopping! This is a well populated area, and prosperous too, so it's hardly surprising that there are so many places of excellence selling good quality products. Here are shopping centres so comprehensive that they will keep you on your toes from the moment the shops open until closing time.

The Arndale Centre at Luton has long been recognised as an example to other shopping centres.

For factory outlet shopping, head for the new Clacton Common Shopping Village - good buys at lower prices!

You will find specialist shops and craft shops too, and a wealth of fascinating antique shops.

### Bedfordshire

#### Luton
**The Arndale Shopping Centre**
Luton LU1 2LJ
Tel: (01582) 412636

This large shopping centre, accessible from Junction 10 of the M1 Motorway, was developed at the heart of Luton in the early 1970s. A recent refurbishment produced a spectacular and exciting environment, a premier shopping location with 110 shops, 10 major stores, an indoor market and 2,300 parking spaces. Anchored by Debenhams Department Store and with most major high street names represented, the Centre offers fashion, books, household items, jewellery, electrical/musical goods and sportswear. The indoor market has 145 stalls covering speciality interests from haberdashery to second-hand books and augments the Arndale Centre's offer. *(D19)*

#### West Thurrock
⊛ **Lakeside Shopping Centre**
West Thurrock Way, West Thurrock, Grays RM20 2ZP
Tel: (01708) 869933
Fax: (01708) 865870
Website: www.lakeside-shopping-centre.co.uk

Voted 'Best Shopping Centre in the UK'. Offering unrivalled retail and leisure facilities. Over 300 shops, including four large department stores, popular high street names plus a selection of boutiques 32 places to eat; 7 screen cinema; watersports lake and award winning children's facilities. Customer service facilities include free pushchair and wheelchair hire, free Shopmobility scheme, shopping lockers, sale of Lakeside Gift Vouchers and the Lakeside Visa Card. The Centre opens seven days a week, 10am-10pm on weekdays and has 12,000 free car parking spaces plus a 250 space coach park. Located at Junction 30/31, off M25, direct trains to Lakeside's Chafford Hundred Station connect with Fenchurch Street (London), Barking and Upminster. *(K/L25/26)*

*Red Lion Walk, Colchester, Essex*

## discovery tours

### Bloomin' Beautiful
- enjoy the spectacular colours and delicate fragrances of some of England's finest gardens.

**Tour 1:**
**Starting point:** St. Albans, Herts *(E21/22)*
**Mileage:** Gardens of the Rose
     & Hatfield House 10m
     Gardens of the Rose
     & Knebworth House 18m

**Morning** - take the B4630 to Chiswell Green, and the sweet-smelling *Gardens of the Rose.*

**Afternoon** - return to St. Albans and take the A1057 to Hatfield. Either visit the 17th c. style gardens of *Hatfield House*, or head north along the A1 to junction 7, and visit the gothic *Knebworth House, Gardens & Park.*

**Tour 2:**
**Starting point:** Colchester, Essex *(R18/19)*
**Mileage:** 34m
**Morning** - take the A120 towards Braintree. After 8m, turn right onto the B1024, then 0.5m later, turn left to the *Marks Hall Estate* and its walled garden. Return to A120 and 5m later (at the roundabout), turn left. At the second roundabout, take the B1018 to *Cressing Temple* and its paradise garden.

**Afternoon** - take the B1018 to Witham and then the A12 south towards London. After 8m, take the A130 to Rettendon and wander amongst the Roses at *The R.H.S. Hyde Hall Garden.*

**Tour 3:**
**Starting point:** Luton, Beds *(D19)*
**Mileage:** 21m
**Morning** - explore nine centuries of garden history at *Stockwood Craft Museum and Gardens.*

**Afternoon** - take the A6 north. After 10m, follow signs to the intricate *Wrest Park Gardens.* Return to A6 and head north to the roundabout, turn right onto the A507. At the second roundabout, turn left onto the A600, then at the third, turn right onto the B658. After 4m, turn left to Old Warden and visit the eccentric *Swiss Garden.*

*The Shuttleworth Collection, Biggleswade, Bedfordshire*

### Wings & Wheels
- transport yourself to the world of planes, trains and automobiles.
**Tour 1: Starting point:** Bedford, Beds *(D15)*
**Mileage:** 29m
**Morning** - leave Bedford on the A603. At the roundabout with the A428, take the road to *Cardington*, dominated by the historic R101 airship hangers. At the T-junction, turn right and remain on this road to Old Warden, and the vintage planes/cars of *The Shuttleworth Collection.*

**Afternoon** - turn right at the exit gate and at the junction with the B658, turn right again. 4m later, turn left through Shefford, to the roundabout with the A507. Turn left, then at the second roundabout, turn right onto the A600. After 1m, turn right to Lower Stondon & visit the transport collection at the *Stondon Museum.* Return to the A600 and turn right to Hitchin, where you take the A505 to Luton. Visit the historic carriages at *The Mossman Collection.*

**Tour 2:**
**Starting point:** St. Albans, Herts *(E21/22)*
**Mileage:** 29m
**Morning** - leave St. Albans on the A1081 (via London Colney) to junction 22 of the M25. From the roundabout, take the B556 to visit the *Mosquito Aircraft Museum* at Salisbury Hall. Return to St. Albans and take the A4147 to Hemel Hempstead. Remain on the road through the town, then join the A4146 to Leighton Buzzard.

**Afternoon** - take a ride on the steam/diesel trains of the *Leighton Buzzard Railway*, then spend the rest of the day relaxing on a cruise along the Grand Union Canal, aboard *Leighton Lady Cruises.*

### Walk on the Wildside
- enjoy a wild adventure, on our animal safari into deepest Beds and Herts.
**Starting point:** Tring, Herts *(B20/21)*
**Mileage:** 27m
**Morning** - visit the unique *Walter Rothschild Zoological Museum*, then leave Tring on the B488/B489 to the roundabout with the A4146 (6m). Go straight ahead, then at the next roundabout, turn right onto the B4540 for 4m to the junction with the A5. Turn right, then after 1m, turn left back onto the B4540, to visit the farmyard animals at the *Woodside Farm & Wildfowl Park*

**Afternoon** - retrace your steps to the A5 and turn right. Follow the road for 8m to Hockliffe, where you turn right onto the A4012 to Woburn. End the day in the exotic animal reserves of the *Woburn Safari Park.*

*Braughing, Hertfordshire*

*Audley End House and Gardens, Saffron Walden, Essex*

## Food Glorious Food

- if you are in search of culinary adventure, then this tour is full of tasty surprises.

**Starting point:**
Southend-on-Sea, Essex *(P24)*

**Mileage:** 30m

**Morning** - start your day in the fishing village of *Leigh-on-Sea*, famous for its cockles. Then its onto *Southend*, where you can take a stroll along the famous pier and enjoy fish & chips in the award-winning gardens.

**Afternoon** - follow the A127 for 7m, then turn right onto the A130. After 3m (at the roundabout), turn right onto the A132 to South Woodham Ferrers. At the 2nd roundabout you reach, turn left and follow the B1418 to Woodham Mortimer. Then take the A414 to *Maldon*, noted for its sea salt production. End the day by taking the B1022 to the rich fruit growing area around *Tiptree* and enjoy a delicious afternoon tea.

## Raptors, Romans & Roundabouts

- a fun-packed family tour, based around England's oldest recorded town.

**Starting point:** Colchester, Essex *(R18/19)*

**Mileage:** 22m

**Morning** - leave the town on the B1022, to visit the excellent *Colchester Zoo*, one of Europe's finest.

**Afternoon** - return to Colchester and visit the Castle Museum, where mum can try on a Roman toga! End the day by taking the A133 to *Clacton-on-Sea* and the fun-packed pier, where you can smash into dad on the dodgems and scare your little sister at the *Reptile Safari*.

## Country Classics

- discover the historic homes and gardens of the rich and famous

**Starting point:**
Saffron Walden, Essex *(K16/17)*

**Mileage:** Saffron Walden &
The Gardens of Easton Lodge 14m
Saffron Walden and
Castle Hedingham 19m

**Morning** - explore charming Saffron Walden, then follow the signs to visit the Jacobean *Audley End House.*

**Afternoon** - two choices, either take the B184 towards Gt. Dunmow, stopping briefly at *Thaxted* with its timbered Guildhall, then continuing for a further 5m before turning right to Little Easton. Then take the first left and follow the road to visit *The Gardens of Easton Lodge*, former home of The Countess of Warwick. Or alternatively leave Saffron Walden on the B1053 to Finchingfield, where you take the B1057 to Wethersfield. Turn left here and follow the road to Sible Hedingham. At the T-junction with the A1307, turn left. Take the next right hand turning (the B1058) and visit medieval *Castle Hedingham*, with its magnificent castle keep.

## Antiques, Auctions, Bids & Bargains

- explore priceless antique towns and stately homes filled with heirlooms

**Tour 1:**

**Starting point:** Hertford, Herts *(G/H20/21)*

**Mileage:** 35m

**Morning** - explore St. Andrew Street, famed for its antique shops. Then take the A119 to Stevenage/junction 7 of the A1(M). Head north to junction 8 and take the A602 to *Hitchin*, which holds a regular bric-a-brac market. Leave on the B655 to Barton-le-Cley, where at the T-junction turn right, then left, passing through Sharpenhoe and Harlington. At the junction with the A5120, go straight across, under the M1 and through Tingrith & Eversholt.

**Afternoon** - discover the art/porcelain collections of *Woburn Abbey*, and browse in the antiques centre. End the day in the village of *Woburn*, exploring the upmarket shops.

**Tour 2:**

**Starting point:** Halstead, Essex *(O18)*

**Mileage:** 29m

**Morning** - explore the speciality shops and antiques centre in *Halstead*. Then take the A1307 to Earls Colne, where you turn left onto the B1024 to visit *Coggeshall*, a mecca for antique lovers.

**Afternoon** - remain on the B1024 south to *Kelvedon* (with its selection of antique shops), where you join the A12 south towards London. After 12m, take the A130 to the antiques village of *Battlesbridge*.

*Colchester, Essex*